In Memoriam:
ITA FORD, M.M.
1940-1980

Presented by the Class of 1961

The Home Front

THE HOME FRONT

An anthology
of personal experience
1938 – 1945

SELECTED AND EDITED BY

NORMAN LONGMATE

1981

CHATTO & WINDUS

LONDON

Published by Chatto & Windus Ltd
40 William IV Street
London WC2N 4DF

Clarke, Irwin & Co. Ltd
Toronto

British Library Cataloguing in Publication Data

Longmate, Norman
The home front.
1. Great Britain – Social life and customs – 20th century
I. Title
941.084′092′2   DA566.4
ISBN 0 7011 2553 5

Selection and editorial matter
© Norman Longmate, 1981

Typeset by Inforum Ltd, Portsmouth
Printed and bound in Great Britain by
Redwood Burn Ltd.,
Trowbridge, Wiltshire.

To D.N.R. and E.M.R.
Too young to remember it.

CONTENTS

PLATES

between pages 146–147

ix

CARTOONS

The Second World War has often been described as the civilians' war, but almost all the anthologies of wartime experience published since it ended have been confined to the adventures of men and women in the Forces. Yet the vast majority of the population never served in the Army, Navy or Air Force, and their struggles, and their contribution to victory, were on very different battlefields – in the workshop, the queue, the farm and the first-aid post. This anthology is an attempt to tell the story of these neglected millions in their own words.

It is right that the soldiers' story should have been told first, for wars are not won by civilians, however hard-working or even heroic. The outcome of the Battle of Britain was not decided by the citizens of Canterbury and Tunbridge Wells, but by the pilots of Manston and Biggin Hill. The real victors of the Battle of the Atlantic were the men of the escort ships and the Merchant Navy, not the Food Office clerks who distributed ration books or the landgirls who helped get in the harvest, vital though their work was. But if the civilian population could not by itself have won the war, it could certainly have lost it. The Forces were able to sustain defeat after defeat in the early years of the war, and still survive to win it, because of the loyal support they received from the Home Front. Had civilian morale collapsed under the bombing, or had there been widespread defiance of the conscription of labour, or the rationing regulations, all the soldiers' efforts would have been in vain. Every housewife who stood uncomplaining in the fish queue, every mother who patiently combed the shops for children's shoes, every weary over-age male who dug his allotment when exhorted to do so and turned out for fire-watching when required, made a positive, personal contribution to victory. The moaners and self-seekers certainly existed, but they were never more than an untypical minority.

I have tried as far as possible to tell the story of the war as seen by the civilians as a continuous narrative, which reflects something of the tedium and weariness of wartime life, as well as its minor triumphs – like receiving an unexpected food parcel – and the occasional high drama, as when a family survived the destruction of their home.

Because it was then, despite the hysteria over Munich, that most people came to realise that war was approaching, and preparations for it began to intrude into everyday life, I have begun with the events of 1938.

Although adopting a basically chronological approach, I have felt no obligation to give the same amount of space to each year. The invasion threat and the Blitz, for example, dictate that 1940 should be treated more generously than the middle years of the war when events already familiar tended to recur. It needs to be remembered therefore that many aspects of wartime experience – the blackout, food rationing, the fuel shortage, crowded trains among others – continued for all, or most, of the six years which followed September 1939. To avoid repetition I have tried to give each year a dominant theme and to collect together the recollections relating to that subject. Thus 1942, for instance, contains most memories about food and 1943 the majority of extracts about the Americans, although rationing began in 1939 and the Americans were a feature of the landscape from early 1942 until VJ-Day. Where there is uncertainty about the date of an incident I have assigned it to what seems the most appropriate year.

The criteria I have adopted in winnowing down to about 80,000 words a collection of passages which was initially at least ten times as long, are as follows. First, while trying to give an impression of civilian life as a whole, I have been influenced by the intrinsic interest of each extract, rather than by its literary quality or the historical importance of the subject covered. (I have, for example, included some of J.B. Priestley's 'Postscripts' not so much because they are splendidly evocative pieces of writing but because they made a deep impression on listeners at the time, comparable to the effects of the launching of the Local Defence Volunteers or one's first air raid.) Second, with only a few exceptions, I have preferred the experiences of ordinary people to those of the more eminent and, where using printed sources, have opted for the less familiar in preference to the already well-known. Third, I have tried rigorously to exclude material already used in any of my earlier books about the war and have only in one or two places, where there seemed no real alternative, selected anecdotes that have already appeared there. I have, however, drawn on the wealth of material sent to me, particularly for *How We Lived Then*, which I have not previously quoted, usually because the story concerned could not be done justice to in the space available. I am grateful to all those who have allowed me to use here material submitted for other books. Fourth, and most important, I have tried to tell the truth, even when this conflicts with more palatable legends which, with the passage of time, have come to be accepted as facts. To suggest that everyone who was asked to help with evacuees did so willingly – or even did so at all – is false. Similarly, I have consciously attempted to dispel the persistent myth that the Blitz was a cheerful and cosy experience, resembling a prolonged, if wet, Bank Holiday, or that there was something ineffectual and humorous about the doodlebugs. Despite all the heroism and friendliness produced by the air attacks on the civilian population, enduring them was basically a grim and frightening experience. Reports of cheerful sing-songs in the shelters may have been necessary in 1940 but the reality was always rather different and now, surely, deserves to be put on record.

It has been a disappointment that a long search has failed to reveal much poetry of quality about the Home Front. A good deal of light 'home-made' verse exists but it now sounds feeble and dated and no poet of real stature seems to have been inspired by the civilians' war. Perhaps this dearth of poetry is itself significant. Apart from an unheroic few who prudently spent the war in America (and whom the public were, in my view, right to regard with contempt, however much of the literary establishment since may have rallied to their defence) most talented writers were in the Forces or helping the war effort in other ways. There was little in daily life at home to inspire those who remained. Apart from the proud summer of 1940, when even the least articulate Englishman became conscious of his rich heritage, the war was not a poetic time. In the phrase of Lady Reading, Head of the W.V.S., the discomforts and sufferings of the civilian population during the Second World War were 'not nice but necessary'. If there was little glamour left on the battlefield between 1939 and 1945, on the Home Front there was even less.

N.R.L.

1938

I believe it is peace for our time.

Neville Chamberlain

30 September 1938

'*Don't dance about on it, Winnie, you might fall through.*'

The ordinary civilian became dimly aware of the worsening international situation in 1935, when Italy invaded Abyssinia, successfully defying world opinion and the League of Nations. In the same year the British government issued its first circular to local authorities on Air Raid Precautions. In 1936 – when Germany openly defied the Treaty of Versailles by seizing the Rhineland and the Spanish Civil War began – rearmament began in earnest. In 1937 the first appeal for volunteers for the A.R.P. [Air Raid Precautions] services was broadcast, but by early 1938 few had come forward and their first exercises tended to be treated as something of a joke. Only in September, with the crisis over Czechoslovakia, did the public realise that war might break out at any moment.

16 February 1938 Great doings in Paddington last night. Mythical enemy bombers wrecked houses, ripped (in theory) fifteen foot craters in the road and sprayed the Borough with mustard gas. It was the first air raid demonstration conducted by a Borough Council in London and was designed to test the Air Raid Precautions service. Girls who had been 'burned' by mustard gas were rushed to the first-aid station in Paddington Central Baths. The first thing to do in such cases is to remove contaminated clothing. Two hundred people in the gallery saw nurses deprive girls of their clothes. The organisers had previously warned 'casualties' to wear bathing costumes underneath. Paddington has been divided into twelve areas for Air Raid Precautions work. In last night's scheme only six areas took part. Home Office inspectors commented – 'Not a bad show for a first effort'.   DAILY EXPRESS

When in the spring of 1938, Hitler moved into Austria, I found it impossible to resist making the small effort of protest that a private citizen could make. Lewis's [the Manchester department store, of which the future Lord Woolton was managing director] had . . . fourteen buyers in various parts of Germany. I cabled to them, telling them to close their books, honourably to fulfil all their contracts, and to return home. A few nights later, I took the occasion of a speech I was making at a Lewis's sales managers' dinner in Leicester, to express my personal alarm and disgust at what was happening and to say that I thought each one of us individually ought to do what he could to warn the people of Germany of the gravity of the position into which Hitler was leading them. I then announced that as far as Lewis's was concerned, we should proceed at once to sell all the

German goods that were in our stores and that we would have no further trading with German manufacturers whilst the German people continued to tolerate a Government that 'for no other reason than that of their faith persecuted one of the oldest races in the world'.

The effect of this speech, which lasted but a few minutes, surprised me. . . . It was not long before people were coming into the stores and asking if the goods they were considering buying were German; they were prepared to pay more for British goods, and many other retailers followed the same line of policy. For the first time, people were given the opportunity of registering a protest in a form that the Germans, apart from their Government, would understand. They did – and they were very angry about it, and months afterwards 'Lord Haw-Haw' threatened that Lewis's stores would be bombed out of existence. Lewis's sold out all their existing stock of German-made goods, regardless of cost. The public quickly came to refuse to buy German goods, and our lead was taken up not only here, but in the Dominions and the United States.

That Leicester speech made me realise how powerful was the latent feeling in the world about German atrocities. For months afterwards I was receiving press cuttings from overseas regarding it, and letters from people thanking me for having, in this practical form, raised a protest. . . .

But it was not all praise. I was sent to appear at Number Ten Downing Street, and there handed what is now colloquially called a 'high-powered rocket'. I was told that the Prime Minister strongly disapproved of my action and that I had no right to interfere in this manner in the foreign policy of the country. I remained respectfully unrepentant, and said that I should continue to exercise my rights to trade where I would, and to say what I thought. Many years afterwards, when the war was over, I received a most beautifully illuminated volume . . . from a Dutch Jew as a mark of his gratitude to me – a Christian – for this particular speech. The significance of the speech was not that Lewis's stopped trading with Germany, but that somebody in Britain expressed, in forthright language, what people were thinking and was prepared to take some risks in doing it.
LORD WOOLTON

The Munich Crisis in September 1938 provided the occasion for what turned out to be a dress rehearsal for the real outbreak of war. Among the

measures taken were the distribution of gas masks and urgent preparations
for evacuation — though only very few children actually moved from their
homes.

Our term [at the Mary Datchelor Girls School in Camberwell] began
on September 20th. The next day the news from Czecho-Slovakia was
very grave, and preparations began for the evacuation of London
children. A meeting of Heads was called at County Hall on September
22nd; and on Friday, September 23rd, as the bell was ringing for
afternoon school, the first batch of instructions arrived from County
Hall, together with hundreds of labels; and in that moment what had
seemed for weeks a remote, shadowy possibility became something
which might really happen.

The first thing we did was to send out invitations for a Parents'
Meeting on the following Monday, September 26th; and the speed
with which the Secretarial Sixth Form typed those notices and some of
the Staff folded them and put them into envelopes was a foretaste of
many similar 'combined operations' in the years to come.

I shall always remember . . . the wonderful atmosphere of trust and
co-operation which filled the Hall on that wet September night. The
Hall was crowded to the doors with mothers and fathers, till there was
hardly room on the platform for me to stand. . . . After I had described the . . . scheme, questions poured in from all parts of the Hall,
which we tried to answer. It was late when the meeting ended, with
a resolution of confidence passed with a spontaneous warmth and
enthusiasm which both overwhelmed and fortified us. As I shook
hands with parents that night, I realised not only the magnitude of the
task we were facing but the co-operation on which we could count in
undertaking it; and the inspiration of the evening helped us in many
difficult times. The absence of fuss and panic, the amazing trust in us,
the steady calm with which parents carried out all the arrangements
we planned, the courage and resource with which the Staff faced the
responsibilities so suddenly thrust upon them, the calmness and good
temper and gaiety with which the School made its plans and went
about its business . . . the confidence which we felt in the plan made
for us by the London County Council, and worked out down to its
smallest detail – all these things forged a new bond of trust
and understanding, not only between the members of the school
community, but also between us and the Authorities and between

Datchelor homes and the School. A year later that bond held – and it held firm all through the years that followed.

From that Monday night we lived in an atmosphere of lists, labels and luggage – lists of girls (about 500 of them) who were coming, lists of girls who were not coming, lists of more than 100 sisters and brothers ('attachments' as we called them later on) who were joining our party in order that all the children of a family might be together, lists of adults who were coming to help; and all these lists had to be altered almost hourly.

By Wednesday, September 28th, our party numbered something between 600 and 700. Things looked very black and the dramatic Debate in the House held out little hope of a peaceful solution.

On Thursday, September 29th, all the 'attachments' and the perishable food arrived and we could have gone off at half an hour's notice; but before Prayers we had word that we should not be going that day. We gave our visitors the opportunity of going back to their own schools, but this they firmly refused to do. So classes were invaded by small or large numbers of boys and girls, many of whom took an active part in the lesson; and a picnic lunch in the gymnasium went with a swing.

Late that night agreement was reached and we knew we should not have to go; so lists were filed, labels put away and luggage taken home. Normal school life began again . . . though some of the girls were heard to say that they 'didn't want a war, but would have liked to go away for about a fortnight and then come back'; and one member of the Junior School, in an article in the Magazine on 'The School Evakuashn', wrote 'On Wednesday they said we would go off on Thursday. On Thursday we went to School and they said we were not going. I was really sorry, I did want to go for one afternoon.'

When we did go, it was for nearly six years. M. DOROTHY BROCK

At three o'clock the next morning [Tuesday, 27 September] (an unheard of, not respectable, secret hour in Auburn) P.Y.C., [Margery Allingham's husband] got a telegram by phone. The message was very much to the point. . . .

It said 'Collect seven hundred gas-masks for your area and fit', and was signed 'A.R.P., Fishling'.

P.Y.C. got up dutifully and fetched out the car. Fishling is eight miles from Auburn [Auburn was, in fact, the village of Tolleshunt

D'Arcy in Essex] and . . . the next we heard of P.Y.C. was at noon, when he phoned in great haste to tell us to send a lorry, book the hall, and get a wireless loudspeaker down there. . . .

Bill, who is an ex-serviceman and lives by the pond, cut his afternoon's work and went off to Fishling with his lorry.

Late in the afternoon P.Y.C. returned from Fishling a little dazed. He had with him a few notes on the back of an envelope and a sample gas-mask, one of the seven hundred which Bill and Charlie the postman were unloading at the hall. . . .

P.Y.C.'s story was simple, and his problem rather startling. In Fishling, he said, the A.R.P. Office was performing miracles. Thousands of gas-masks were being assembled by volunteer labour. . . . Other volunteers were driving the things out to the villages and distribution centres in the town. The amount of work was tremendous and the strain terrific. One of their executives had fallen dead at his post at two in the morning. P.Y.C. had hung about getting all the information he could and had managed to get a short intensive course in gas from the A.R.P.O.'s [Air Raid Precaution Officer's] assistant, who had given him the information between incessant telephone calls.

We all went over the notes he had made. The salient factors were these: the masks were a complete protection to the face and lungs if properly put on, everybody ought to have one in the next twenty-four hours, the area of our operations was roughly five square miles, and there was nothing yet for babies. P.Y.C. added that the thing they had impressed upon him most was that there was to be no panic.

At first the problem appeared to present great difficulties. . . . However, we were wrong. From the beginning the entire operation went with astonishing smoothness. . . . Four hundred and fifty people out of six hundred of us turned up quietly to the village hall in the pouring rain at the appointed time, two hours after P.Y.C. came back, although the message was only passed round by word of mouth.

The hall, which is only a glorified army hut, has two main rooms, the smaller containing a billiard table. They put the masks on the table, and Albert's father and Charlie sorted them into the only two sizes we had – Large and Medium. Albert had got his big loudspeaker into position, and P.Y.C. and Sam, who had taken charge of the gathering, got everyone to listen to the Prime Minister's speech. . . .

After it was over P.Y.C. began to explain the more personal aspect of the gathering. . . . He and Sam were on the stage together in the big room and were framed in an exceedingly dusty and shabby red curtain. Immediately behind them was a dilapidated forest glade with a tear in the sky and scraps of paint flecking off all over it, while a single electric light bulb with a prosaic green shade hung indirectly over their heads. Between them was a very shaky card table and one small creaking chair. Sam sat on the chair and put on the gas-mask, while P.Y.C. did the talking. . . . Meanwhile the rest of us were letting people into the inner room, fifteen at a time, and fitting their masks. . . . All this time the rain was pouring down on the roof as if it had come from a hose, and there was the problem of how to take the things home through the lanes without getting them wet. People went hurrying away with them clasped to their bosoms like puppies under their coats. . . .

All the [next] morning the 'shopkeeping' at the hall went on. Some of the more frail elderly ladies who had not felt up to joining the scrum the night before came in with embroidered shopping bags and bent their sleek little grey heads meekly for the rubber monstrosities and asked very gently for a good recipe for getting mustard gas off the skin.   MARGERY ALLINGHAM

1939

It is reported from Oslo that the Norwegian Nobel Committee
has decided not to award a peace prize for 1939.

Newspaper Report, November 1939

'But apart from this, life is going on just the same as usual.'

*Although war was averted by the Munich agreement, which gave Hitler all
he had demanded without making him fight for it, buying off the Germans
proved no more successful than buying off the Danes a thousand years
before. After Germany had occupied the whole of Czechoslovakia in
March 1939, no one except the astrologers and the* Daily Express, *which
both predicted that there would be no war, really believed that the peace
could be saved. The year gained by Munich – assuming in fact that Hitler
would have attacked then had the democracies stood up to him –was not, as
is often said, wasted. Although rearmament remained painfully slow,
strengthening the nation's passive defences was a main part of the government's policy, and A.R.P. went rapidly ahead.*

SMALL CHILDREN'S RESPIRATOR
INSTRUCTIONS FOR PUTTING ON

To put the respirator onto a child:

1.   Stand the child in front of you with its back towards you so that its
head rests against your body.

2.   See that the hook and eye on the head harness straps are undone.
Put your left thumb under the bottom and middle straps on the left
side of the head harness, and your right thumb under the bottom and
middle straps on the right side, and hang the respirator from your two
thumbs.

3.   Catch the chin of the respirator under the child's chin and then
stretch the head harness over the head.

4.   See that the respirator is straight on the child's face and that the
chin is properly in position. Then join the hook and eye on the two
bottom straps to secure the respirator in place.

NOTE: Most children quickly learn to put on the respirator themselves. They should be taught to do it in the way described above.

ANTI-GAS PROTECTION OF BABIES AND YOUNG CHILDREN, *1939*

*In May 1939 the well-known travel writer, H.V. Morton, set out to take
his last look at England in peacetime.*

I thought I would go and look at the house, now called Quebec House,
where Wolfe lived when he was a boy. It belongs to the National
Trust, and is shown to the public on three days in the week. It stands a
few yards out of the town [Westerham], at the bottom of the hilly road
leading to Sevenoaks, a dignified mansion of Kent brick, with three
gables and three storeys . . .

The door was opened by a middle-aged lady in a cheerful chintz overall . . . We were joined by a second lady in middle age, and also in a chintz overall, and before long the three of us were good friends, and I was shown many rooms in the Wolfe mansion which are not usually open to visitors. . . .

Having shown me all the Wolfe treasures in Quebec House, the two ladies took me into a room which was probably the old kitchen. It has an immense fireplace in which you could roast an ox. Looking up the chimney, I saw that it had been boarded, and I said that no doubt this had been done to stop the draught.

'Oh no,' said one cheerfully. 'That's not the reason why we boarded it up. This is our gas-proof room. You see it has a stone floor and stone walls, and we were told by the A.R.P. that this is the best room in the house for the purpose. We have to make the windows absolutely gas-proof too.'

I came back from the savage age of Wolfe to our own civilised era and looked with interest at the first gas-proof room I had seen. It seemed utterly preposterous that the two charming ladies in chintz overalls should in the year 1939 be preparing to save themselves from poison gas. I wondered what Wolfe, who was always very outspoken on military matters, would have said could he have known the true significance of the boarded chimney in the kitchen at Westerham.
H.V. MORTON

As war drew closer A.R.P. exercises became more frequent and – in intention at least – more realistic.

We were having a grand-scale Civil Defence exercise in Chelsea. It was June 19th, 1939. . . .

Mrs Freeth, my housekeeper, and I had both been given our parts to play. I was to be a casualty, she was to take shelter on a piece of pavement marked with white-painted lines to indicate that here (when built) would be the air-raid shelter for our area. . . .

The exercise was timed for twelve noon, and Mr Harold Scott, the Commissioner for Police, had ordered that all traffic should be stopped for fifteen minutes – it was said that he himself would be present. Friends who had trained with me in first-aid and who were acting as wardens appeared for the first time in uniforms. They caused a lot of ribald comment. Brown overalls with A.R.W. [Air Raid

Warden] in yellow on the breast pocket brought jeers from many onlookers. The uniforms, mass produced, did not fit – and some of the women's seats were on a level with their knees. I felt sorry for some of my friends with trim, neat figures having to appear in public in them.

The sirens wailed – the anguished lament of a soul in torment – and we all took up our positions with combined grumbling and that fear of ridicule ingrained in us all. It *did* seem ridiculous to have to lie flat on a piece of marked pavement pretending to be a casualty, but it seemed to me that to do so was the easiest way out of an argument as to whether I was to be in the First-Aid Post or in the Control Report Centre in the Town Hall, I having taken the training for both. Mrs Freeth, worried about some special dish in the oven, thought it a ridiculous way of wasting a morning. She had Vicki, my dachshund, in her arms, being determined that if the dog couldn't stand there with her in the allotted space she wouldn't stand there either. It was a point on which our warden was not prepared to argue. Whether dogs or cats would be allowed in shelters he was unable to say, but to Mrs Freeth's argument that as the shelter wasn't yet built Vicki had just as much right to stand on the pavement as she had there was no answer. . . .

At the given signal I lay down on the pavement awaiting the attention of my fellow V.A.D.s in the Mobile Unit. . . .

I could just see Mrs Freeth and Vicki standing patiently in the imaginary air-raid shelter. Vicki was frantic because I was lying on the pavement, which she thought suspicious to say the least of it. The First Aid Party arrived. My leg (broken in two places) was strapped. My wounds were bandaged with many giggles and much chaffing, and I was taken in charge to await an imaginary ambulance. Vicki's struggles became so frantic when she saw me being tied up that Mrs Freeth called out that she had better take her home. 'Stay where you are, the raid is still on,' shouted an authoritative warden. Mrs Freeth and Vicki stayed. Ambulance bells clanged, whistles blew, fire engines raced, rattles sounded – it was absolutely maddening not to be able to see what was happening. Only one eye was left free of bandages and my lowly position made visibility poor. The flurry of violent activity went on in the deathly silence of the traffic-less streets. Comments, some jocose, some ribald, some angry, were being freely exchanged all round us. 'Lot of tommy-rot, won't be no air raids here. All this silly play-acting', I heard fellow-casualties grumbling.
FRANCES FAVIELL

On 21 August Germany announced that she was about to sign a non-aggression pact with Russia. During the next few days the armed forces were mobilised. On Friday 1 September evacuation began. Among the thousands of schools affected was Dulwich College Preparatory School, the headmaster of which had enterprisingly built a camp for his pupils on land belonging to a relation.

At last, on 31st August, we were told that the next day was our zero hour. . . . The school was provided with a large banner embroidered with P 246 in large letters, and I and other members of the staff had imposing arm bands emblazoned in the same way. . . .

Next morning we stood-to at 8.30. The children were divided into their various groups, each with a member of the staff in charge and were told to keep in their group whatever happened. . . . I then addressed all the fond parents telling them that the way in which they could be of the greatest assistance would be to go away at once. This they very nobly agreed to do, and after the boys had given three cheers for their parents and the parents had given a somewhat forlorn answering cheer they moved off and we were left to our long vigil. . . . Hour followed hour of intolerable waiting. . . . At last, just before 6 pm, the messenger arrived telling us that we were entraining at West Dulwich station at 6.35 pm.

. . . I went first, armed with tin hat, army respirator, arm band, first-aid haversack and a large megaphone. Immediately behind, borne on poles by two of the bigger boys, was our banner P 246, and behind came the children with their suitcases, haversacks and gas masks, each hut group marching beside its master or mistress.

Once in the train we all sat back with a sigh of enormous relief. The strain of entertaining 135 boys from five to thirteen-and-a-half years throughout all those long hours had been terrific and, excellent as the children's behaviour had been, the younger ones were getting rather fractious towards the end of the long day. The train gave us all a respite and we felt that something at last was happening. On we went, rather slowly because we were following a very intricate time-table and had to make a cross-country journey through Sevenoaks to Tonbridge and Paddock Wood. By the time we got to Paddock Wood it was dark and had started to rain. Eventually, well after nine o'clock, we pulled into Cranbrook station. Here it was that the hut system came into its own. We found on arrival that we had come in for the

first blackout in Britain. Cranbrook station was three miles from the
camp and the only transport we had was my father-in-law's Morris,
my own Triumph, which Muff [J.H. Leakey's wife] was driving, and
a large lorry which had been used that day for evacuating sheep from
Romney Marsh. The owners had not had time to clean it! Matters
were made more difficult by the fact that the train was too long for
Cranbrook station and the driver kept puffing up and down in a
distracted manner trying to find somewhere the boys could get off on a
siding.

The children at last managed to get decanted into the pitch black
amid pelting rain, and I started to get some sort of order. Flashing my
torch and screaming 'Hut 7, come to me,' I got the small children off,
packed with their teachers, in the odoriferous sheep lorry. Next I got
the smallest hut into the two cars packed four deep and the remainder,
mostly bigger boys, started marching down the road on their three
mile trek. The van and cars ran a shuttle service and picked up a hut
group at a time on the road so that eventually only a few of the bigger
boys had to walk more than two miles. We finally arrived at the camp
to find more difficulties. The police had descended on Muff and her
helpers and told them that, as we had no blackout, on no account were
any lights to be used. After a tremendous amount of trouble they
allowed us to have one small hurricane lamp in each hut and two in the
dining hut. We managed to give the exhausted children, who had
been on the go for nearly fourteen hours, a hot meal and finally dossed
them down on their straw palliasses and blankets. By 11 pm they were
all bedded and fast asleep.   J.H. LEAKEY

*All told one and a half million 'official' evacuees left the cities in the first
few days of September, plus an unknown number of people travelling under
their own arrangements. This was by far the largest such movement of the
whole war.*

A few days before the war was declared my parents told me I was to be
evacuated; plucked from our small and ordinary house slumbering
behind dusty privet in Muswell Hill and dispatched to the alien
countryside. I received the news with indifference. How was I
to know that I was never again to live within its semi-detached
walls? . . .

I was nine years old, nearly ten. . . . One night we went up to town to see *Band Wagon*. When we left the the theatre the sky was crowded with searchlights, sprinkled with stars. Paper sellers' voices were hoarse with the crisis and troops were cushioning a building with sandbags.

Next day they labelled me, addressed me and packed me off to the country.

I paraded with the other children from Tollington School outside Hornsey station as heavily loaded as a soldier in full marching kit. A gas mask in a white tin box stuffed with sticky plaster, anti-burn cream and iodine pulled me down one side: a haversack crammed with sandwiches and apples balanced me on the other. Brown paper parcels hung from my belt like grenades – emergency sandwiches, spare socks if my feet got wet, a mackintosh cape, a slab of chocolate. In my pocket were labels displaying my school, home address and destination; in one hand I carried a brown suitcase containing clothes, in the other a wad of comics.

It was a restless morning, full of haze and expectation. . . . We wrenched ourselves from loving hands to scuffle and punch, flattening opponents with a swing of a parcel or a buffet with a gas mask case: mothers admonished us with unexpected patience and chatted to each other in strained tight phrases. . . .

The carriages were Victorian, gold-lettered first, second and third class, windows streaked and stained yellow, seats hard and narrow. Above the seats in wooden picture frames, straw-bonneted girls strolled seaside promenades with white-flannelled young men.

Our teachers . . . marshalled us into queues and classes. Mothers sidled alongside, tying knots, straightening caps, tucking loops of hair beneath peaks. . . .

'Look after yourself, darling,' my mother said. 'Don't forget to eat your sandwiches . . . And don't forget to send that card as soon as you can.'

"All right,' I said, feeling the stamped, addressed card already smeared with chocolate. 'I won't forget.'

She had a handkerchief in her hand now; so did some of the other mothers as the queues shuffled towards the carriages. The mistresses fed us into compartments and the doors closed. I had a last glimpse of the mothers, some already walking away with heads bowed, some waving handkerchiefs, mine with handkerchief pressed to her face. There was a sudden thrust of pain, a blade parting flesh, a momentary appreciation of fireside security and maternal love, and then steam curtained the window.

When I next looked out of the window we were approaching another suburb and the boy next to me was trying to steal my chocolate.

They took us by bus from the station at Abbotsley, Huntingdonshire, to the school hall. There pyramids of buns, bottles of fizzy lemonade and worried groups of foster mothers awaited us. . . .

With a dark leggy boy called Kenneth Francis – an ancient enemy – I was led away by a sadly pretty housewife with pale cheeks and straight hair . . . to a council house clean and scented with the varnish smells of new furniture and hot-pot cooking.

That evening Kenneth and I, briefly at peace, walked up the long vegetable garden and sat in a sloping field of clover. There we rolled and shouted, sucked the honeyed petals of clover, embraced the countryside and sneered at the soiled grassland we had left behind.

We walked down a lane between hedges loaded with blackberries and garlanded with bryony. Beneath the hedges the ditches were choked with twigs, leaves, brambles, mist and hedgehogs. The lane led to a stream where tiny fish darted and trembled in hollows pressed in the mud by cattle hooves, where water boatmen skated and wild irises grew and – or so it was said – a kingfisher sprinted through the evening air.

We raced a few twigs, tested the leaks in our wellingtons, made a dam, stoned a long-dead water rat. When we turned to walk back along the lane it was crowded with hostile animals. They chewed and lowed and lowered their horns and walked remorselessly towards us . . . .

Suddenly the white council house was remote, the country cruel, home the other side of the world . . . .

We went to strange beds and lay with fists clenched. Our toes found tepid hot water bottles and our fingers silk bags of old lavender inside the pillows. An owl hooted, wings brushed the window. I remembered the London sounds of distant trains and motor cycles, the creaking limbs of the mountain ash, next door's dog, the droning radio, the fifth stair groaning and the ten-thirty throat clearing; I remembered the familiar wallpaper where you could paddle a canoe through green rapids or drive a train along sweeping cuttings, a shadow like a nose on the ceiling and the curve of the bedstead rail which had seemed as permanent as evening cocoa.

We sobbed in awful desolation but never again mentioned those first war tears to each other.

Our foster parents took their new duties seriously. They were God-fearing, clean and healthy, and they led us in the ways of godliness, cleanliness and good health.

Mr Storey was young and strong, with glistening dark hair, sinewed forearms and reserves of patience as deep as the village pond. He wore dark blue overalls, worked as a mechanic and played cricket every summer Saturday. . . .

Sometimes Mr Storey took us on a rabbit shoot with his friends and a black and white clown of a dog called Toby. . . .

Mrs Storey did her best to warm the strangeness around us and prevent the bouts of night-time despair. She was gentle and worried and, like my mother, had dietary remedies for all ills. They all originated in the garden – in bags of mint, wafers of onion, rubbings of chives, sniffs of rosemary and lavender. But her real panacea was a full belly. And the first return of vague security centred around heaps of garden potatoes, garden carrots and garden parsnips almost hiding the meat of the rabbit. . . .

Another factor which charmed us into accepting our new way of life was sanitation. There was no chain, no cistern: it was hardly credible, rather disgusting, decidedly intriguing.

We had to walk out into the frosted night to find the toilet; the wooden seat was icy. . . . Late at night we saw Mr Storey journeying to the end of the garden. At first we suspected him of poaching, burying loot, or signalling to the enemy from the clover field. Later we found that he was merely emptying night soil from the shed – hence the fat yield of tomatoes. . . .

The bath was made of galvanised iron and hung by day from a peg in the kitchen . . . Mrs Storey, aproned and anxious, spouted torrents of steaming water into the bath. . . .

'Shall I wash you down?' she asked doubtfully. 'What did your mums do?'

'My mother washed me,' I said.

'And mine,' said Kenneth.

'Oh.'

The three of us looked desperately at each other for a moment.

'But I think I can manage,' I said.

'And me.' Kenneth said.

'Oh, well, I'll leave you to get on with it,' she said.

Relief all round.

DEREK LAMBERT

Not every foster-parent proved equally welcoming, especially when the expected air raids failed to materialise. This was the start of what became known as the 'phoney war', when in the West nothing seemed to be happening. Already a drift back of evacuees to the cities was beginning.

I was fourteen when war broke out, and was a pupil at Bolling High School, Bradford, Yorkshire. On Friday 1st September 1939 I was evacuated with a body of teachers and schoolfellows to Nelson, Lancashire. . . .

My bosom friend and I thought ourselves very fortunate indeed to be – eventually – (around 8 pm) billeted together at the T—— homestead. Mrs T. was nearly seventy-three (she had her birthday during our brief stay, this is how I remember), her husband a year or so older. . . . Very soon the 'phoney war' . . . together with our demanding appetites and tiresome loquaciousness (J. and I were members of the Labour League of Youth whilst Mrs T. had always been – as she repeatedly, pugnaciously, informed us – 'true blue'), wore down what feelings of goodwill and protectiveness that lady might have borne towards us, so that one day when we returned from the local grammar school there was a note on the kitchen table in the deserted house: 'Both girls to pack and go to Mrs D., —— Road, Nelson.' Not without difficulty, for even in a month two adolescent girls can collect much 'clobber', we dragged ourselves and our possessions over a mile to Mrs D's modest property. In response to our knocking she opened and glared around the door: 'I don't want you! I'd like you to go away! But I suppose you'll have to come in! But I don't like it!' Mrs D., a lady of sixty-seven, and a childless widow, had apparently, through possessing a vacant bedroom, been *commandeered* by the billeting officer to offer succour to the two refugee Bradfordians whom Mrs T. . . . had been obliged to reject. Mrs D. gave us a late high tea of pearl barley and carrots, all the time reiterating: 'I don't want you, you know! Two growing girls! I can't be bothered at my age! It wouldn't trouble me if you both ran away tomorrow.' I still think she quite consciously put the idea into our heads.

Accordingly, the following day, leaving all our luggage behind, we 'ran away', or, rather, walked away (having 3½d. between us) in the vague direction of Bradford, 32 miles distant. We wrote what we considered highly dignified letters of farewell explaining our predicament and conduct to the evacuation authorities and our German language teacher, who had been evacuated with us and who was our form mistress. (She never spoke to either of us again.) Eleven footsore miles out of Nelson we got a lift on a Bradford-bound lorry from a cheery driver who, fortunately, was not a rapist. A couple of hours later we burst in on our startled parents; we none of us realised the furore our unconventional departure was to cause. . . . I later wrote to a boy I knew in Nelson – he had . . . lent us a road map – describing our homeward journey in somewhat colourful terms. The boy's father was a reporter on the *Burnley Express* . . . and the whole letter was subsequently printed in this paper under the headline 'Two Little Girls from School'. This all infuriated the education and evacuation people. Both J's and my own mother later visited Mrs D. to collect our luggage; that lady, who must have gone through a disturbing time, was now effusive about us – 'two such lovely girls!' and entertained the mothers by playing *Tales from the Vienna Woods* on the pianola and giving them potted meat sandwiches.   PAT CROSS

In expectation of an immediate flood of air raid casualties, the great London hospitals were largely cleared of patients and most of the staff were evacuated to the country.

I had started my training to become a State Registered Nurse in the West London Hospital, Hammersmith, and had completed just nine months of my training when war was declared.

What excitement was in the air! Immediate evacuation to the country – where we knew not. We were placed in charge of the Sister Tutor. The double-decker London buses were put to good use and so we said our farewells. 25 lbs. of luggage, no more, was the warning. These, I'm afraid, were idle words, and so we staggered out with bundles, wireless sets, and suitcases, that looked as though they would never make the journey!

1939

We arrived at a large mental hospital in Hampshire (in fact it was Park Prewett Hospital, Basingstoke) about lunchtime. Great confusion everywhere. We certainly were not expected, and nowhere was prepared for us. After spending the afternoon in the bus, it was decided to find somewhere for us to sleep. All dormitories and corridors seemed crammed but at last a corridor was found and this was our home. . . . Our furniture consisted of a bed and chair only. About fifteen nurses in our corridor and somehow one managed to keep more or less with one's pals.

The dining hall was the scene of much activity – rows and rows of nurses and still more queues and queues waiting to be fed. We were all allocated to different wards. The poor Sisters in charge had no idea which nurses belonged to her ward as we were all from different hospitals. Hundreds and hundreds of nurses and not a single patient.

Our days were spent in making dressings, cleaning, and learning how to use primus stoves (for sterilisation). When not doing these things we were engaged in making and eating stacks of dripping toast. Most of the hospital rules were broken. Windows that only opened two inches were the entry and exit of many nurses. The toilet facilities left much to be desired, no bolts on the lavatory doors and always company when having a bath as there were two baths to every bathroom. Keys were used instead of taps and these, I regret to say, were often taken half way through running a bath, and then, behold, a flooded bathroom and no one to own it.

When we first arrived, no blackout was prepared, so it was straight to bed after coming off duty, or out (of course against orders). Dances were given, and frowned on by the senior sisters in charge of the various hospitals. Most of the London hospital students, as well as nurses, were in residence at the hospital and the 'local' was the scene of much activity. Several of the students arrived there by various 'invalid carriages', some of which had to be seen to be believed.

Much bother was caused by the students changing the signposts to the opposite direction which, of course, led to much confusion – and bitter words by the local police, but as these same 'brave lads' had helped to fill sandbags at the local police station all was forgiven.
BEATRICE JOBBINS

We sat around, a rather dazed group of men and women who had been hustling for two days to obscure purpose, just enrolled in a service [the

Ambulance Service] about which we knew almost nothing, waiting for we knew not what. It was a lovely house, Whistler's house on Chelsea Embankment, with the four big chimneys of the power station dominating the view, but we hadn't a radio. Our Commandant came in, very reliable and very beautiful; a reassuring combination. She said:

'I don't know if you've heard the news. The Germans have marched into Poland. I should think we'll be for it any time now.' . . .

There was . . . a rather solemn feeling during the last few days before the war and the first few days after it started, of:

> *Look your last on all things lovely*
> *Every hour*

People looked with extraordinary attention upon familiar sights; the sun on a pane of glass, the towers of Westminster. Everybody has some vivid irrelevant picture; with one it is dinner at the Zoo just before the invasion of Poland, and the magic effect of flood-light on the rose flamingoes; with me it is sitting under the mulberry tree in Whistler's garden, to watch the dawn, with all the swans in the world gathered on the river. The most inarticulate people, bus drivers, demolition men, would actually mention beauty; didn't the barrage balloons look kind of nice, silver and gold in the sky with the sun on them; had one been to Hampton Court because that did take some beating. We believed that everything we had known was going to be wiped out.   THEODORA BENSON

Among the early casualties of the war was the infant television service.

The morning of Friday, 1 September, 1939, found me in a rehearsal-room in a mews off Marylebone High Street, extremely occupied with Somerset Maugham's play *The Circle*, which I was to produce for television on the following Sunday. It was my first production of a full-length play in the new medium, and I was proportionately nervous and excited. But I fear that neither my mind nor the minds of the excellent cast were altogether on the considerable problems implied by work in front of a dummy television camera. . . . I doubt if any member of our little group had started *The Circle* rehearsals with much conviction of actually performing the play on 3 September. None the less, the shock was considerable when just about noon I was called to the telephone, informed that Alexandra Palace was closing down, and instructed that the B.B.C. 'emergency period' had begun. I had just put down the receiver when an office messenger arrived with various 'properties' for the play, including two tennis racquets and a number of balls. I have occasionally wondered what happened to those racquets and balls – if they were ever collected from Marylebone Mews, or if they remain there to this day, forgotten relics of a dead world.

For me, as for many others connected with Broadcasting, the announcement of the 'emergency period' implied an immediate change of base. The B.B.C. was by no means unprepared for war and . . . on the assumption that London would, immediately after war was declared, be deluged with bombs . . . most of the programme divisions were . . . to be scattered about the country. And my own department – together with the recently recruited Repertory Company – was booked for Evesham, at that time referred to only under bated breath as 'Hogsnorton'. . . .

The months spent at Evesham were not happy ones. No doubt there were many admirable technical reasons for the choice of the place and of the actual houses in which our work was done. But they were not obvious to the harassed programme official, deafened by typewriters operated upon parquet floors; nor to the wild-eyed producer trying to cope with the peculiar acoustic qualities of metamorphosed stables and billiard-rooms, and the vagaries of hastily wired studios. . . .

Not that the house lacked its picturesque qualities. Originally the property of a former Pretender to the throne of France, its walls were hung with deep blue liberally sown with *fleurs-de-lis*. Indeed, the royal device was everywhere – even on the bath-plugs and the weathervane. There was a large and rambling garden, including a bear-pit; a drive lined with noble trees, appropriate rather to coaches and curricles than to the bicycles to which we had all, willy-nilly, to resort; and lawns with a superb prospect south and west, on which, one felt, peacocks should have paced and spread their tails, rather than actors frowning over scripts. It was, of course, before the days of the Home Guard, but a rumour of sabotage intended by the I.R.A. constrained us to a system of nightly patrols of the grounds. Clad most uncomfortably in heavy mackintoshes and sou'westers, and armed with huge wooden clubs, which we could hardly lift, we would squelch through the shrubberies at intervals during the night. We must have been audible about a mile away, and in the face of any professional mischief-maker our armament would have been about as useful as an arquebus. But the proceedings . . . gave us a very necessary reminder in our retreat that there was a war on, however 'phoney'. While starlight over the river, and the displays of searchlights wheeling and flaring away to the north, combined with the days of an Indian summer to insist that all beauty had not died with the end of the old world.   VAL GIELGUD

Saturday, 2 September 1939 12 o'clock. As I write this there is raging outside a terrific storm, almost continuous lightning and thunder. Nature is providing the finishing touches to these poignant, horrible days. The waiting, listening to news bulletins every hour, the instructions for complete blackout at nights, general mobilisation yesterday – khaki-clad boys everywhere – the speeded up evacuation of 3,000,000 children and invalids from the cities, all these things have come to us – a supposedly civilised people. Warsaw has been bombed, German tanks and aeroplanes have been shot down and war is once more striding across our world. This storm makes one feel that perhaps God is wishful of reminding us that our little wars are as nothing compared with his awful power, but it is too late now, we are too deeply immersed in it. I am to go on duty at the local Report Centre for eight hours tomorrow – so I'll be working with the rest of 'em I suppose – though sitting in a cellar waiting for the raids we all dread is a funny way of 'doing one's bit'. I'm less likely, however, to be a coward if I have something definite to do. The blackness in the streets is so strange, one feels that one must be quiet and secret all the time and walk upon one's toes. . . . Here's the storm again, tearing its way across the sky above us – I wish it would stop and we could have some sleep, as we should be able to do, without fear of raids for tonight at any rate.   VIVIENNE HALL

Neville Chamberlain announced the declaration of war in a broadcast at 11.15 am on Sunday, 3 September. Immediately afterwards the air-raid warning was sounded.

We were using an underground studio [in Broadcasting House], as the rule was for a 'state of emergency'; and the only sirens we could hear were the B.B.C.'s internal ones. We could hear nothing else. They were the loudest, most ear-tearing, most soul-lacerating things I have ever heard . . . there was one every few yards along all the corridors. . . . As you passed, each siren seemed to scream like a dog in hysteria, as if it had some inside premonition of destruction and were bounding and shaking itself to get free. They lasted the regulation two minutes, also; and by the time they had died down, there was a groove cut in your brain that could hold nothing in the subsequent silence but din.

. . . I proceeded to the Concert Hall. The instructions were that everyone in the building was to go straight to this huge chamber in the middle of it as soon as the sirens sounded. We found a large assemblage there, all festooned with gas-mask cases, and sat down in the comfortable stalls. Familiar faces appeared in curious A.R.P. disguises. The House Superintendent stepped forward and asked all those sitting under the balcony to come forward, as the balcony was structurally unsuited to air raids. This caused a ripple of amusement and people went on talking quietly. Nobody showed any signs of nervousness. By and by we began to hear bangs and bumps, some loud, some more distant. My neighbours began to discuss direction, but couldn't agree. We wondered what it would be like if we had to sit with gas-masks on. . . .

The bangs and bumps continued; and I realised that I had no knowledge on which to speculate how loud a bomb should sound, if I heard it. . . . I had no idea whether what I was hearing was being concentrated on the Thames docks, or whether on leaving the building I would find Portland Place a mass of rubble.

After what seemed hours, the 'Raiders Passed' was sounded; and those going off duty were allowed to leave the building. Outside all appeared normal and untouched. There was the little car waiting for me in the middle of the road. I got in and started towards Regent's Park.

There were several barrage balloons in the sky. . . . We were very proud of our own particular protector, which swung almost over our block of flats on the north side of Regent's Park.

It was a lovely sunny day, with blue sky and a few white clouds. As I faced up the street I sensed the beauty of it, and the illogicality of destruction and pain and fear on such a day. Then my inside turned to water. The balloon on the other side of the Park was black, not silver. . . . Anticipation told me that the fire and smoke from our destroyed home had been so great that even the high balloon had been blackened and singed. Imagination told the rest. I stamped on the accelerator.

Inside the park I overtook a lady driving a baby Austin. There was nothing else on the road. For some reason I felt she was a woman doctor. I was doing over fifty, but she kept parallel with me. Neck and neck we raced round the Outer Circle until she shot out at Hanover Gate. I decided she was trying to get somewhere before someone died from loss of blood. . . . For my part, I kept on, peering through the trees for feared signs. All was still normal.

And the flats were still normal; and my home was still normal, and when I asked my wife if she had been scared, she said:

'Scared? I nearly died of laughing.'

'Laughing?' I said.

'Yes,' she said. 'There was a little man selling Sunday papers over by the railings; and when the sirens went, he made a dash across the road toward the shelter, and then dashed back toward the railings and swithered in the middle of the road whether to leave his papers and save his life or save his papers and lose his life.'

It was not long before we learned it had been a false alarm . . . and I can only suppose that the bumps and bangs were the shuttings of different doors and the balloon was in the shadow of a cloud. Both were lessons I never forgot. JOSEPH MACLEOD

I had just left school [at the age of sixteen] in July and had obtained a job at Bulmer's Cider Works as a junior clerk. . . . I started there, oddly enough, on the 4th September, at fifteen shillings a week. . . . On the 3rd September we were all in bed drinking tea and someone switched on the wireless and we heard Chamberlain announce war was declared. My immediate reaction was to get dressed up in my Sunday best: smart, blue edge-to-edge coat and matching blue and white dress with dirndl waist, navy shoes, bag and gloves and blue beret. Off I went out into the High Street. I stood like a fool on the edge of the pavement waiting for the soldiers to march off to war. You see, I had seen films of the 1914–18 war and heard and read of the fond goodbyes and romance of the lads going to war, of every girl looking her best and trying to be brave and naturally thought the men would be marching through Hereford streets and the brass band would be leading – great excitement.

Nothing happened. A few people passed looking worried, a few were coming home from church, otherwise the streets were literally deserted. Oh, I thought, they are at the station, so off I tripped to the main line station to wave goodbye. Arrived at the station – nobody there – no soldiers, not even any trains – nothing. I cried all the way home. My relations thought I was upset about the declaration. . . . In fact I was crying because the glamour of war, as I had seen it on film, wasn't true and someone had lied.   JEAN DENHOLM

The war rapidly emptied the universities of most of their male students. To keep his former pupils in touch with what was happening in Cambridge the senior tutor of Trinity College, Cambridge, began a series of regular letters to them.

8 September 1939   We have sent away some of the more important pictures and books; the Porters' Lodge at the Great Gate is strutted and sandbagged as our chief Wardens' Post, cellars in Whewell's and Nevile's Courts have been made into quite good shelters, and something is being done to the cellar under Hall, which isn't so good for the purpose but will serve at a pinch; as it contains a good deal of beer some may even prefer it. We started with a false alarm of a raid some days before war began. This was due to a warden in Chesterton switching on the siren instead of switching off the electric light, but he stopped soon enough not to cause me (at any rate) to get out of bed. On Sunday, the first day, there was a real alarm . . . which blasted me out of bed at 2.45 and there have been others since. They have been tiresome, but not useless, for they have given us an opportunity of seeing defects in our arrangements which may presently be useful. The College Wardens take it in turn to be primarily responsible and my hours are 11 to 2 at night. I go to bed, but have disposed at hand clothes suitable to the purpose and can get to my post in about three minutes with my gas-mask, a tin hat (much too small and very uncomfortable, but there is a shortage of larger sizes) and in my pocket a copy of the *Inferno*, which seemed a suitable book for reading while waiting for something to happen.   A.S.M. GOW

We didn't stay long at Whistler's house with the garden and the mulberry tree on Chelsea Embankment. Our job was to drive stretcher-bearers to incidents, and we were drafted to Civil Defence

Depots. At first Depot 1 was a vast furniture repository, hideously cold and uncomfortable, a tall, concrete building with stone floors, fantastically adorned at one end of the great main hall on the ground floor with some theatre scenery in storage of a musical comedy rose garden.

We expected the raids at once. The drivers slept, men and women, in their clothes, ready to jump up, on mattresses in a stone passage, rather unfortunately ventilated by holes just three inches from the floor. Every morning we thought with wonder: 'Another night, we've got through another night.' We expected to feel rather flurried when things happened, because we weren't trained, and were still mugging up first-aid and the whereabouts of every smallest street in Chelsea, and getting used to night driving in blackout. . . .

One of the doctors who gave us a first-aid lecture sticks in my mind as a very reassuring man. The lecture was frighteningly illustrated with coloured pictures passed round; blue asphyxia was particularly arresting. He had really faced up to the fact that one didn't go about with a cork on one for putting between the teeth of epileptics, nor even necessarily a strong knife for cutting down suicides by hanging. We all agreed that we should attack first-aid with far more fortitude and less flurry because of his line, that we'd probably have no luck with it, anyway.

'Man unconscious with gas escaping. Well, naturally, you're supposed to turn it off at the main, but of course you won't be able to find the main . . . You're pretty well obliged to try artificial respiration for a longish time; it doesn't really matter what method you use, as it's almost sure to do no good, but Schaeffer's is recommended. . . .'

We drank innumerable cups of tea, smoked endless cigarettes (there were plenty then) and got to know each other. . . . The drivers were well-to-do people who could contribute their own cars before the Borough got round to providing any, the stretcher-bearers were all sorts, the officers were mostly tradesmen. We . . . had never mingled our lives so intimately, and it widened all our horizons. A little man with a very cockney accent said to me after a ping-pong tournament that he'd always known 'gentlemen' were all right and just like him, but had never felt it before. . . .

For a long time we were waiting eagerly for casualties. Our first was a drunkard who lost his way home in the dark on a fine quiet night and fell down the steps of a public lavatory. Our next was an aggressive stranger in a pub, whom a group of us there had got round to hating till he smashed a glass with an emphatic gesture and cut his hand. Never was such eager competition to help a human being and practise our first-aid.

After the bitter cold first winter we got moved across the road to more comfortable quarters, a big school in parts of which Ambulance people and nurses and the Rescue, Shoring, and Demolition men were already installed. The R.S.D. men added a new element, though we didn't see so much of them as the squads we were actually to drive. For some reason they were a much tougher crowd than the stretcher-bearers, with a lower average of education; talkative enough, but not really so articulate; noisy, friendly, and cheerful, singing and shouting at breakfast while the rest of us looked sour. . . . They always seemed strong and well and hearty. After one had been kissed by all the R.S.D. under the mistletoe at a Christmas or New Year dance one really needed a face pack.   THEODORA BENSON

A number of men joined the Auxiliary Fire Service on the outbreak of war when their own jobs disappeared. The anonymous author of The Bells Go Down *had previously worked in a film studio.*

During our exercises last week we had sheet jumping. This was the first time I'd done it. . . .

We went down on the tender to a training centre somewhere in the north of London, and there in the middle of a yard was a tower some fifty feet high. We had to climb up the tower one after another and jump first from ten feet and then twenty feet into the sheet.

The slogan is: 'If you don't want to do it again, don't look down. . . .' In other words the correct way of doing the jump is to walk off the tower looking straight in front of you. . . .

It is a very strange sensation and when you land in the sheet it doesn't hurt a bit. As soon as it is over you feel wonderfully excited, and almost as if you'd had a number of quick, strong drinks.

As I was sailing earthwards . . . I remembered childish nightmares in which I'd been falling, and I can honestly say that the nightmares were far more frightening than the real thing.

After the sheet-jumping we had hook-ladder exercises. . . . With the aid of two hook ladders, two firemen can scale the face of a building in a few minutes. Some of the champions . . . can do six floors in one minute, so I was told. *THE BELLS GO DOWN*

Nothing caused more ill-feeling between the public and the wardens and police than enforcement of the blackout, which had begun on Friday 1 September.

I became involved with the police the day after war was declared . . . I had moved [with a Civil Service department] from Whitley Bay to Newcastle-on-Tyne four days before, taking possession of my new flat on the Monday evening after business. When I went to turn the light on the merest glimmer appeared from the electric bulbs. The Electricity Department had switched my 210 voltage to 105. The blackout curtains were drawn and the light was insufficient to unpack my boxes of china and books. The flat was a studio one with picture windows all round, high up on the hill which overlooked the Vickers Armstrong factories. I drew one curtain and sought for a candle, placed it on the top of a packing case, surrounded it with cardboard and started work.

A few moments later there was a sharp knocking on my door and a stern voice called, 'Open in the name of the law!'

'Who is it?', I stammered.

'The police,' came the reply.

I staggered to the door between obstacles, knocking my shins against a case and wondering what crime I had committed. A burly policeman stood outside. Without preliminaries he pushed his way in.

'We've been informed you are signalling to enemy planes and giving the location of the armament factory. Ah!' He had caught sight of the glimmer of light from my packing case and he strode forward and fell over a case of books. It didn't improve his temper.

'But it's only a candle,' I said.

'It's placed strategically to throw a beam of light for miles around,' he said pompously and promptly blew the candle out. We stood in the darkness. . . .

'What am I going to do?' I said frantically. 'I only moved in today. I'm unpacking.'

'You can go to bed,' he said brusquely, as he stamped across the room.

'Mind the packing cases,' I called out after him. The slam of the outer door was the only answer.   NELLIE TURNER

Because of their strict enforcement of blackout regulations the Special Constables were particularly unpopular: they were regarded as 'not like the

real police', and suspected of having an officious desire to throw their weight about.

Illuminophobia: The popular name for this complaint is 'Special Constable's Palsy', its cause being the shock to the nervous systems of S.C. personnel induced by shafts of light, spots of imperfect blackout before the eyes, and uncurtained bathroom windows. The symptoms are violent, producing a quickened step, a dilated eye, rapid pulsation, swelling of veins in the neck, and a succession of snorts, followed by loud angry cries. *THE SPESHUL.*

When walking in the blackout, whichever side of the pavement they take, walkers are involved in unexpected risks: on the one side Belisha beacons, lamp-posts, pillar boxes and sand bins; on the other, sandbag promontories. The middle of the pavement is the only safe place and . . . I suggest that the better rule at night would be that walkers northwards should use the west and those walking southward the east pavement. . . . It does not matter much at night which side of the street one walks since there are no shops or other attractions. *Letter in THE TIMES,* 8 November 1939.

Although we were in a relatively safe area, blackout was very strict. I went, one evening, to ask for a friend who was ill. They lived at the other end of the town, and at the top of the hill. There was a public park which cut off a bit of the road and an appreciable part of the climb, but my mother thought it no place for a woman in the dark, and I promised not to cross it. I climbed farther up the hill, and took the bus to the centre of the town. I expected to alight at the door of a bank, but in the darkness all I could make out was a high wall. I groped for the window-ledges, but found none. I was completely lost. The bus had moved on, there was no one about; I simply did not know which way to turn. I continued along the wall for a short distance till I stumbled off the kerb and my hand felt a wooden gate. Then I had it. The bus had taken the right fork at the end of the High Street, and landed me at the doctor's back door. . . .

The next time I visited that house . . . coming back, I decided to walk home, and to risk the park. As I veered left towards the gate, I saw ahead of me, and already committed to the uphill fork to the bus stop, a young man in plus-fours, as he passed under the dim light of one of the infrequent street lamps. When I changed direction, so did he, and fell into step a few yards behind me. I didn't quite like it, but I kept steadily on, expecting him to pass me with his presumably longer stride, but he didn't. We got into the park where it was completely dark, and still the heavy step kept the same distance, till the further gate drew near. Then he suddenly began to run. 'This is it,' I thought, but he ran on past me; and then I saw that 'he' was a tall young girl who had decided to sail under my convoy. She had outgrown her coat, and may have had no coupons to replace it, but she had let down her skirt, and the effect, in the poor light was that of the baggy plus-fours of these days. HELEN ANGUS

I took Mary out and we had supper at a nice place in Frith Street – [station] 33's ground I couldn't help thinking. There was a slight difficulty when I went into the restaurant in my fireman's uniform, and the waiter said he wasn't sure the management would like it. I was just getting into a temper when the manager himself came over and said he didn't really mind a bit . . . but it was quite clear that he'd rather I hadn't come in at all . . . After we'd spent money on the meal and a bottle of wine, even the waiter thawed towards me and explained in confidential tones that it was only his duty to do as he had been asked by the management. *THE BELLS GO DOWN*

Although the news-readers stayed in London, many BBC departments were evacuated.

Bristol in September, 1939, was a strange place. Upon this comparatively small Regional Broadcasting Centre there descended suddenly three whole Production Departments, Variety, Music – including the full Symphony Orchestra – and Children's Hour, with their attendant administrative and announcing staffs. All this crowd of people had to be found offices in which to work, studios from which to broadcast, and – equally important – beds in which to sleep. . . . We in Variety Department had at our disposal about twenty-five actors and actresses, two orchestras and a few sets of band parts, and with this very small equipment we set to work to provide 120 hours of entertainment a week. . . .

The Regional Headquarters in Whiteladies Road was not very large – just a block of offices and three studios – so that we found ourselves housed all over Clifton, and the studio problem was tackled by wiring up every Parish Hall in sight. My office turned out to be a dormitory in one of Clifton College Houses, and as I looked out over the famous Close immortalized by Newbolt as being bathed in a 'breathless hush', there were on all sides the sounds of pianos hammering out popular tunes or composers' efforts as they wrestled with building programmes, while on the Close itself the silver shape of a barrage balloon, with its attendant crew, took the place of the Cricket Eleven, and the whirring of the motors replaced the peacetime sounds of bat meeting ball. Round my office walls still hung the usual photographic groups of College teams, and as I looked at them I wondered what those boys were doing now.

Most of us at this time were doing two or three programmes a day, and we were all, performers included, rushing about from studio to studio on newly-purchased bicycles, rehearsing and broadcasting, snatching meals when and how we could, sitting up half the night writing or discussing ideas for further programmes. I was given a list of shows which I was to prepare and put on, and among them there appeared the following:

Tuesday, 19th September, 1939 9.30 – 10 pm
IT'S THAT MAN AGAIN . . .

We had no idea how this seemingly simple little programme idea was going to develop; it was just another job. . . . The thing was to get a new slant on the 'story' presenting Tommy [Handley] to a wondering war-struck world. As it was a time when everybody in the land, from the highest administrator down to the humblest A.R.P. type, was being given a new title which generally resolved itself into the appropriate initials, we thought it would be in keeping if we made Tommy a V.I.P. of some sort. Finally, we decided that nothing less than Cabinet rank would meet the case, so we created the post of *Minister of Aggravation and Mysteries*, housing this new encumbrance in the mythical *Office of Twerps*. (The Office of Works which had an office next door to the B.B.C. were somewhat pained at the slight confusion that arose later when the programme became popular and the mail got mixed up!) . . .

We felt that we, too, ought to be known by the fashionable initials, but unfortunately the combination derived from Min. of Ag. and Myst. or yet the Office of Twerps were unsuitable. So we proceeded to think out something else on the same lines. Tommy, who is given to doodling on blotting pads, had printed the title of the show IT'S THAT MAN AGAIN, and then proceeded to black in heavily the capitals at the beginning of each word. Suddenly, he said 'I've got it – ITMA!' And thus the Minister of Aggravation and Mysteries became ITMA overnight. . . . On the 19th September, 1939 at 9.30pm . . . ITMA had its real First Night. After a two-hour rehearsal – a long one for those early days of war – we took the floor in the Clifton Parish Hall before a small audience mainly composed of people on the staff. Outside there was the blackout, responsible for many a black-eye, for somehow one was continually walking briskly into lamp-posts or parked cars. Wardens were being very strict about even the tiniest glimmer of light, and we had to creep into the various studios round a complicated system of screens and curtains, carrying our gas-masks wherever we went. But once inside the building all was gaiety and light, and a sort of party-spirit pervaded the atmosphere. For one thing there was no stage, so that the audience and the artists were all together on the same level, and when they were not actually speaking their lines or performing, the cast sat down often on grand piano or floor, thus giving the whole thing a very informal air. Thus it was on the First Night of the show that was destined to make radio history. Tommy's first words . . . set the topical pace at which we have tried to keep the show going every since:

'Hello Folks! It's Mein Kampf again! Sorry. I *should* say: Hello, Folks! It's that MAN again! That was a Goebbled version a bit doctored. I usually go all goosey when I can't follow my proper-gander.' . . .

These radio people who inhabited the first ITMA series were not, perhaps, so memorable . . . as those who followed. But there was among them the supreme telephone character of them all – the notorious *FUNF*. Here was the embodiment of all the nation's spy-neurosis, a product of the times. True, he was an ineffective comic spy, the enemy agent with feet of sauerkraut, but he crystallised the contempt tinged with unacknowledged fear with which the British people faced a new enemy. . . .

Those . . . blood-curdling guttural tones, so soon to be heard being reproduced all over the country, were actually obtained by Jack Train speaking into a glass tumbler.

We got the name Funf quite accidentally. We were searching for something short and sinister, and . . . one day I heard my small son trying to recite the German numerals to the Austrian woman refugee, a Doctor of Law from Vienna, who was living with us at the time. 'Eins, zwei, drei, vier, fünf . . .' he went, and there he stuck. 'Fünf . . . fünf . . .' 'FUNF!' I shouted. 'That's the name we're looking for!' and Funf he became, and 'Foonf' he was pronounced. . . .

Everywhere one went, Funf kept cropping up. In the blackout, two people would collide. 'Sorry. Who's that?' one would say, and like a flash would come the answer 'Funf!' Perhaps a workman would accidentally drop a brick down near a mate below. "'Ere, who threw that?' And from somewhere up in the scaffolding a raucous voice would bellow 'Funf!'

. . . Tommy laughed him to scorn, and the nation laughed with him, for Tommy's contempt for Funf expressed the people's contempt for the enemy, from Hitler himself down to Haw-haw.
FRANCIS WORSLEY

In 1939 many families still had servants and did not intend to allow the war to upset the social order.

The following were the pre-Blitz air raid arrangements in a big house that I know well, in a danger area in the Home Counties. The spacious cellars were arranged so:

First Cellar: for the elderly owner and her guests; Wilton carpet, upholstered arm-chairs, occasional tables, a ration of best bitter chocolate, a bottle of expensive brandy, petit-beurre biscuits, thermos jugs, packs of cards, a Chinese lacquer screen concealing an eighteenth-century commode.

Second Cellar: for female servants; wicker-work arm-chairs, an oak table, an old phonograph (complete with horn), a half bottle of cheap brandy, plain biscuits, tea-making apparatus, a Japanese paper screen concealing sanitary accommodation of a bedroom type.

Third Cellar: for chauffeur, boot-boy, gardeners, and stray neighbours; a wooden bench, wooden table, an electric bell connected with first cellar in case owner should wish to summon masculine moral support; water biscuits. No brandy, no screen.
SYLVIA THOMPSON

HOW TO SAVE YOUR DINNER IF AIR RAIDS COME: Housewives may be called away from their cooking, in these troubled times, by many interruptions. An air-raid warning, an accident, a sudden call for help in packing-up for someone who has to leave home at a moment's notice – all these out of the way events may call a housewife away from her stove in the middle of her preparations for dinner.

With these interruptions in mind, the Stork Kitchen has been making experiments so that we may help you by telling you what to do if you have to leave your cooking at a critical moment.

If an air-raid signal, or any other interruption, takes you away from your kitchen for an indefinite time, the first thing to do is to stop the heat; that is, turn off the gas or electric current or close the dampers of a kitchen range. If you do this your food cannot get burnt.

Meat is easiest to deal with. Leave a roasting joint in the oven. The heat that will remain for some time in a gas or electric oven will be enough to go on with the cooking for a time, but not enough to burn the joint. When you come back to the kitchen, you may find that the meat is cooked. If it needs more cooking, start the oven again, baste the meat well with hot fat, and finish the cooking. Your own common sense and your knowledge of how long the meat has been in the oven will help you here.

Stews will take no harm at all from an interruption in cooking. Turn on the heat again and bring them slowly to simmering point; then continue cooking until the meat is tender.

Puddings may need a little more attention. Milk puddings can stay in the warm oven, and will probably be cooked by the time you come back to the kitchen. If the rice or sago is not cooked, continue the cooking a little longer. Baked puddings, like Apple Sponge, Cake Pudding or Queen of Puddings can be treated in exactly the same way.
STORK MARGARINE WARTIME COOKERY BOOK

As autumn gave way to winter the novelty of caring for evacuees, and of living in the country, began to wear off.

Wherever diet is mentioned, it is in identical terms. The children are used to being fed on 'pieces' (bread and margarine), fish and chips, tinned food and sweets. This comment is not confined to the areas with very poor housing conditions. Vegetables (other than potatoes) and puddings were unknown to many children. It is frequently remarked that the children 'looked at the country food at first with dark suspicion' but soon became accustomed to it. In many areas it is apparently the custom to give the child some pennies and for it to buy biscuits or fish and chips and eat it in the street. There are frequent reports of children being quite unaccustomed to having to sit down to meals and using knives and forks; when they are hungry they are given hunks of bread and margarine which they eat sitting on the doorsteps or elsewhere. Some children said they had never seen their mother cook anything and had no hot meals at home . . .

EXTRACTS FROM REPORTS

Walthamstow. 'Bread and lard are a usual breakfast for a number of children when at home . . .' . . .

Leeds. 'A number of the children . . . were surprised that we had "Sunday dinner" every day.' . . .

West Bromwich. 'A hot meal was an unknown quantity with some. A "roe and a penn'orth" seemed the favourite meal.'

Grimsby. 'Their chief food at home was in most cases fish and chips, more often the latter without the fish. Milk puddings were unheard of and some did not even know what a pudding was.' . . .

Manchester . . . 'Few children would eat food that demanded the use of teeth – in almost every case could only eat with a teaspoon.'

'Practically all disliked fresh vegetables and pies and puddings of fresh fruit, plums, damsons, etc., were quite unknown to them . . .'

Liverpool. 'One little girl of 5½ remarked one day that she would like to have beer and cheese for supper.'

'Most of the children seemed under-nourished when they arrived, yet some were troublesome to feed, not liking stewed fruit, vegetables and jam. Children had been used to receiving a penny at home to buy their own dinners. One used to buy broken biscuits, the other Oxo cubes.'

'Most of them seemed quite unaccustomed to ordinary everyday food and preferred a "piece" or a bag of chips on the doorstep.'

Newcastle. 'Those from the most neglected homes had no idea of eating at table, but were expert in making anything into a sandwich, fingers being preferred to forks.'

'Soup seemed to be unknown to some of the children. One mother admitted they never had soup, while two boys (10 and 12) attempted it with a knife and fork.' . . .

Lambeth. 'The children did not seem to have much idea of proper meals; they used to whine for a bit of bread. . . . A large number, even from apparently well-off homes, were quite unused to sitting down to table or to using knives and forks. They were used to having their food handed to them to take out, or eat anywhere.'
TOWN CHILDREN THROUGH COUNTRY EYES

Many private companies, as well as government departments, moved their offices to the country on the outbreak of war.

In 1939 I was employed as shorthand typist in a firm selling automatic vending machines, with its head office in City Road, E.C.1. The managing director had the foresight to acquire on a lease a manor house in the Oxfordshire village of Bodicote, and in the last few days of August and the first two days of September the office staff and equipment were evacuated there by lorries and private cars . . .

On the 1st September, 1939, I was driven by car in the late evening to the village, leaving my parents, and younger sister at home in Hammersmith. (My fiancé, who was in the Territorial Army had been called up on the 16th August.) I remember we sang on the way, although I was anxious about the imminence of war and also ignorant of the whereabouts of my fiancé. In the blackout, I remember noticing cats' eyes on the road for the first time.

On arrival at the Manor House we found conditions rather congested, as some thirty staff were accommodated in addition to some rooms having to be used as offices. In my bedroom were a double bed which had to be shared by three girls, two single beds, occupied by one girl in each, a dressing table and a wardrobe. There were so many to be accommodated and to be found room to work that four of us had to have our desks put in a greenhouse, and I remember working there among tomatoes growing all round the walls. This was not unpleasant except in sunshine, when it was very warm; however, the side windows could be propped up for ventilation and the roof was white-washed to reflect some of the heat.

The boss's main concern was with his accounts – instalment accounts kept on trays of index cards in heavy steel cabinets. Work was commenced rapidly on digging an air-raid shelter in the garden, all the staff taking a hand in this in the preparatory phase. When it was finally completed the girl typists and clerks had to take turns, two each evening, in pushing these heavy cabinets from the house into the air-raid shelter for safety, and this was rather tricky as there was a narrow sloping entrance to the shelter with a sharp bend in it. Marrows were grown on top of the shelter. . . .

We played table tennis in the evening and tennis in the garden, as there was a large lawn. The surrounding country was also very pretty for walks. But there was not much in the way of facilities for girls to do washing or get it dry in wet weather, with only one bathroom for the men and one for the girls (both with W.C.). There was a nice little pub opposite the house, a small village church – the vicar of which rode a bicycle, mounting from a step at the back in the old-fashioned way and leaping off backwards. There were two cinemas in the nearest town two miles away, and a bus service once an hour but not after 10 pm (Later we always walked both ways when we went to the cinema.) As the winter drew on conditions in the Manor House were very cold and we often went out for walks to get warm, in the evenings. . . .

On New Year's Eve, 1939 the boss took a party of five or six of us girls over to the house of the head salesman which was in a village about 14 miles away. After a very successful party he tried to drive back but the car stuck on a ridge in the deep snow and we all tried to push it off. One girl dislocated her knee doing this, and a doctor was sent for. . . . Eventually we gave up and all slept on chairs etc. and the next day a farmer brought horses to pull the car off the ridge, but most of the girls had by then made their way back to our village, some walking all the way. . . .

When food rationing started we were all given our small portion of butter which we kept in individual dishes in the sideboard in the communal dining room. This was often attacked by mice but we had to eat it all the same because it was all we had. There were also mice in the bedrooms and one girl had a large hole eaten in a woollen dress.

On going home for the weekend we would of course travel back as late as possible on Sunday night, and . . . usually had to walk the two miles back to the Manor House, and sometimes were pestered by soldiers or airmen on the way. However, we managed to keep out of trouble! Sometimes we caught the midnight train from Paddington and by the time we were walking back into the village the birds were singing their dawn chorus. . . .

We enjoyed country walks and bicycle rides (the boss did provide three bicycles) and we learned horse riding cheaply because the proprietor of a riding school taken over by the Military kept his horses in the Manor House stables for a nominal rent, plus manure! For town girls it was the first time we had really enjoyed the country and we particularly liked seeing it by moonlight, and especially so in the snow.   GLADYS BURNIE

Christmas accelerated the return of evacuees to the cities, but conscientious parents heeded official plans to 'leave them where they are' and went to visit their children instead.

Christmas, 1939. Carol singers mingled with air-raid wardens, search-lights tried to sweep the Bethlehem stars from the sky. Soldiers and civilians waited uncertainly for total war or peace: children waited for parents and Santa Claus.

Toy shops were filled with khaki howitzers, scale models of war-ships, tin helmets, marbles, fret-saws, biplanes to be made from balsa wood and crashed in the back garden, guns and more guns. . . .

Some children went home that Christmas . . . the majority stayed in their billets and waited . . . and wondered if our fathers, mothers, brothers and sisters would arrive.

Mine did. They came on Christmas Eve with heavy suitcases and secret parcels. They were so familiar, so dependable, it was suddenly ridiculous to have doubted that they would come. There was my father, compact and neat and seasonally rosy, my mother resolutely determined to improvise a happy family Christmas despite Hitler. . . .

We adjourned to a tall house in the centre of the town where my parents were to stay. . . . We were greeted cordially and shown up to a bedroom occupied by a large bed, a washstand and a gas fire with glowing stumps and cold white crowns among its broken clay teeth. We kept our overcoats on and sat on the bed.

'Let's play a little game of something,' said my mother brightly.

My father wound his scarf tighter round his neck and fished in a suitcase for Happy Families, a game which he had detested through-out my childhood. He won and we played draughts and I-Spy although there wasn't much to spy. The flames in the fire shrank to small blue cones and frost patterns crystallised on the windows behind the curtains. . . .

We shivered closer together round the fire now plopping and grumbling gaseously to itself. . . .

'Might as well go to bed,' said my father. 'I'll take you back to the Lovells and we'll meet in the morning.'

'All right,' I said.

As we rose there was a knock on the door. 'May I come in?' said a woman's voice. In she came, the temporary landlady. 'We wondered if you'd like to come downstairs now,' she said. 'We thought you'd like to be together for a little while at first.'

Down we went to plum-pudding warmth and selfless hospitality; to mince pies, carols, small presents and a tree with a fairy on top. The Spirit of Christmas thawed and accompanied us and the spectre of war retreated amid so much human decency.

Next day among the presents there was a gun which detonated strips of paper with gunpowder ferocity, a fat red annual, tins of toffees, a fountain pen soon blunted on the scouts' hall floor, crackers filled with sparklers and firework serpents. . . .

On Boxing Day my parents took me to the cinema with my foster-parents, suddenly said good-bye – and left us there. The film starred Anna Neagle but I didn't much care for it.   DEREK LAMBERT

1940

Dining-room customers who wish to go to the shelter
should tell their waiter, who will present their
bill immediately.
Notice in an Edinburgh hotel

'My husband got a load of sand and made it all just like the seaside for them.'

1940 was a year unlike any other in British history. Looking back, it seems scarcely credible that any country should have survived such a succession of disasters as now fell upon Great Britain – and should have ended the year not merely unbeaten, but with spirits higher than at the beginning. Everything about 1940 was memorable, even the weather, with the finest spring and summer in living memory following the most bitter winter on record. In April the complacency of Chamberlain and his colleagues was at last exposed when Hitler overran Denmark and easily defeated the British forces sent to stop him occupying Norway. In May and June he overwhelmed Belgium and Holland even more rapidly, drove the whole British Expeditionary Force into the sea and totally defeated France.

Ironically, the democratic institution of Parliament, which Hitler despised, now saved Great Britain and the world and ensured Germany's eventual defeat, by overthrowing the discredited Prime Minister and his largely imcompetent colleagues and replacing them with a real leader and a real government. The accession to power of Winston Churchill on 10 May 1940 was Germany's first major defeat of the war. The second and third followed rapidly after, when the R.A.F. defeated the Luftwaffe in the Battle of Britain, and the citizens of London and other cities endured the Blitz with morale, if not unshaken, at least unbroken. By December doubt, defeatism and the man associated with them were all dead. A mock batting order published at this time showed almost every nation in Europe 'bowled by Hitler', but at Number Ten 'Britain: Not Out' and as Last Man: 'America: Still to Bat.'

With no fighting in progress, except at sea, the civilian had to demonstrate his patriotism in strange ways:

A TOILET ROLL THAT IS 100% BRITISH MADE
Up to now practically all paper for toilet rolls has been imported. We are now able to offer one made entirely in Kent . . . Sale price, dozen 5/11. (*D.H. Evans's* Winter Sale Catalogue, *February 1940*)

Suddenly the war in the West began in earnest. Almost overnight even invasion became a very real possibility.

The Whitsun week-end . . . began on Friday, the 10th of May . . . Auburn heard on the early morning wireless bulletin that the invasion of the Lowlands had begun and later on, during the day, the windows began to rattle faintly in their frames as they used to all the time when I was a child and there were big guns in Belgium before. . . .

I took the precaution of putting my only valuable, my manuscript (which represented, if nothing else, at least six solid months of my living time), in a biscuit tin, and Christine, who felt we ought to bury something, began to look about for some silver or some china we could hide. She gave this up in disgust in the end and was cool with me when I suggested we bought something for the purpose. I thought the sort of things which would be valuable if the worst happened were pails and blankets and tinned beans and soap, but none of these things seemed suitable for burying. . . .

As the week-end went on the big drama obtruded more and more into our tight little lives. An order came through . . . decreeing that all Wardens' Posts should be fully manned and that the men should patrol at dawn and dusk to keep a look out for parachute troops. Word was coming through from Holland that these were sometimes disguised as 'nuns and other familiar figures'. Now a nun is not a familiar figure in Auburn and the arrival of one by bus, much less by parachute, would have occasioned considerable interest, not to say suspicion, so the information had a touch of pure fantasy about it very hard to stomach at first. . . . However, all the Wardens went out dutifully in the grey times and scouted along the little green hedges as secretly as only the native can.

The rest of us in the house took turns at minding the telephone for raid warnings when they were out. . . .

All through the days, which were green and luxuriant, Auburn looked and felt, save for the far-off mutter of the guns, just the same as usual in the Spring, and the familiar little jobs cropped up as usual. . . .

It was the new jobs which seemed so melodramatic and were yet somehow so reasonable. Grog turned the house upside down looking for our only firearm. It was a .22 Winchester dated about 1890 and we had no ammunition for it, which I for one was glad about because the whole contraption looked dangerous to me . . . I found an Arab sword . . . in an umbrella stand. It was about five feet long, for use on camel back, and a bit rusty, and we discounted that also. . . . The odd scraps of gossip I heard were enlightening. Some of the tales might be thought ridiculous but all were gallant. There were anecdotes of staunch elderly ladies setting aside their shears and trowels and training their old gardeners as stretcher-bearers or arranging trench refuges for the children next door. There was no hint of panic: on the contrary, rather a sort of grim enjoyment.   MARGERY ALLINGHAM

1940

On 14 May the new Secretary of State for War broadcast an appeal for men to join an unpaid, part-time army to protect their own localities.

Over the wireless in our cottages in Wilmington we heard Eden's appeal for Local Defence Volunteers.

Wilmington is one of the small Sussex downland villages scattered in the area between Lewes and Eastbourne, and right in the middle of what was then considered a dangerous invasion area.

The news stirred the villagers. A man named Royston in the next cottage to mine went with me first thing next morning to the police station at Hailsham to see if we could help in organising a squad for our village. We were received with some surprise. A constable listened smilingly to our tale. Oh yes, he had heard something about volunteers, but he didn't quite know what was going on, and we had better see the sergeant. The sergeant had heard the news over the wireless, but he had no further information. Anyhow, he would make a note of our names and addresses. One or two other men arrived at the same time to offer their services.

We heard nothing more. Then a day or two later the vet who ran an animal hospital in our village and who had been a major in Egypt in the last war told us he had been asked to enrol volunteers from ours and neighbouring villages.

Well, this being a democracy, the chaps decided we had better talk it over. A meeting was arranged at the village pub, the *Black Horse*. The boss there (since killed bombing Germany) and I commandeered a car to tour the district and rope people in. The car was a small Ford belonging to a villager who had jacked it up for the duration. He had removed the battery. Roy Reynolds, mine host from the pub, was a bit of an electrician, and he scrounged a secondhand battery from a friend's garage at Polegate and we soon had the car going. We really had no right to pinch that car, and it wasn't insured anyhow, but in those days we did many things not in the book. The owner was a good old sort who didn't mind. He was too aged to serve himself, but he would do anything in his power so long as he wasn't asked to climb ladders, which his doctor forbade.

We went to remote farms and cottages. Sometimes we were received with considerable suspicion as a sort of 'press gang'. . . . Generally speaking the response was excellent, and at the end of the day we had about fifteen names of potential recruits in our penny exercise book, and a few others ready to consider giving their support.

47

At the *Black Horse* meeting the major-vet put me up to talk. There were shepherds, farm hands, gardeners, village shopkeepers, a retired civil servant from India, a retired schoolmaster, and one or two folk who worked in London and had cottages in downland. We held a subsidiary meeting at another village over the hill. Men came in from their work in the fields, and we stood round a farm waggon in a farmyard and discussed things and elected a local section leader, calling him Corporal. Communications were the difficulty, so we went to the big house of a local Colonel to get him to agree to let us use his telephone. The Corporal's wife (a domestic there) could answer if need be. . . .

Then came the 'election of officers'. . . . The local section leader must obviously be a chap always there in the village, so the choice fell on Roy, mine host at the pub.

'He's the best rabbit shot in the neighbourhood,' said one of his backers.

I was to be sort of secretary-help and in charge of communications – my headquarters at the start to be the telephone box at the pub. The problem of a parading place in case of alarm was easily solved. There was a unanimous vote for the yard at the *Black Horse*. Then we decided to have a round-up in the village for funds for things we should want. An appeal was put in the village shop window, and wives and sweethearts – as well as we – went round collecting.

That brought in, as far as I remember, about fifteen pounds. We spent four pounds on a ramshackle old car (we had to return the commandeered one) to take our patrols in relays to our first remote outpost on the Downs; also to fetch in people who lived in out-of-the-way corners. . . .

We raked over the whole district for firearms. I think a few people were scared at our enquiries as they had overlooked the need for taking out gun permits. We built up an armoury at first in one of the upper rooms at the pub. . . . Eventually we were sent eight Ross rifles, and with these and four shotguns and one revolver we made a brave show on our first real parade one Sunday morning in a field behind the pub. We spent some more of our funds buying ammunition for the shotguns.

At first our job was to keep vigil on the Downs from dusk to dawn, and report back to the real troops in the rear if we saw parachutists or anything else suspicious.

Our chief observation post was an exposed hilltop, which meant a long walk from the village and a stiff climb at the end. It was all right in the summer, but we felt we should need shelter in the bleak winter. So a deputation went to a gypsy encampment and bargained for an old caravan. We got it for, I think, under five pounds, using the funds subscribed in the village. We spent a bit more money on paint for camouflage, which to my mind made the gypsy caravan more conspicuous than ever after our amateur efforts. A farmer lent us a horse to fetch it. We had about five miles to go. Then at the village we borrowed another horse, and, with the help of about half a dozen of the squad, and the village women and children cheering us as we sweated, we pulled, pushed and shoved the broken-down caravan right to the top of the Downs. That job took hours. . . .

Quoted by CHARLES GRAVES

Sunday afternoon, May 26, 1940 Inaugural meeting of officers of No. 3 Company at C.D.'s house. Mutual introductions. Met a few old friends. No. 2 Platoon allotted the area of the Leeds (Cobble Hall) Golf Club and some of the surrounding country. Tea served, then we were dismissed to get on with the job. . . .

May 26–29 My second-in-command (Mr F.T. Day, Captain of the Club) and myself had a busy time recruiting. Club steward very useful in passing the word on.

The bar became a desk for filling in forms. . . .

Four-ball cliques joined up together, did their guard together, and often finished up with a round of golf before going to business.

May 29 First guard mounted.
Dress – golf gear.
Arms – a stout stick.
Guard room – Club lounge. Easy chairs for sleep.

May 30–31 Guard now armed, two members having brought .22 rifles. Had to reprimand one man very severely for rabbiting in the early morning when he ought to have been on the lookout.

May 31 Received 6 S.M.L.E. rifles and 100 rds. .300 s.a.a. This was a red-letter day. The bearing of the men completely changed under the influence of a little arms drill. Club tea room handed over to us as permanent guard room. Drying room given to us 'for the duration' for use as armoury. Blankets, beds, mattresses, gum boots and oilskins given to us by various members of the Club who were either too old to serve or already in C.D. services. . . .

We had to stand a lot of chaff from the other Platoons because of the rather *de luxe* conditions under which we were doing our guard. The Council and Staff of the Golf Club did everything they could to help, and their attentions were sometimes embarrassing. On one occasion the Orderly Officer (whose own Platoon was very badly housed) arrived at about 22.30 hours just as a waitress, looking very prim in white cap and apron, brought into the guardroom a tray with sandwiches and coffee, for the Sergeant of the Guard. . . .

We had the assistance of the green keeper and his staff in the making of a bomb-practice range and bayonet fighting assault course. . . .

Golfers as a class are ideal for Home Guard work, but, they sometimes find it difficult to forget golf. For instance, at first their reports had a smack of golf in them, e.g.

'Flares seen over the 13th green.'

'Flashing light at 105 degrees from the 7th tee.' . . .

During the first few weeks we used to eke out the rota of guards by employing the services of some of the old men of the Club as telephone orderlies. . . . When our strength was such that they were no longer required, they were very disappointed. One pleaded very hard to be kept on, although he was quite unfit to be enrolled properly. You see, there is a bar, a billiard table, and some good bridge to be had at the Golf Club. CAPTAIN T.E. MASON, quoted by Charles Graves

The L.D.V. were . . . at the start . . . more of a menace than an asset. I remember one night being called over about 1 am to visit the little boys at Benenden as one of them was rather ill. I climbed into the car cursing at the thought of a three mile drive in the middle of the night. As I was turning down Golford corner an uncouth youth, flourishing some sort of musket of ancient vintage, held me up. As he seemed extremely uncertain how to manipulate his weapon he filled me with an agony of nervous apprehension. 'For God's sake put that bloody thing down,' I said, 'I am sure you will do either yourself or me severe damage if you are not careful.' He meekly obliged and laid the musket on the ground. He then asked to see my papers, and bent over unarmed, reading them by the light of my side lamps. Then having given me back my papers he picked up his blunderbuss and allowed me to go on, obviously feeling very pleased with himself over the whole affair.   J.H. LEAKEY

If one man, other than Winston Churchill, put into words the spirit of the time it was J.B. Priestley in his broadcast Postscripts.

9 June 1940   I don't think there has ever been a lovelier English spring than this last one, now melting into full summer. Sometimes, in between listening to the latest news of battle and destruction, or trying to write about them myself, I've gone out and stared at the red japonica or the cherry and almond blossom, so clear and exquisite against the moss-stained old wall – and have hardly been able to believe my eyes. . . . Never have I seen (at least, not since I grew up) such a golden white of buttercups and daisies in the meadows. I'll swear the very birds have sung this year as they never did before. Just outside my study, there are a couple of blackbirds who think they're still in the Garden of Eden. . . . I've looked out of my house in the country on these marvellous days of sun and blue air – and I could see the blaze and bloom of the Californian poppies and the roses in the garden; then the twinkling beeches and the stately nodding elms – and then, beyond, the lush fields and the round green hills dissolving into the hazy blue of the sky. And I've stared at all this – and I've remembered the terrible news of battle and destruction I'd just heard or read – and I've felt that one or the other couldn't be true. . . .

But sometimes, too, I've felt that the unusual loveliness of our gardens and meadows and hills has come home to us because these things are, so to speak, staring at us – as you see so many women now staring at their soldier husbands, sweethearts, sons, just before the trains take them away. It's as if this English landscape said: 'Look at me, as I am now in my beauty and fullness of joy, and do not forget.' And when I feel this, I feel too a sudden and very sharp anger; for I remember then how this island is threatened and menaced.
J.B. PRIESTLEY

16 June 1940   A night or two ago, I had my first spell with our Local Defence Volunteers or 'Parashots'. . . . Ours is a small and scattered village, but we'd had a fine response to the call for Volunteers; practically every able-bodied man in the place takes his turn. The post is on top of a high down, with a fine view over a dozen wide parishes. The men I met up there the other night represented a good cross-section of English rural life; we had a parson, a bailiff, a builder, farmers and farm labourers. Even the rarer and fast disappearing rural trades were represented – for we had a hurdle-maker there; and his presence, together with that of a woodman and a shepherd, made me feel sometimes that I'd wandered into one of those rich chapters of Thomas Hardy's fiction in which his rustics meet in the gathering darkness on some Wessex hillside. And indeed there was something in the preliminary talk, before the sentries were posted for the night, that gave this whole horrible business of air raids and threatened invasion a rustic, homely, almost comfortable atmosphere, and really made a man feel more cheerful about it. . . .

Well, as we talked on our post on the hilltop, we watched the dusk deepen in the valleys below, where our women-folk listened to the news as they knitted by the hearth, and we remembered that these were our homes and that now at any time they might be blazing ruins, and that half-crazy German youths . . . might soon be let loose down there. The sentries took their posts. There was a mist coming over the down. Nothing much happened for a time. A green light that seemed to defy all black-out regulations turned out to be merely an extra large and luminous glow-worm; the glow-worms, poor ignorant little creatures, don't know there's a war on and so continue lighting themselves up. A few searchlights went stabbing through the dusk and then faded. The mist thickened, and below in all the valleys, there wasn't the faintest glimmer of light. . . .

So we talked about what happened to us in the last war, and about the hay and the barley, about beef and milk and cheese and tobacco. Then a belt of fog over to the left became almost silvery, because somewhere along there all the searchlights were sweeping the sky. Then somewhere behind that vague silveriness, there was a sound as if gigantic doors were being slammed to. There was the rapid stabbing noise of anti-aircraft batteries, and far away some rapping of machine-guns. Then the sirens went, in our two nearest towns, as if all that part of the darkened countryside, like a vast trapped animal, were screaming at us.

But then the sounds of bombs and gunfire and planes all died away. The 'All Clear' went, and then there was nothing but the misty cool night, drowned in silence, and this handful of us on the hilltop. I remember wishing then that we could send all our children out of this island, every boy and girl of them across the sea to the wide Dominions, and turn Britain into the greatest fortress the world has known; so that then, with an easy mind, we could fight and fight these Nazis until we broke their black hearts.   J.B. PRIESTLEY

During the invasion scare of 1940 . . . a group of us [at Smarden in Kent] were summoned to a meeting to discuss any public feeding arrangements that might be necessary if the invader *did* come. Mrs R., a famous voluntary local caterer, was asked if she would undertake the organisation of public meals. She looked seriously at the chairman and said: 'Well, everyone must wash up their own knife and fork!' Good old Mrs R. – Germans or no Germans – down to the practical details of the moment. I asked her later: 'What would you do if a German soldier appeared at your back door?' Her answer: 'I should say to 'im, I should say: "What are you a-doin' of 'ere?" '
LETTICE RATHBONE

Three depots for jam-making were organised by the Women's Institute. In those strange days, when parachutists were expected by day and night, a serious jam problem arose. Was it wiser to hide one's store of jam under the floor or somehow sealed up in a quarry hole or was it better to imitate a Jael-like housewife who kept a hammer ready for a last-minute smashing, in hopes of the dire effect of powdered glass on jam-starved Germans? *WAR HISTORY OF THE LANGTON MALTRAVERS WOMEN'S INSTITUTE*

As one nation after another surrendered to Hitler, a curious mood of elation swept the country, as though all Great Britain's misfortunes so far had been the result of having allies.

On 17 June poor France fell. That day, as we trudged past Greenwich on our way to Canvey Island, a tug skipper yelled gaily across the water: 'Now we know where we are! No more bloody allies!'

In peace time, on a friend's yacht, I had studied the International Code of Flag Signals, and noted in my diary a few odd 'groups'. There was QUH – 'Have you any women on board?' and LWV – 'Have dead rats been found on board?', and the extraordinary query LVI – 'Can you suggest any means whereby my radio apparatus could be made serviceable?' After a visit to the *Lobster Smack* that day I remembered another. I had often wondered in what circumstances it would be used, but this seemed to be a suitable occasion. I hoisted ATI – *'There is no need for alarm'*. It was not exactly what we felt, but the signals officer replied BDV – 'Approved', and made it a general signal to the little fleet. Few could read it, but it got about, and I think we all felt better.   SIR ALAN HERBERT

The fall of France affected our work. Invasion seemed more than likely, at any moment. Instructions would have to be given by announcers under such circumstances that no voice could succeed in issuing false instructions even if the enemy seized a station. Therefore the public must recognise our voices. . . .

We were called together to agree the best formula. One was required which would be neat, accurate and memorable; preferably something new, which could make a hit with the public and be burlesqued on the halls and in the comic papers. This plan was deliberate and succeeded. The formula finally chosen was, 'This is the B.B.C. Home Service. Here is the News, and this is —— reading it.' I suggested 'read by ——' because that avoided the repetition of 'this is'. But the other served the purpose better, and certainly caught on.

Yet I never got used to my own name. It sounded indecent to me. I couldn't forget that I was bursting into a room where two or three people were sitting in chairs talking. Never in private life do I burst into strangers' rooms and say 'Stop talking. I'm Joseph Macleod. Listen to me. There's been a great naval victory at Cape Matapan, and Jim's ship has been mentioned.' And yet after some months we were their intimate friends, and many of them had a feeling that we knew all about Jim in his ship.

And after a few more months, one learned to drop the voice in shops when one gave one's name. Otherwise people turned round and stared.

That had its pleasant side, too: and one would be a hypocrite if one denied it. It was pleasant, when there were said to be no oatcakes, to know that one's wife had only to give the name, and oatcakes would turn up next day for 'his' breakfast. It was pleasant to hear a new friendliness in a strange voice when one ordered theatre-tickets or a dinner-table by telephone. It was pleasant, and still is even now, to watch the changing expressions of a face in exchanging names or jobs with fellow-travellers on a railway journey. There was an immediate interest, a deep psychological quickening, a welcome, which not only warmed one's heart, but also was fascinating in its revelation of character. . . . A group of W.A.A.F. on the Isle of Islay claimed threepence off me. I had stated that the fighting in North Africa had been bloody. I was reading the News, so to speak, in their barrack room; and they had a Swear Box. A penny a swear, N.C.O.'s twopence, visitors threepence. I sent them some cigarettes.

A well-known popular composer and musician wrote that a certain goodnight of mine, in a form I sometimes used during the Blitz, had given him an idea for a song. Later he sent me a copy. It was 'Good Night, Good Luck, and Carry On. . . .'

I had a letter from a group of nurses in Edinburgh. They said they always listened to the Midnight News; and from then on, I always read it to them. . . .

Somehow it had become the custom of all of us to say 'Good-night' twice. . . . Once or twice I tried saying it only once, and had a lot of complaints. Some said it made them feel lop-sided and they couldn't get to sleep.   JOSEPH MACLEOD

From early July German aircraft became a familiar sight in the skies above South-East England.

'Enemy activity' was steadily on the increase; for now we were well into the opening phases of the Battle of Britain. Air-raid warnings in our area [Tunbridge Wells] averaged twelve or thirteen a day, and seldom any longer were they false alarms. Time after time we would hear the heavy rumble up among the clouds which betokened a formation of German bombers, and there you would spot them as they sailed across the intervening patches of blue sky, dainty and silvery like little moths in the August sunshine, with still tinier moths that were their protective fighters weaving in and out and making rings around them as well-trained dogs encircle a flock of sheep. And then often would be added the sound of our intercepting aircraft as they came tearing across the sky to do battle. Faint bursts of machine-gun fire would reach our ears, and sometimes a shower of the 'empties' would descend upon us . . . to bounce off the roofs and rattle all over the streets, whereupon there would be a frenzied rush of children scrambling to fill their pockets. . . . There was a period when the pupils of the Maidstone Grammar School had to go over every foot of their football-ground before each game in order to clear it of splinters. . . .

The red-letter days were, of course, those when the exchanges overhead produced visible results in the form of Nazi airmen floating to earth. First you would discern a white speck against the blue, apparently stationary. But the speck would grow larger until you could make out its umbrella-top shape, and then at last you would be able to see the minute figure dangling beneath. And what a rush there would be in the direction of the spot where the figure seemed likely to descend. Sometimes there was more than one. On one memorable occasion I saw five on their way down simultaneously, and the difficulty then was to decide in which of the five directions to rush. . . .

I saw my first Nazi at close quarters during those memorable days. My wife and I had just finished lunch when we were startled by a 'zoom' that ended in a loud crash. Rushing to the window, we saw a column of black smoke rising above the tree-tops, and a few moments later began a crackling fusillade that reminded one of the Fifth of November. 'Machine-gun ammunition popping off in the bonfire,' I decided. We jumped into the car and drove towards the smoke and noise, and soon we were overtaking a throng of cyclists and pedestrians all heading in the same direction.

The scene of the crash was on a golf-course, and a good-sized crowd had arrived there before us. . . . The German fighter-bomber had hit the tree-tops in its descent, and there it lay, sprawling broken-backed on the greensward. . . . It was consuming rapidly in its own flames, and the empty cartridges-cases leaped out of the pyre in all directions. The police had formed a cordon. Sternly they ordered the mob to keep its distance, but the small boys were too much for them. They dived and ducked through the cordon singly and in dozens, cheerfully contemptuous of the awful penalties attached to interfering with captured enemy property. . . .

Beneath the trees . . . lay the Nazi airman. A First-Aid Party was in attendance. Tender hands were bandaging his cut forehead and broken leg. He was silent now, but I learned afterwards that when first dragged from his burning 'plane he had made noise enough until one of the men said to him: 'Be a man and shut up, can't you? You asked for it, and now you've got it.' Not another squeak had come from him after that rebuke. . . .

Meanwhile the police were examining his effects. . . . They drew forth in turn a carton of Californian dried raisins, a large slab of Cadbury's chocolate, and – crowning insult – a packet of twenty Gold Flake. Many of the men who had thus far kept silence could no longer restrain their feelings when they caught sight of those Gold Flakes. They might be able to forgive the German for having come over with the intention of blowing them to bits, but not for having brought with him cigarettes looted from our abandoned stores in France.

HUBERT S. BANNER

14 July 1940 The other day I made the strangest journey I ever remember making in this country: I went to Margate. . . .

The start wasn't unusual except that we all had a lot of passes and permits, and we took tin hats along with us too . . . Some people despise tin hats – but not me. I remember them first arriving in the trenches – and very glad we were to see them too.

Well, we set off for Margate – and for some time it was all quite ordinary, but after that it soon began to seem rather peculiar. Along the road there were things that weren't quite what they first appeared to be . . . the Bren guns seemed to be getting mixed up with the agricultural life of north Kent. The most flourishing crop seemed to be barbed wire. Soldiers would pop up from nowhere and then vanish again – unless they wanted to see our permits. Some extra large greenish cattle, quietly pasturing underneath the elms, might possibly have been tanks . . . then as we came nearer the East Coast, the place seemed emptier and emptier. . . . A field would have a hole in it, made at the expense of considerable time, trouble, and outlay of capital, by the German Air Force. An empty bungalow, minus its front door and dining-room, stared at us in mute reproach. An R.A.F. lorry went past, taking with it the remains of a Heinkel bomber. . . .

But there we were at last – on the front at Margate. The sun, with a fine irony, came bounding out. The sea, which has its own sense of humour, winked and sparkled at us. We began to walk along the front. Everything was there: bathing pools, bandstands, gardens blazing with flowers, lido, theatres, and the like; and miles of firm golden sands all spread out beneath the July sun. But no people! – not a soul. Of all those hundreds of thousands of holiday-makers, of entertainers and hawkers and boatmen – not one. And no sound – not the very ghost of an echo of all that cheerful hullabaloo – children shouting and laughing, bands playing, concert parties singing, men selling ice-cream, whelks and peppermint rock, which I'd remembered hearing along this shore. No, not even an echo. Silence. It was as if an evil magician had whisked everybody away. There were the rows and rows of boarding-houses, the 'Sea Views' and 'Bryn Mawrs' and 'Craig-y-dons' and 'Sans Soucis' and the rest, which ought to have been bursting with life, with red faces, piano and gramophone music, and the smell of roast beef and Yorkshire pudding, but all empty, shuttered, forlorn. A most melancholy boarding-house at the end of a row caught my eye – and that one was called 'Kismet'. Kismet, indeed!

In search of a drink and a sandwich, we wandered round and sometimes through, large empty hotels. The few signs of life only made the whole place seem more unreal and spectral. Once an ancient taxi came gliding along the promenade, and we agreed that if we'd hailed it, making a shout in that silence, it would have dissolved at once into thin air. An elderly postman on a bicycle may have been real or yet another apparition.

At last we found a café open, somewhere at the back of the town, and had no sooner had our roast mutton and green peas set in front of us, than the sirens began screaming. But after all this strange ghostliness, an air-raid warning didn't seem to matter much; and we finished our mutton and had some pancakes. The 'All Clear' found us in a small bar about two miles away, where one of the patrons – a fat man in his shirt-sleeves – observed placidly: 'Well, I fancy there ought to be another one just about six.' After noting this evidence of the 'terrible panic' among the remaining inhabitants of the south-east coast of Britain, we returned to contemplate, still under its strange spell, this bright ghost of a Margate. . . . This Margate I saw was saddening and hateful; but its new silence and desolation should be thought of as a bridge leading us to a better Margate in a better England, in a nobler world. We're not fighting to restore the past; it was the past that brought us to this heavy hour; but we *are* fighting to rid ourselves and the world of the evil encumbrance of these Nazis so that we can plan and create a noble future for all our species.

J.B. PRIESTLEY

Now everyone began in their different ways to prepare for the worst.

August 1940 Have you packed a kit-bag or basket ready to take into the shelter with you, along with your gas-mask, when the sirens sound? It is a good plan to have ready: (1) some cotton wool (for swabbing cuts); (2) absorbent gauze for dressing a cut; (3) a kit-bag to hold all these oddments; (4) a triangular bandage in case of fractures; (5) safety pins; (6) sal volatile; (7) tannic acid jelly for treating burns; (8) sticking plaster; (9) bleach ointment for blister gas casualties; (10) small bandages; (11) boric lint (for application to wounds); (12) scissors; (13) Elastoplast dressings; (14) ear plugs to deaden noise (cotton wool does just as well); (15) iodine; (16) a metal mirror and comb; (17) a bottle of antiseptic; (18) a pencil for use in making a tourniquet; (19) a jemmy (a useful tool in case of the door jamming, or if there is some debris to clear); (20) toys for the children; (21) a reliable torch (include a spare battery as well); (22) chocolate; (23) chewing gum to soothe the nerves of smokers who must not smoke in the refuge room. Some cold food and something to drink might also be added to this list. *HOUSEWIFE*

The babies who are being born now, or who are going to be born during the next few months, are certainly arriving at an exciting time in the world's history.

It is I think, reasonable to affirm now that no one place in the British Isles is safer than any other, so the best place to have baby is wherever you would have had him if there hadn't been a war at all. One would naturally avoid the more isolated coastal villages, since they seem rather to invite invasion; but, anyway, such places are probably all forbidden areas, so that point would not arise. . . .

Plan the whole of baby's outfit with the possibility in view of having to journey with him hastily from one place to another. . . .

A Moses basket will act as cradle *and* store for napkins; a large rubber beach bag or waterproof rucksack will hold wet napkins till they can be washed. A suitcase (if you've disposed of the napkins elsewhere) will take all baby clothes and a necessary change for yourself. A miniature hammock made of netting with a webbing strap at each end slung over your shoulder and fastened behind your back with a buckle, is an excellent thing in which to carry a baby if you have to walk any distance. The hammock takes most of baby's weight, and there is only his head to support on your arm.

At this particular time I would advise an all-knitted layette, as it takes less room in the suitcase and doesn't need any ironing. I would also advise you to accustom baby to taking a *little* bottle feed after his 2.0 pm breast feed. It need only be an ounce, so that he gets accustomed to it.

The point is that, however courageous you are, the actual noise of an air raid is apt to be very upsetting, and you may find yourself without milk for a few hours; then baby can have a full feed of the dried or evaporated milk to which he has become accustomed, and will return quite happily to the breast when, with returning serenity, your milk comes back.

Whether you've decided to have baby at home or away, it would be a wise precaution to have all your own requirements, sanitary sheets, mackintosh, nightgowns, sanitary towels and all the small etceteras you have prepared, fitted into a large suitcase, so that if your own house, for any reason, becomes uninhabitable, you can slip over the way and have your baby in the house of some hospitable friend. You'll be surprised and gratified to find how completely a confinement takes your mind off 'enemy operations'. *HOUSEWIFE*

As autumn approached there were many 'invasion' scares. This one occurred in 'a small fishing village on the south-west coast'.

In the evenings . . . members of the local contingent of the Home Guard used to assemble in the village inn for a chat. The leading lights were the vicar, who was seventy-two years of age, the village postman, and a fisherman who was in charge of a coastguard hut situated near the beach. They were all extremely enthusiastic, including a local farmer, who decided one evening to show me how well he could slope arms, but in his excitement he forgot that the inn ceiling was very low, and on bringing his rifle to the slope, promptly smashed the only light in the bar, putting the place in darkness. Several nights later . . . I was woken up in the early hours of the morning by the tolling of the church bell, and a shrill voice shouting below my bedroom window 'Invasion, sir, invasion!' I got up in a great hurry, put on a few articles of clothing, seized my cap and overcoat, and went out to see what was happening. In the road I found a collection of sinister looking figures, including the coastguard auxiliary, who announced that the enemy had landed, and that as I was the senior serving officer present they expected me to take charge of the proceedings. At this point the local policeman appeared, and asked me for my identity card. Quite right, too, as I suddenly realised that I must have looked a suspicious object, dressed in my pyjamas, and with an old blazer under my service coat. There were now whispers of 'Perhaps he's a Jerry or one of them fifth columnists', and similar remarks, until the situation was happily restored by the production of my identity card.

A moment later a farm hand ran up to say that the Germans had landed in force at the village of R——, about three miles away. After a short conference, during which everyone spoke in a subdued whisper, it was decided that the right thing to do would be to send out a patrol. Having called for volunteers, the vicar, accompanied by the publican, set off together on their mission and disappeared into the night. After giving orders to the rest of the party, I made my way to the village post-office, which I had announced would be my headquarters. Here I found the postmaster with a terrible-looking axe. His great idea seemed to be that he must smash the telephone at all costs if, as he said, 'things looked like getting serious'. Several attempts were made to get in touch with the village of R——, where the Germans were said to have landed, when in rushed a Home Guard in a state of great excitement. 'They are landing on the beach, sir, there's hundreds of them.' I told him to wait a moment while I collected one or two stalwarts, and we would then accompany him back to his post. When I returned I found that the messenger had gone, and so we were forced to grope our way through the sandhills without the help of a guide. We had not gone very far before we heard some terrible cursing and swearing just in front of us, and there was the missing runner with his foot caught in a rabbit snare. . . . After we had set him free we set off again, and a moment or two later we were peeping over the top of a sand hill not far from the beach. I crept alongside the look-out man, who pointed to the beach and whispered 'There they are, sir, hundreds of them'. There were hundreds of them, but they were not Germans. 'You silly ass,' I said, 'don't you know what those are? They are stakes placed on the beach to stop German aeroplanes landing at low tide.' The man was a local farmer, whose work never brought him near the shore, and so it was the first time that he had seen the alterations which had recently taken place. *HISTORY OF THE 8TH (BURTON) BATTALION, STAFFORDSHIRE HOME GUARD*

The Home Front

At last the massive air raids which everyone had expected a year earlier were launched against London and other cities. They were to become known as the Blitz.

September 7th was one of those beautiful early autumn days which feel like spring, and can make even London streets seem fresh and gay. There was hardly a wisp of cloud in the pale blue sky. At 4.43 pm the sirens wailed, and the population trooped to the shelters. The women were frankly fussed and ran, grabbing their children by bits of shirt or jacket; one woman rushed down, her hair a pile of soapsuds straight from the Saturday afternoon shampoo; the children were excited; the men made a point of swaggering in front of their women-folk, and walked slowly and soberly. But nobody was seriously frightened. There had been repeated 'alerts' and a few actual bombs dropped during the preceding weeks. Something might possibly happen this time, but probably not.

Within a few minutes a large V-shaped formation of planes flew over us, heading to the south-east. The tiny machines glinted in the sunlight and looked more like a flock of geese migrating before the winter than hostile aircraft. Soon they were followed by a smaller formation, each silver speck leaving a gossamer tail curving gracefully behind it. The old soldiers were very knowledgeable and told us they were 'ours'. Later that phrase, 'It's one of ours,' became one of my chief superstitions so often was it followed by the whistle and crump of bombs.

But that afternoon the danger was still remote from us. It was the East End that was 'getting it'. From where we were [in central London] we could see the miniature silver planes circling round and round the target area in such perfect formation that they looked like a children's toy model of flying boats or chair-o-planes at a fair. It was almost impossible to imagine that they were doing damage. Occasionally there would be a few puffs of Ack-Ack, but they were too low to interrupt the rhythm of the formations. As one set of planes flew off, another V-formation would fly in, stretch out into a 'follow-my-leader' line, and circle round as its predecessor had done.

Presently we saw a white cloud rising; it looked like a huge evening cumulus, but it grew steadily, billowing outwards and always up-wards. A fire-engine went by up the main road. The cloud grew to such a size that we gasped incredulously: there could not ever in history have been so gigantic a fire. Another fire-engine raced by, then a third, then a fourth, clanging their bells frenziedly as they shot across the traffic lights; our local sub-station turned out, nearly every fire appliance in London was heading east.

As evening drew on, the barrage balloons turned pink in the sunset light; or was it the firelight? They looked pretty enough, but the enormous cloud turned an angrier red, and blackened round the edges. From our vantage-point it was remote and, from a spectacular point of view, beautiful. One had to force onself to picture the misery and the havoc down below in the most overcrowded area of London; the panic and the horror when suddenly bombs had fallen in the busy, narrow street markets and bazaars, and on the rickety houses.

We were only four miles from this horror, but no one had any conception of what it was like. When the 'all clear' sounded at 6.15 pm people left the shelters saying 'About time too', little realising what lay in store for themselves . . . I felt, myself, that that was today's raid, and that we should probably have another tomorrow, but went off to Soho for dinner that evening. It was not, technically, one of my nights on duty. . . . I was annoyed when the siren went again before we had even reached the coffee.

When we came out of the restaurant we stopped aghast. The whole sky to the east was blazing red. The afternoon spectacle was completely dwarfed; it seemed as though half of London must be burning, and fifty thousand firemen would not be able to put out a fire of that size. In Shaftesbury Avenue, five miles from the blaze, it was possible to read the evening paper. Some planes were overhead, but one still had the false confidence of the afternoon that the docks were the target, and that these machines had empty bomb racks. With a whine and a crash a bomb fell somewhere near Charing Cross and the pavement trembled. It was the first time that I had heard a bomb, and in that instant I realised that the whole of London was a target area, and that Piccadilly and King's Cross were as important as the Albert Dock, and any street might get its share. We had to walk most of the way home; it was an unpleasant journey, but one could hardly be missing on the first real raid. . . .

By 10 pm the shelterers were growing exasperated; if it did not stop soon it would be past 'closing time'! By midnight they were frightened. Very few of them had imagined that they would have to sit in a shelter for more than an hour or so; neither for that matter, and more inexcusably, had the authorities. They had not brought rugs or blankets or provisions, some even had no coats, as it had been a warm evening. The wooden benches round the walls were packed, and the remainder had to stand, or sit on bits of newspaper on the concrete floor: the overcrowding was appalling, and the air stank. . . .

I found the bombs terrified me less than did the people in the shelters. It had not before occurred to me that a warden would be expected not only just to poke his head round the door to see if there was anything wrong, but to chat to one and all, and try to cheer them up. In all the nine shelters that came within our province I knew only two people slightly. I was horribly embarrassed, and . . . stood awkwardly by the door, smiled stupidly, and could say nothing. One of the good things about the war, however, was the friendliness that the common danger evoked, and comparatively soon I realised that the mere sight of a tin hat gave people a spurious sense of confidence, and that they were really pleased to see one. Whereas before few of us had even known our next-door neighbour, within a week people called 'good morning' to one from their bedroom windows, and we chatted in the grocer's as though we were villagers. Later, I had cause to visit every shelter in the borough, and I doubt if many people have as large and varied a circle of acquaintances as I collected.

By 3 am the raid was heavier than ever and the bombs were much closer – they came down with a tearing sound as well as a whistle; they did not fall, they rushed at enormous velocity, as though dragged down towards the earth by some supernaturally gigantic magnet. Planes began to circle steadily and monotonously overhead, just as we had seen them circling over the East End in the afternoon. It was alarming to feel that this time it was we who were the target: sticks of four, sticks of six, came crashing down, and still the planes circled above, and the houses rocked and trembled. I was alarmed. One hadn't got a chance. For half an hour the bombs pounded down all round us; as one struck another started on its downward journey, and we crouched in the doorways thinking that the next one *must* get us. But we were wrong; neighbouring sectors were hit; ours was let off unscathed. . . .

At dawn the 'all clear' went, and groups of pale and jaded people trailed back to their homes to snatch a cup of tea before leaving for work. They were cold and exhausted and subdued; 'D'you think we'll get another tonight, Miss?' they asked. It was as well that they could not know that they were to get 'another' for fifty-seven nights on end, and after that some raids that were going to make this night's look like child's play.   BARBARA NIXON

Much was heard of the heroism of the East End under repeated bombing.
Not all of it was true.

After the terror of that night people [in the East End] started to flock towards the tube. They wanted to get underground. Thousands upon thousands the next evening pushed their way into Liverpool Street Station, demanded to be let down to shelter. At first the authorities wouldn't agree to it and they called out the soldiers to bar the way. I stood there in the thick of the crowd with my mother and father and brothers and sisters [from Stepney] thinking that there would be a panic and we would all be crushed to death.

It was the worst experience I had up until then and I wanted to rush out of that crowd, but I was jammed tight. I would have preferred to take my chances in the street with the bombs. Anything was preferable to that crush. I shouted my head off, went limp and was carried along by the surging masses, trying to hold on to my slipping identity. The people would not give up and would not disperse, would not take no for an answer. A great yell went up and the gates were opened and my mother threw her hands together and clutched them towards the sky. 'Thank God. He heard me'. . . .

'It's a great victory for the working class,' a man said, 'one of our big victories.'

And though I felt ill and my heart was beating over-fast, all the family were thrilled to know that people had taken over the underground and made the government acquiesce.

So I dashed with the crowd into the underground and saw the solidarity of the surface disappear as an endless stream of people crushed in after us. We were underground people with the smell of disinfectant in our nostrils and blankets under our arms, standing jammed, shoving and pushing each other. No laughter, no humour. What sort of victory had we achieved? Every family for itself now, and my mother tried to encompass all her family with her bulk, a family that had emigrated into the bowels of the earth. Dignity and joy left the world, my world. Shuffling down I felt as if we were fulfilling some awful prophecy. A prophecy that no one had uttered to me. Something that everyone knew but didn't want to talk about.

The soldiers downstairs forced us to get into trains, to go further up the line. Liverpool Street, being the closest geographically and umbilically, was the most popular. So we were forced to move on and we tried the next station along the Central Line, and then the next and the next. . . .

Some people feel a certain nostalgia for those days, recall a poetic dream about the Blitz. They talk about those days as if they were time of a true communal spirit. Not to me. It was the beginning of an era of utter terror, of fear and horror. I stopped being a child and came face to face with the new reality of the world.

I would scoot out of the train ahead of the family and under the legs of people, unravelling the three or four scarves tied around me. And I bagged any space I could along the platform. The family followed, and we pitched our 'tent', then we unravelled and unwound and relaxed. And out came the sandwiches and the forced good humour. Here we were back on the trot, wandering again, involved in a new exodus – the Jews of the East End, who had left their homes, and gone into the exile of the underground. Our spirits would rise for a while, we were alive for another night, we would see another dawn. . . .

But I wasn't only miserable, for seizing advantage of my mother's preoccupations, I managed to get some money out of her. And I got bars and bars of chocolate out of the chocolate machines and weighed myself incessantly. Here was a new life, a whole network, a whole city under the world. We rode up and down the escalators. The children of London were adapting themselves to the times, inventing new games, playing hopscotch while their mothers shyly suckled young babies on the concrete. And I used to ride backwards and forwards in the trains to see the other stations of underground people.   BERNARD KOPS

Wardens and other Civil Defence workers now learned rapidly what no exercise could teach them.

My first incident occurred one afternoon in the second week. . . .

It was a grey, damp afternoon in late September, ten days after the start of the air-blitz on London. I was bicycling along a shabby street in a district some miles from my own. . . .

Suddenly, before I heard a sound, the shabby, ill-lit, five-storey building ahead of me swelled out like a child's balloon, or like a Walt Disney house having hiccups. I looked at it in astonishment, that bricks and mortar could stretch like rubber. At the point when it must burst, the glass fell out. It did not hurtle, it simply cracked and dropped out, allowing the straining building to deflate and return to normal. Almost instantaneously there was a crash and a double explosion in the street to my right. As the blast of air reached me I left my saddle and sailed through the air, heading for the area railings. The tin hat on my shoulder took the impact, and as I stood up I was mildly surprised to find that I was not hurt in the least. . . .

For no reason except that one handbook had said so, I blew my whistle. An old lady appeared in her doorway and asked, 'What was all that?' I told her it was a bomb, but she was stone-deaf and I had to abandon bawling for pantomime of a bomb exploding before she would agree to go into a surface shelter. After putting a dressing on some small cuts on a man's face, I turned back towards the site of the damage. . . .

At four in the afternoon there would certainly be casualties. Now I would know whether I was going to be of any use as a warden or not, and I wanted to postpone the knowledge . . . I was not let down lightly. In the middle of the street lay the remains of a baby. It had been blown clean through the window, and had burst on striking the roadway. To my intense relief, pitiful and horrible as it was, I was not nauseated, and found a torn piece of curtain in which to wrap it. Two H.E. bombs had fallen on the new flats, and a third on an equally new garage opposite. In all this grimy derelict area, they had struck the only decent habitations.

The C.D. services arrived quickly. . . . I offered my services, and was thanked but given nothing to do, so busied myself finding blankets to cover the five or six mutilated bodies in the street. A small boy, aged about 13, had one leg torn off and was still conscious, though he gave no sign of any pain. In the garage a man was pinned under a capsized Thorneycroft [lorry], and most of the side wall and roof were piled on top of that. The Heavy Rescue Squad brought ropes, cleared away the debris, and heaved and tugged at the immense lorry for an hour. They got the man out, unconscious, but alive. He looked like a terracotta statue, his face, his teeth, his hair, were all a uniform brick colour.

Eleven had been killed but a larger number were badly injured – an old man staggered down supported by two girls holding a towel to his face; as we laid him on a stretcher the towel dropped, and his face was shockingly cut away by glass. . . .

By now the news had travelled, and women back from shopping, girls, and a few men from local factories, came running and scrambling over the debris in the street. 'Where is Julie?' 'Is my Mum all right?' I was besieged, but I could not help them. They shouted the names of their relatives and scanned the faces of the dusty, dishevelled survivors. Those who found that they had lost a relation seemed numbed by the shock and were quiet, whereas a woman who found her family intact promptly had hysterics. . . .

A little later I left: there was nothing apparently that I could do. . . . I felt discouraged and depressed. My bicycle was bent, but since the wheels would go round, I clanked and wobbled on it back to my own Post.   BARBARA NIXON

Returning one night from one of these visits to Catherine, [a friend in hospital] I took a short cut through a side street from the hospital. There was no transport and walking was the only way of getting back to Chelsea. There was the usual raid on, and it had been very noisy, but now it was quieter and only occasional bursts of gun-fire shook the silence of the streets. Passing a gap in a terrace I saw a little group of people bending over what seemed to be a hole in what had been the basement of a house but which now appeared to be filled in with debris. A car stood in the road with the notice 'doctor' on it. It was dark, but I could see that there were three men bending over the hole and one woman. The woman wore nurse's uniform.

As I hurried by she turned, said something to the others, then called to me, 'Nurse.' I went over. The man bending over the hole straightened up, but I could not look at him because of the appalling sound coming from the hole. Someone was in mortal anguish down there. The woman in nurse's uniform who was tall and very largely built, said sharply to me, 'What are your hip measurements?' I said, above the horrible moaning from the hole, 'Thirty-four inches.' One of the men took a piece of stick and measured it across my shoulders, then across my hips, and then put it across the hole. 'Easy – an inch to spare each side,' he said.

'Will you let us lower you down there to help that man trapped and in great pain?' he asked. 'We're all too large for the hole – and we daren't widen it until the Heavy Rescue Squad come to shore it all up.'

'What must I do?' I asked fearfully, for I was tired already, and the black hole was not inviting.

'Just do as you're told, that's all,' said the large nurse.

'All right,' I agreed.

'Take off your coat,' said the doctor. I took it off. 'And your dress,' he said. 'It's too dangerous – the folds may catch in the debris and bring the whole thing down – better without it.' I took off the dress. 'Fine,' he said shortly when I stood in the 'black-outs', as we called the closed black panties which most of us wore with uniform. 'It'll have to be head first. We'll hold your thighs. Go down first with this torch and see if it's possible to give a morphia injection or not – I doubt it. Ready?'

'Yes,' I said faintly for I was terrified.

'Better hold the torch in your mouth, and keep your arms tight to your sides,' he said. 'Can you grip the torch with your teeth?' I nodded – it was as if I was having a nightmare from which I would soon waken. 'Ready?' Two wardens gripped me by the thighs, swung me up and lowered me down over the hole. 'Keep your body absolutely rigid,' said the doctor.

'Don't be afraid – we'll hold you safe,' said the large woman. 'I ought to be doing this – but I'm too big.'

The sound coming from the hole was unnerving me – it was like an animal in a trap. I had once heard a long screaming like rabbits in traps from children with meningitis in India, but this was worse – almost inhuman in its agony. The torch showed me that the debris lay over both arms and that the chest of the man trapped there was crushed into a bloody mess – great beams lay across the lower part of his body – and his face was so injured that it was difficult to distinguish the mouth from the rest of it – it all seemed one great gaping red mess.

The blood had rushed to my head from being upside down. Fortunately I had done some acrobatic dancing and had been held in this manner previous to being whirled round in the dance, so that keeping my body stiff was not too much of a strain, but the stench of blood and mess down there caught the pit of my stomach and I was afraid of vomiting and dropping the precious torch. There was plenty of room for my arms at the bottom of the hole so I took the torch cautiously from my teeth and began trying to soothe the remains of what had once been a man. He could still hear, for after I had repeated several times the formula we had been told to use to reassure trapped casualties, 'Try to keep calm – we're working to get you out. You'll soon be all right. . . . Very soon now,' the horrible screaming stopped, but the gap which had once been a mouth was trying to say something . . . it was impossible to catch what it was . . . so unintelligible were the sounds. 'Pull me up,' I called, and put the torch back in my mouth and kept my arms rigidly to my sides as they hauled me up. On my feet I felt violent nausea and vomited again and again. They stood back, and the doctor handed me a huge handkerchief.

'All right?' he asked when it was over. I was deeply ashamed, apologised, and told him what I had seen. 'Have to be chloroform,' he said shortly. 'Have you seen it given on a pad?' I nodded. He took the bottle with a dropper from his case and a cotton mask.

'I'll hold it in my mouth,' I said. 'When I'm down, if someone shines the torch down I'll be able to see.' The terrible screaming had started again down there. All I felt now was the urgency to stop it. 'How many drops?' I asked.

'All of this,' he said grimly, 'and hold it over the face as near to the nostrils as you can judge. Try and keep yourself from inhaling it – be as quick as you can.'

I took the pad and the small bottle in my mouth. The big nurse lay down on her stomach by the hole – I thought it was asking for trouble for the whole structure was perilous and one false move could bring the whole pile down on to the trapped man and extinguish what small flicker of life remained there. But she did it very cautiously and carefully, so that she could shine a torch down for me. 'Ready?' asked the two tough-looking men in overalls. I nodded. They gripped my thighs and swung me upside down and lowered me again into blackness.

'I'm back again, you see,' I said to the terrible anguished thing down there. 'The doctor has given me something to help the pain – they'll soon be here now to get you out.' I was dropping the chloroform on to the pad now. 'Breathe deeply – can you?' A sound as from an animal – a grunt – came from the thing which had been a face. I held the pad firmly over him. 'Breathe deeply . . . deeply . . . deeply. . . .' There was a small convulsive movement of revulsion . . . another fainter one – and then the sounds stopped. All was quiet. The chloroform was affecting me, and it was all I could do to call 'Ready' and they hauled me up. I disgraced myself by violently vomiting again and again – this time intensified by the chloroform and the stench of blood, for there were other bodies down there – I had seen the pieces. The big nurse held my head, and hastily pulled my

70

dress back on me and then buttoned me into my coat.

'All right?' asked the doctor, taking my wrist professionally. 'Breathe deeply yourself now – go on, several big deep breaths.' I recovered quickly, and said I'd be getting along – it was very late.

'I'd drive you home,' he said, 'but we're wanted elsewhere. That'll keep that poor fellow quiet until the rescue squad arrive to take over so that I can get down myself. Thank you, nurse. You did very well.' All I wanted was to get away – I was going to be sick again.

'Run along while it's quiet,' advised one of the wardens. I went – but I did not run. All the way back to Chelsea I vomited at intervals. An awful shivering had taken hold of me – and nothing could stop it. I had never seen anything like that horror in the hole. . . .

I lay in bed and I thought of all those times we V.A.D.s had been dropped into holes for the rescue men to practise on us – and I thought of the times my sister and I had had a craze for acrobatic dancing and learned to be held upside down by the thighs or ankles. Who would have thought that such things would ever have been so useful?
FRANCES FAVIELL

For the hard-pressed fireman and Civil Defence workers the Blitz brought a dramatic change of attitude on the part of the public.

I couldn't stand any more of . . . not seeing Mary, so I 'phoned up her unit and arranged for her to come out with me. We went to the same restaurant (it's still there) where we went before, and instead of being greeted by the manager and the waiter as doubtful characters, he ushered us both to the best table and waited on us personally, saying: 'Nothing can be too good for a London fireman!' . . . When I asked for the bill, he waved airily at me and said: 'Have this on the house . . . it's a pleasure. . . .' *THE BELLS GO DOWN*

Our little pub at the corner of Lancaster Gate Terrace underwent many changes during that last fortnight in September and the first fortnight in October. It was a popular pub, because nearly all the people in the Terrace lived in single rooms, and found in its cheerful atmosphere a common meeting-place. Also one could get hot steaks and chips there of an evening, or if one preferred to sit up at the bar, there was an excellent choice of cold dishes to be had. . . . At first Australian and Canadian soldiers used to fill it and one could hardly get near the bar. After the first week of September these soldiers from the Dominions seemed to be spirited away from London. The casuals, too, dropped off, for most Londoners were beginning to accustom themselves to eating and drinking as near their homes as possible. So gradually the *Crown* came back almost to its peace-time atmosphere, when most people in the bar knew each other. Among the people I used to eat or drink with there was a young War Office psychiatrist, who grumbled that so far he had not had enough to do since leaving private practice; a quiet young naval officer who worked at the Admiralty; a blonde girl who worked in a Government office, and a starry-eyed brunette who was a school-teacher. . . . The psychiatrist was the first to bring us a bomb story, so for a few days he was more important in the bar than the town-crier in a mediaeval village. For he had been in the Medical School at Millbank when it was hit. He had not been greatly disturbed by it, and in fact, as London was his first experience under fire, he was rather proud. We drank a lot that night as guns roared outside and bombs swished down somewhere, but not on our pub.

If, however, there was anyone in that pub who had not had a bomb story, one October night conferred on them that honour. All along bombs had been falling somewhere in the district. We were near Paddington station, and we gathered that Paddington was the objective (if, in fact, the Germans had any particular objective those days in London, except to release their bombs and go). Many fell harmlessly in the Park. We rarely heard them swish down, for there was such a buzz of talk and blare of radio-gramophone records inside that only the guns penetrated it. In fact, the guns developed into a rather dramatic background for a gay evening. But this night, when we were all sitting up on our stools at the cold-dinner counter, we heard the terrifying crash before the swish. The explosion was terribly near, and threw some glass over us, but no one was hurt. Instinctively we all dived under the counter, and when we rose, the starry-eyed girl, nervous but laughing, called out, 'Who was down first, the Army or the Navy?'

After that, however, bombs seemed to come nearer and nearer to us. The night after, one washed out about five houses and a cheerful little pub only a hundred yards away; faces at the bar were drawn and there was not a lot of talk. Grim-faced rescue squads, who had been engaged on a gruesome task the whole day, were among those at the bar. They drank their pints silently, and went out through the gunfire to carry on with their task.

Cooking arrangements were now being gradually curtailed, and the steaks and chips disappeared from the menu as various gas mains were cut. Sometimes the lights went out in the pub as electric cables were hit, but usually they came on again in about half an hour. The grey-moustached waiter . . . was unhappy when the steaks and chips and hot meals went. He used to like to place it in front of you with a flourish to show you that everything was as usual, though guns were popping outside. . . .

As bombs drew nearer to us, and gunfire became almost an uninterrupted symphony during the hours of darkness, many of the regular customers at our pub fell away. In fact, a number of people were leaving the Terrace and moving fifteen to twenty miles out of London, mostly to the north and west, so that they could get more sleep at night. . . . Some people arranged to sleep overnight at their business places, if adequate shelter was provided. So the crowd that gathered at the bar of the *Crown* grew thinner and thinner. The psychiatrist was moved out of London, the young naval officer too disappeared, and the blonde Government clerk was asked to sleep in her offices, where a deep shelter was provided. The starry-eyed girl remained, and she and I used to eat at the pub pretty regularly. Gradually she found that the guns were beginning to get her down, and would not leave her room if the barrage was very intensive.

As the customers fell away, our landlord, a tough-looking Cockney, started to close earlier. The siren sounded every night somewhere between eight and nine, which just gave us enough time to finish our evening meal before the symphony started. Sometimes it began just as we were in the middle of the meal, but the pub remained open until we were finished. Then the owner and his staff went down the neighbouring Tube station to shelter. A new crowd of customers started to patronise us – the Tube shelterers. They usually staked out their claims about six o'clock. I would see them hurrying along the Terrace, carrying deck-chairs, eiderdowns and blankets as I returned home of an evening. . . . If the siren did not sound as early as usual, the men-folk in the Tube came upstairs to have one. Many of the shelterers came from the other end of London. In the early stages of the bombing they had travelled from station to station looking for a place on the platforms. Once they had found one that suited them they made a habit of being in at the 'early doors'. . . .

The dull, heavy, rain sodden weather of October had now set in, and I used to look forward to the cheerful atmosphere of this pub, where you forgot bombs and guns with a few beers and a lot of talk. The weather seemed to make no difference to the raiders, and many a time as I came along the Bayswater Road when the clouds were low, and the rain was driving hard against the pavement, I could still hear the drone of the bombers, sometimes very low. These nights it was good to push open the door and emerge from the black-out into an atmosphere of light and music with a hubbub all round you. One felt safer inside, though there was no reason in the world for the feeling, except that to be among people makes danger seem less. But the next bomb that whistled down in that district put an end to that pleasant call on the way home. I was not there at the time. It was not a big bomb, but it dug itself deep in the pavement, and did something to the foundations of the building. Apart from glass and woodwork hurled inside, causing a few more injuries, there was no damage. The interior was intact, but a few days later I saw an official notice up outside the window: 'These premises have been closed in the interests of public safety.'   JEROME WILLIS

But it was on the East End that the real weight of the attack was still falling. Among those coping with the post-raid chaos was the mayor of Stepney.

We resolved to occupy the People's Palace, the theatre in the Mile End Road where I had listened to opera while the first bombs fell. This place was big enough to give us elbow-room in handling the masses of homeless who were already tramping in like a retreating army, seeking our assistance. It was universally known, central, and – an important point – served by plenty of roads. . . .

The hours of 9 pm to 5 am were spent, if possible, in a shelter; in my case an Anderson. . . . One could get two hours' sleep after 5 am; then a wash and clean-up and a good breakfast (amazing how food and hot coffee or tea put heart into one); then a day's work till six or later; then a hearty night-meal, followed by an hour's sleep before the sirens went again.

When we first set up business at the People's Palace . . . our very first task was to arrange for the evacuation of mothers and small children who had been rendered homeless, and, after those, for mothers and children who wished to get out of London. . . .

I see myself, dog-tired after a terrific day's work, dragging wearily out of the People's Palace and seeing in front of me a great area of deserted prams in the evening light, with the drifting smoke of nearby burning houses dimming them. . . . The mothers had brought their babies in prams – and, of course, we had not foreseen that – and, as they could not take the prams with them on the overcrowded trains, they just had to leave them there in front of the building, so that it was, by evening, hardly possible to get in or out except by climbing over a great expanse of them. . . .

You must try to picture the bombed-out as I saw them. White-faced, their homes and lives shattered, often with the grime on their faces runnelled with tears for husbands or children or other dear ones newly dead – or just missing – beneath fallen rubble. Or maybe not identified, because how can you identify a bit of an arm or some charred rags?

They had crept out of the shelter of underground stations, perhaps, or church crypts or brick shelters. Some of them had only night attire on, because that was how they had been blown into the street by a bomb that wrecked their houses. Many glided along as if they had risen from the dead.

They came past houses with no windows and no roofs, houses split and frontless, sectioned, maybe with the furniture showing on each floor.

Here is fair-haired Mrs Caroline Wright of Frances Grey House, a block of flats in Ocean Street. She is wearing bedroom slippers and has a baby on one arm and a cardboard suitcase under the other. Her husband is in the Army. There is a time-bomb down her street and it is roped off. . . .

'Time bombers', as they were called, were one of those problems that had not been foreseen. No billets were provided for them at first because, after all, their houses were still standing . . . temporarily.

So Mrs Wright comes to us. I am not a married man, and the mysteries of napkins are out of my depth; but the W.V.S., that magnificent body of selfless women . . . are here in the basement of the new Council offices, sorting bundles of clothing to provide a new frock for seven months' Harry Wright, and more napkins and food. . . .

There are clothless tables down in that basement, and on those tables are laid hundreds of slices of bread and jam for breakfast, and hot tea, and a hot meal a head for all who need it at midday, and bread and jam for tea. At nights the tables are pushed against the walls and row on row of stretcher beds are placed there for the time-bombers to sleep on till better accommodation can be found for them. . . .

Though our 'guests' in the basement did pretty well for meals, I and my staff were not so well off. For periods when the stuff had been coming down heavily we had no lighting, no gas, no cooking apparatus, no drainage, no water to wash our hands, no telephone.

On one occasion every telephone message we wanted to send – or receive – had to go from the one telephone in that part of Stepney that Goering seems to have missed. It was in Harry Lewis's tailor's shop opposite. . . . Presently a very large crater turned up just outside, so that anyone hurrying out in the dark could fall into it; and, in fact, it was perfectly easy to go headlong over the rubble at any time. Lewis's shop was later destroyed by fire; but, by that time, the ant-like industry of the public services had got our own telephone working again. . . .

W.V.S. ladies, cooking on oil-stoves that they had brought from somewhere, cheek-by-jowl with us as we worked over our endless forms and interminable crowds of people. They cooked our dinners just beside our elbows; and if we stuck too hard to our work they came round and fed us. Teachers – those wonderful teachers; Council staff; voluntary helpers of no organization; old men and women; bombed-out children messengers; clergy; nuns, publicans and sinners.

Trestle-tables everywhere, with hundreds of parcels of clothing on them, being swiftly sorted; blitzed victims passing in and out of my office and receiving a signed chit for whatever they required, and taking it down to the tables to have clothes fitted; records being improvised to prevent people taking advantage and getting more than they required; . . . Council lorries rattling through the cratered streets to pick up furniture from smashed houses, or furniture that was being so generously given to replace some of what had been destroyed; and, as a background to it all, the sirens wailing every few hours, and the drone of bombers overhead, and the whine and crash of bombs, and the everlasting sour smell of smoke. . . .

FRANK. R. LEWEY

Conditions in many shelters in the early days led to a public outcry. The most notorious of all was in the Isle of Dogs, Poplar, which was noted by an American journalist.

We went down a long damp flight of stairs at the bottom of which we found a small cubby-hole office with a counter window in it, several policemen and wardens standing about. . . . Suddenly we came into a great cavernous room. It had been the sub-cellar basement of some commercial establishment and along one side were rows of wagons – flat-bottomed wagons with enormous wheels. In parts of the cellar there were counters raised a few feet from the ground.

It was impossible to take in the whole room. . . . You cannot take in the concept of thousands upon thousands of people sleeping in a dim-lit cave. The room into which we had just arrived was simply carpeted, blanketed, draped with people.

They lay in long rows the length of the counters. They filled the wagons with arms and legs and heads sticking over the tops. They sat propped against the wheels of the wagons. They balanced miraculously on the couplings. They were under the wagons, packed into each other. I remember an old lady, bolt upright, in a kitchen chair with a black shawl wrapped around her.

In the open places they lay in rows with just room enough for us to walk down aisles lined by badly shod, twisted, sprawled feet. It was still only about ten o'clock but about half of them were asleep. Most of those who were awake looked up with only mild curiosity. Many men had their hats on. A woman was sitting undoing her hair. Two women near her were whispering together. Here was a little island of reclining camp chairs. The people in them were old and fat and looked tired, even asleep.

We walked on and on, up one row and down another. It took the conversation and the questioning out of us. We just walked. . . .

The standard toilet unit in an East End shelter is a three foot square of floor screened to perhaps 6 feet high by burlap [canvas] tacked to a little wooden frame. The front side is simply a curtain, pushed aside to enter. Inside there is a bucket with chemicals in the bottom. Signs tacked on the front say 'Men', 'Women'. They smell. In this shelter of 8,000 people there were six of these burlap-screened conveniences for men, six for women. All that I saw were on the floor where the people slept.

We went back through other rooms as full of people. The whole experience shocked so that it numbed.

We drove back to the Dorchester [from the Isle of Dogs], not talking much. . . . We went in in our steel helmets, past the people who slept in the lobby. A waiter who was just leaving took us down. We went past the empty kitchen and around a corner into what were once the Turkish baths. And there they were, the sleepers in the Dorchester shelter. A neat row of cots, spaced about two feet apart, each one covered with a lovely fluffy eiderdown. Its silks billowed and shone in the dim lights in pale pinks and blues. Behind each cot hung the negligée, the dressing-gown. By each cot the mules and the slippers. Alongside, the little table with the alligator-skin dressing case. The pillows on which the heads lay were large and full and white. . . . They did not sleep as well as the heads slept in the Liverpool Street tube. Even though it was 3 am and we tiptoed, most of them raised off the pillows and eyed us defensively. There was a little sign pinned to one of the Turkish-bath curtains. It said, 'Reserved for Lord Halifax.'
RALPH INGERSOLL

21 September 1940 Just as common sense dictates that one does not stand under a tree during a thunderstorm, so it is reasonable that those who can should seek shelter from present dangers. . . .

Queen's Hotel, Penzance . . . for a sense of security cannot be beaten . . . Torquay. You can sleep at the Grand Hotel, for the drone of an aero engine is rare and sirens even more infrequent.

Sundridge Park, Bromley . . . An up to date hotel in every respect, even to an exceptionally strong bomb-proof shelter.

Station Hotel, Perth. Free from alarms.

Advertisement for 'Sanctuary Hotels Recommended by Ashley Courtenay' in *THE TIMES*

You and your neighbours can easily make your brick street shelter into a place where you can spend many hours at night, not only in comfort but under conditions where your family's health and your own will not suffer. . . . There is a great deal you can do at little or no cost to make the shelter healthy and homelike. You can begin by getting some old rolls of wallpaper – shopkeepers often have some they are willing to sell for a few pence. Paper the walls of your shelter and whitewash the ceiling.

A home-made heater can be made with two large flower pots and a candle . . . A balaclava helmet, such as every soldier knows, will keep draughts off your head . . . By far the best bedding for any shelter is a properly made sleeping bag. . . . Take any Army or similar thick blanket about seven feet long and six feet six inches wide . . . line with muslin or cotton material making pockets, which should be well stuffed with old newspaper.

MINISTRY OF HOME SECURITY LEAFLET: *YOUR BRICK STREET SHELTER THIS WINTER*, 1940

Animals, too, had to 'stick it out' in London. Professor Julian Huxley, secretary of the Zoological Society of London, notes the following reactions of animals and birds to air raids.

Most animals quickly accustom themselves to raids and after a night or two pay no more attention to them.

Camels at the Zoo didn't even get up when a bomb fell within ten yards of their cage.

Rooks, jays and magpies get very excited during bombing, and moorhens take shelter, but swallows and robins don't seem to mind them a bit.

Hens are put off laying, but not guineafowl.

Dogs and cats vary in their reactions about as human beings do.

Two cases have been reported of dogs which unfailingly distinguish between friendly and enemy aircraft.

Two dogs and a cat can differentiate between the Alert and the All Clear.

If bombs drop close one cat will awaken its mistress, who is deaf.

Other cats choose their own air-raid shelters, to which they repair during a raid.

Many animals, particularly dogs, ducks, parrots, geese, gulls, owls and pheasants, are aware of aircraft before human beings hear them.

Parrots imitate sirens.

Animals generally regarded by their keepers as incurably nervous, such as antelopes and giraffes, do not seem unduly worried by bombs.

Chimpanzees don't mind guns, but shriek at the sound of sirens.

BASIL WOON

On one of those days [in the basement shelter of an East End vicarage] I asked a woman whether she prayed when she heard a bomb falling.

'Yes,' she answered; 'I pray, Oh God! Don't let it fall here.'

'But,' I said, 'it's a bit rough on other people, if your prayer is granted, and the thing drops, not on you, but on them.'

'I can't help that,' she replied, 'they must say their prayers and push it off further.'   REV. H.A. WILSON

The most destructive weapon of all was not high explosive but fire. The Germans dropped many thousands of small, one kilo, incendiary bombs in every major raid and ordinary civilians rapidly became expert in dealing with them.

Richard and I were married during one of London's heaviest daylight raids. Because of this none of our guests turned up for the ceremony — and, what was more important, neither of the witnesses did. We went out into the deserted street and found two taxi-drivers, who were philosophic about bombs – saying that bombs or no bombs they had to eat and what was the use of staying alive if one's stomach was empty? They acted willingly and charmingly as witnesses, and afterwards tossed up as to which of them should drive us to the Guards' Club where we had invited our friends to lunch. The All Clear sounded before we reached there and most of the guests turned up, although some were late because they had been on duty during the raid. . . . When we got back to Cheyne Place, Mrs Freeth [the housekeeper] had tied a white ribbon round Vicki's [the dog's] neck and had put flowers everywhere and Mr Ferebee [a neighbour] had sent over some champagne.

In the evening some friends came in to drink our health, but the sirens went very early and most of them had to rush away on duty. We spent the first night of our marriage putting out incendiaries. . . . It was exhilarating, especially as we drank champagne in between the bouts of fire-fighting. When there appeared to be a lull in the dropping of these small fire bombs we decided to go to bed. There were now high explosive bombs being dropped and the barrage was very noisy. One bottle of champagne had been opened but not drunk, and as we appreciated the fact that French wines were already scarce we put it in a pail of ice, intending to drink it last thing before going to bed – but we forgot it.

In the early hours of the morning we were both awoken by a loud explosion in the room. 'It's a fire-bomb come through the window,' I said, for the plop was exactly like the plopping explosions of the small incendiaries which we had now become accustomed to extinguishing. But there was no sign of a fire-bomb – the champagne cork lay on the bed and the ceiling was splashed all over with champagne. I was astonished that it could explode to such a height and make such a mess.   FRANCES FAVIELL

Although concentrated on London, the Blitz was extended during the winter of 1940 to many provincial cities.

Along with the rest of the city centre of Coventry, our flat was reduced to rubble on the night of 14/15th November. We took such necessities as we could find, put them on a borrowed handcart and pushed them to my father's house on the outskirts of the city. Two days later, a chauffeur-driven car arrived to drive us anywhere we wanted to go. The managing director (of my husband's firm) had sent it, plus two weeks' pay.

We were very dirty, with clothes heavy with dust. There was no water in the city and my father and brother had collected a meagre daily ration of fresh water from a well on factory premises outside the town. We used it sparingly for absolute essentials, so washing meant a small bowl of water for hands and face, between six of us. There was certainly none to spare for hair-washing, though even with brushing Peter and I had hair greyed with dust, so we looked very unkempt in our fine limousine. We were driven in a wide detour round the wreckage of Coventry, until gradually we came to countryside, villages and towns, quietly drowsing in the normality of Sunday, worlds away from what we'd left.

No shops or cafés were open, so we drove on until we reached Bath. . . . By that time in the afternoon, I, being in the early stages of pregnancy, was weak from exhaustion. The chauffeur drove to a palatial hotel in one of Bath's Regency crescents. He and Peter helped me from the car, up the steps to the hotel lounge, where I sank into a chair. The residents were having tea. After an astonished, horrified glance at our appearance, they pointedly ignored us. . . . The plate of postage-stamp sized cucumber sandwiches made us smile, for we were in no mood for dainty picking – we were *hungry*, so a plate of tiny scones was also brought. As that was all there was, it had to do until we could get a real meal.

At a nearby table sat an old woman, heavily made-up and dressed in a feathered hat and an expensive dress. Her claw-like, red-tipped hands completed the illusion in my weary mind that she looked like a parrot. As she pecked at her food, she gave morsels to the small pekinese on her lap. In a stage whisper she spoke to the pekinese, lamenting the breakdown of standards caused by the war, when one must eat in the same room as *most* disreputable-looking people who knew no better than to share a table with a chauffeur. What *was* the world coming to? . . .

As we got up to leave, someone glanced from the window, noticed the registration plates on our beautiful car, and realised we must be from Coventry. Instantly we were the centre of excited attention, with the parrot-woman particularly making much of us. We learned that the Sunday papers had been full of pictures and news of the city's devastation and there we were – real live heroes and heroine who had experienced it all. MEGAN RYAN

I was twelve years old when the war started. On 21st December 1940 we were bombed out. . . . We were in our usual place under the stairs. My sister and I (fully clothed as the raids became more severe, with overcoats at hand) and our dog lay on a mattress and slept when possible. My mother and father sat in the pantry which was also under the stairs. My brother was at sea – my special hero *he* was. The raid started as usual at tea-time. It was always a rush to get tea over and 'pots' cleared away before the siren went. . . . After a dreadful night, with mobile A.A. guns going off around us and a tremendous number of bombs and incendiaries falling, we heard different explosions which were later found to be landmines. Soon after these, all resistance from A.A. guns seemed to end. We could only hear bombs and the thud-thud drone of the German planes. . . . It was bright moonlight and the first 'near miss' blew our windows in at the back of the house. The bomb didn't whine, it just sounded like a gust of wind before the explosion. My father dashed into the kitchen and could see the windows blown out and the curtains in shreds. He shouted 'The blackout!' and threw a kettleful of water on the dying embers of the fire in the grate. There were always lulls in the raids and during one of these my father had a look out and saw the whole area seemed to be on fire and there were lots of people shouting and firemen and wardens terribly active. We stayed in our places under the stairs and soon afterwards . . . a bomb fell in our back garden and I must say I was scared stiff. We stayed where we were and everything seemed to be falling in on us. We were quite unharmed, but my father said we mustn't move until the bombing stopped. Water started running down the stairs and the hall became flooded, but we were not wet. At dawn when the raid was over we looked out and found the hall full of water and our hats and coats floating about. The stairs were covered with rubble and my father went upstairs and said the water tank was broken and leaking, and that all the beds were covered with rubble and broken glass. The front room furniture had been thrown all over the room and the windows were blown out from a bomb which had had a direct hit opposite us. The road was full of rescue workers and I saw a friend of mine carried by a blanket and the blanket was over her head and I knew she was dead.

As we were wandering around the house my brother came running home – he had sailed up the River Mersey and seen both sides of the river on fire and he wondered if we were still alive. He started looking round the house and found a large unexploded bomb in the side passage between our house and next door. He told my father, who reported it to one of the A.R.P. men and shortly after the police came and ordered us all out. We collected a few belongings and my mother gathered up some food in a basket and we left our house, walking in rubble and crunching broken glass. It was light now and the sky was red with the reflection of fires. When we reached the top of a hill on our way to knock up some friends and ask if we could stay for a while we looked back over the river and Liverpool seemed to be on fire. There was a sugar refinery and oil storage tanks on fire and through it all we could see the tower of the new Anglican cathedral safely standing.

We stayed a day at the friends' house while my father went to the Town Hall with all the 'refugees' to find out what to do. It turned out we couldn't return to our house for any belongings until the unexploded bomb was removed, and also my father had to find somewhere for us to live, as our house was too damaged. He was very angry and hated all Germans anyway, dating from the 1914–18 war. He kept blaming the German schoolboys who had been at our local schools on exchange visits before the war. He had refused to have one, and now he was certain they had taken home photographs and maps of Merseyside and the docks and shipyards. . . . He had bought his house after the 'last' war and had struggled to pay for it and now the 'bloody Huns' had bombed it to blazes. He wished he could get his hands on one – he'd murder him willingly. That is the only emotional scene I remember and I agreed with him, too!   ISABEL KIERNAN

The Blitz had brought a flood of evacuees to remote areas like North Wales, where up to now many families, unaffected by the war, regarded what was happening elsewhere as no concern of theirs.

I had been for a time in a luxury hotel in Wales, and was sick and tired of seeing, and being one of, a bunch of idle women. There were no war factories, no canteens, nor any kind of work; in fact, war had not, at that time, even approached the country. . . .

We heard the bombers roar overhead, we watched the dull red glow as a city burned, and then it started, and the quiet Welsh villagers were asked to open their doors. It is hard for those who have seen the horror and devastation of a blitzed city to understand the reluctance of most of these people to share their homes, but the villagers had not seen; what they did see was a stream of dirty, foul-smelling humanity. These poor bewildered women came, each with two or more children, expecting to find hospitality and ease for their pain. Some were fortunate, others were met with curt disapproval, and many were housed in churches and schoolrooms until the local policemen and billeting officers could take each family to their new homes, armed with the necessary warrant. . . .

I had through all this period been helping in a small way with other members of the W.V.S. and now saw an opportunity of doing a real job. I would take a house and fill it with as many children as I could look after. The local council were delighted with my suggestion . . . The council would provide beds, bedding and the barest necessities of furniture, provided I would undertake to have as many children as the house would comfortably hold, eight to arrive in one week. . . .

With the help of friends I . . . scrubbed and scoured, polished and moved furniture, cleaned windows and put up curtains. During these days our work was constantly interrupted by well-meaning or curious visitors. 'The County' called in unlimited numbers. 'My dear child, how wonderful of you to take on such a noble work.' 'Is it true that you are preparing to receive so many children? I think it quite heroic.' 'We must help you all we can. I think you are wonderful.' 'Anything we can do for you, just let us know . . .' Lady J. insisted that I call upon her for any help. I could count on her. . . .

Puddings . . . arrived from Lady J. in large washing-up bowls, enough to feed an army, and cakes and buns besides. I . . . cut mountains of bread and jam, so the whole effect was quite festive. Then I dressed with as much care as I would have given to a great occasion. I wanted to look my best, I wanted to be as my own children love to see me, hair shining, navy blue slacks and sweater, and lots of lipstick.

It was after five, and the children's train was due in at five-thirty. From the top window I could see the little station down by the sea, less than a mile away . . . What would the children be like – boys or girls? . . . I vaguely pictured them as my own pair away at school – rosy, clean, happy, normal children. . . . Then a large black car turned into the gate. . . .

Lady J's chauffeur was in the hall with a child. I was conscious only of blackness. Somewhere underneath that blackness was a boy, lonely, afraid and desperately unhappy. I felt it immediately. . . . I was on my knees untying the string of his gas mask, wound tortuously round his black fingers. I heard the chauffeur's voice, 'I'll be going back for the young ladies now, madam. We thought we'd best get rid of 'im first.' He was gone and I was talking to David, feeling faintly sick at the smell of his clothes and body. Then with the speed of a whirlwind I was overwhelmed with what seemed dozens of little girls, nearly as black as David, but all with merry faces, and an occasional bright curl escaping from the inevitable pixie hood. Pandemonium reigned. The ladies stood just inside the door, smiling with content-ment at their job, well done. . . .

The little nurse saw the ladies out, and came back to help me to get some order. All but David were flying madly up and down stairs, into every room, screaming with excitement and delight. Coats and hats were on the floor; pillow-cases, the regulation luggage, were half emptied on the floor and one young lady was already sampling the bread and jam. Somehow we got their hands washed; it was like chasing puppies to collect them together, and then they were sitting down to tea.

By this time two small girls were fighting, one had been sick in her plate and two had wet their knickers, but the table was empty of food. For the first time I collected them round me for a talk. David was still sullen and had, I noticed, eaten little. The girls were cheerful and communicative. . . . The sisters, Betty the elder, round-faced, very sensible and seven years old, ready to help and full of ideas about how we should manage until we got some help; June, just five, with the merriest, cutest little face, very coy, obviously the family beauty, showing off a good deal. 'We like being vacuated, me mum's glad to get us out of it and she's coming to see us when me dad's called up'. Aileen, the plainest child I've ever seen, with hair cut round a basin well above the ears, full of confidence, and clutching two very black handkerchiefs. 'Look, me mum gave me two 'ankies, one's to wipe me nose and one's to wipe me tears, but I 'aven't 'ad no tears.'

I was tired and worried, and I realised that I hadn't thought or spoken about anything but children for over a week. I'd go to the village inn, have a drink and perhaps talk to someone. . . .

At my entrance a grim, forbidding silence came over the little bar. With silent disapproval the landlord served me with a drink, and his wife came out to see so strange a sight – a woman alone, drinking in the bar. Cautiously she questioned me.

'You must be the one who's come to look after the evacuees?' Slowly she thawed, and we talked of many things. I left, feeling relaxed and ready to face any new problems at the house; little realising that I damned myself in the eyes of all those who had looked upon me with some respect and perhaps a little admiration. . . .

When Kathy came to help with the bathing that night she seemed to be in high spirits. 'I hear you went to the pub last night – a bit risky, wasn't it? – you can't get away with that kind of thing here, my girl. I'd have gone myself, but I don't want to be turned out of my digs. Is it true you were an actress? The village is agog. . . .' I couldn't understand the attitude of this young woman – why had she allowed herself to be swayed by these people? I didn't realise then how completely one could be crushed – one's spirit almost broken by a handful of people shut away from the world by those mountains, oblivious to the sufferings or joys of those outside. They farmed their land, they sold their produce in their tiny stores, they fleeced the unfortunate few who took refuge in their lovely village, and on Sundays they prayed – oh, how they prayed. The five little chapels were packed several times a day with those solemn black-clothed figures eager to promote their salvation, even more eager for the new week, when they might be in at the kill of any who dared to offend. . . .

My first real battle was with the rector of the English church . . .
the children had been sent regularly to Sunday School at home, and
. . . they seemed to look forward to it.

I dressed them in their best, and they went off, looking clean and
happy. They evidently enjoyed it. . . .

Following their third attendance I received a call from the vicar,
who rather timidly asked if I would refrain from sending the children
to Sunday School. 'You see, we already have more work than we can
do. My daughter manages to take a small class, just a few, you know,
but she can't possibly manage the added number.'

'But surely,' I said, 'you have among your congregation someone
who would help your daughter?'

He shuffled, and fumbled for words. 'It's so difficult – I hardly like
to ask – Sunday afternoon, you know. . . .'

Next came the barber. I sent all the little boys with sixpence each –
the price given on the list in his window – to have their hair trimmed.

They returned crestfallen and still shaggy. The price for the Welsh
was indeed sixpence – for evacuees ninepence. Off I went to interview
the gentleman in his tiny shop. Why, I asked, were my children asked
to pay more than the stipulated price? He withstood all my raving at
this injustice and attempted robbery. He had enough customers –
besides it was a risk he would be taking to cut the hair of these little
English – they are so dirty. If I cared to pay him a certain sum each
month he would come and cut the hair at the house; it would be after
his working hours, of course, and he would expect to make a little
extra. . . .

We also had a feud with a tiny shop not far from the house. I gave
each child a few coppers and told them, for the comfort of the
shopkeeper, to go in twos or threes for their sweets. The first three
were served, the others came back, some swearing, others in tears –
she would not serve them, she hadn't enough sweets. Off I went, and
after looking at the rows of bottles and boxes, I approached her. Why
do you refuse to serve my children, you have sweets here, the children
have money, is there any justification for your refusal? The old lady
spoke English badly, but made me understand she did not want her
stock depleted in such a way. . . .

There followed a tirade in Welsh, and as I left she managed to
scream: 'I shall have nothing in my shop, nothing to sell, I am telling
you, if you stay here, nothing I tell you, you *locusts*.'

The only shoemaker in the village refused to mend their shoes unless I paid first; after some argument I handed over twenty-seven shillings. I asked parents to refund this money. Some paid, others ignored my letters; Enid's mother wrote that if I was going to ask for money every five minutes, she'd have to take the children home.
NORAH BARING

By Christmas the regular occupants of particular shelters formed little communities of their own. Some organised special celebrations.

Christmas parties made extremely hot work, but were really enjoyable. Parents and residents in the street or square concerned clubbed together with cash, or half a pot of jam here, and a bit of margarine there, to provide a tea for the children. ('Bring your own cup.') There were singing and dancing and a film. Some of the wardens made toys from debris wood. We scrounged the paint, and a number of snappy trucks, tanks, and boats were turned out. The pleasure they gave was immeasurable.

On one occasion, when it had been firmly decided that the party should be for the twenty children of that shelter only, I arrived with the correct number of toys in a sack, only to find that the loud-mouthed but soft-hearted Mrs Thompson, who ran the canteen, had admitted eighty. There was no escape, and I could not hide the inadequate sackful, as I had been spotted long before I reached the entrance. The remainder of my progress was hampered by children clinging to my clothes, hanging round my neck, standing on my feet. I despaired of ever effecting a distribution without a riot from the sixty toyless ones. We decided on a lucky ticket system. . . .

I started the distribution with a clear space round me, maintained by other wardens. But when I produced a pink-spotted wooden horse that you could sit on, not all the wardens of the borough could have held the mass assault that ensued. Nevertheless, we avoided any fights, and there was not much wailing, as we managed to find a threepenny bit each for the unlucky ones. The only casualty was my voice. The boys dashed off to try their boats in the static water tank nearby, and came back wet, announcing haughtily that the aircraft carriers were not really seaworthy.

On another occasion the W.V.S. provided a four-foot long cracker with small toys inside. The shelter concerned was better controlled by

its marshal, and was in a less poor quarter. All the children had shiny faces and wet, smooth hair; some had shiny party frocks. I hid the cracker till late in the proceedings hoping that they would be tired by then. We collected the children under ten. There were too many, so we reduced it to those under eight. I produced the cracker. With piercing squeals all the little tots fell on it, and me, like tigers. If I had not been wearing a leather jacket, I doubt if I should have retained my shirt. Within thirty seconds there was not a shred of cracker left.
BARBARA NIXON

On the night of Sunday, 29 December 1940 the Germans made a deter-mined, and largely successful, attempt to burn down the City of London. Everywhere shops, offices and warehouses were deserted and, because the tide was low, little water was available from the River Thames.

The typewriter is treading flakes of soot into the paper as this . . . is being written. Every now and then, like the opening of an oven door, as the wind changes, a gasp of hot breath comes in through the seventh-floor window, a breath foul with the reek of burning London. At three in the morning [of Monday, 30 December], with the curtains drawn back and the light turned off (although no warden could notice if it were not), it is possible to see to type in a light as bright as an angry sunrise. Fiery confetti spatters the papers on the desk with singe-marks. A spindrift of fine spray from the firemen's jets follows them reassuringly. Now there is another muffled roar, like the blowing of a Bessemer blast furnace, and a fountain of flames, crested by a plume of sparks as vivid as the fire-belch of a Roman candle, leaps to the high heavens; another building has been clean-gutted. Something flutters like a stricken bird against the window, hovers burning, then sizzles on the spray-damp sill; it is a charred form, delivered by the fire from a near-by printers; it says, 'Last Will and Testament'.

The Second Great Fire of London is raging furiously.

Goering's arson-squadrons have done their work thoroughly. They flew in with the blackout, at the hour when, in peace-time, the Sunday bells would be ringing for Evensong. . . . From the spotter's post on the roof of a tall building I watched the fire-bombs come hurtling down and white magnesium fires leap up . . . to turn red as buildings caught alight. There were the thuds of the heavy oil-bombs, followed like a visible echo, by the upsurge of flames. An occasional high explosive would make the fire-haze vibrate. As the fires married and multiplied, London became as clear as daylight. Against the luminous reef of smoke-clouds, the barrage balloons became gilded blobs. . . .

'It is going to be a warm night,' said the spotter, conversationally, just as he would say when his perch was rocking with high-explosive explosions, 'It's going to be a noisy night.'

Suddenly the guns were silenced; with the curtness of a conductor flicking his baton, the overture completed. And the night was divided between the roar of the bombers and the clangour of the fire-bells. . . .

Downstairs, a colleague had been brought in wounded. As a journalist, he had been 'out on the job'. . . . He had been driving through the shower of bombs when he saw one crash through the window of a radio-shop and start blazing up. He and his driver immediately jumped out and dashed into the window to put it out. A bomb exploded, and he was hit. It was the old but true story of the wallet which averted death. The splinter was deflected, but tore open his side. He insisted upon returning to his newspaper office to report before going to hospital. . . .

On the ninth-storey roof I saw such a sight as none has seen since Samuel Pepys took boat at Tower Hill and from the river saw London ablaze in 1666. The building was ringed with fires. As one ventured to the edge of the roof the flames reached out like fondling arms from nearby buildings. The roof-tops of Fleet Street seemed a stockade of flames. The Middle Temple library was hopelessly alight. Johnson's London, those narrow back courts which are the hinterland of Fleet Street, was a flaming acre. Part of the *Daily Telegraph* building was burning furiously. The spire of St. Bride's, parish church of journalism, was a macabre Christmas tree festooned in fire, and its inner pillars burning like candles. Other Wren churches were torches. St. Paul's was etched against a lurid sky; the fires seemed to be lapping round its dome. Fires in Cheapside; fires by St. Martin's-le-Grand. Stationer's Hall Court, Ave Maria Lane and Paternoster Row a furnace fed by their own books; fires across the river, charring Little Dorrit's London; great fires that fused into greater until it seemed that puny man could never master them. Standing on that roof one felt like a Smithfield Martyr must have felt as the faggots were lit around him. . . .

Over the stricken city hung dense clouds of smoke, lit up as the smoke of a railway-engine is from the fire-box. . . . And upon us descended a blizzard of snow-fire – flakes that stung and scorched. Familiarity with the district added to the dread. . . . One suddenly realised that that building threatened by a change in the wind was a paper warehouse, or a varnish works, or a celluloid store, or a photographers' wholesaler stocked with film. . . . And as each in succession caught, there was a kind of routine. Flames licked round the walls as though they were sampling a fresh tit-bit; then thrust through the windows and attacked the stores hungrily. Beams caught alight. The roofs slowly sagged as though they were gelatine, and then crashed with a roar. A container would explode and add fresh fuel to the flames. Floors would be eaten through and collapse in succession, and then, with each new gift of stores, the fires would leap up. The wind from the south-east acted like a forced draught, and a fountain of fire, with a jet of sparks, would spout fifty feet or more and then suddenly subside. Gradually, the flames would be confined with a lantern-effect within the walls of the building.

. . . 'A nice tidy job, if I may say so,' said one A.F.S. man, ex-motor-salesman, talking . . . about the fire he and his mates had just put out. . . .

'Has it gone midnight yet?' asked another Auxiliary as he wrestled . . . with a serpentine hose-pipe. I told him it had. 'Then it's me birfday,' he said. . . . And with that he darted up an alley with the length of hose – I watched him disappear into what looked like a furnace door, and had not the nerve to wish him many happy returns of such a day.

A heavy bomb had fallen in Holborn and had wrecked the windows of a famous store. The shop warden when I arrived was propping up, with mock gallantry, a wax model which looked as though she had swooned. He emerged out of the window into the lurid glare of the fires, and, as he chatted to me, industriously swept up the clutter of plate-glass.

'Let's look on the bright side, chum,' he counselled. 'We were going to have a salvage sale anyway.'   RITCHIE CALDER

At one branch in the City of London, where the plate glass windows had been blown out in the first days of air attack, and most of the glass dome lighting the office had fallen pane by pane, the roof and upper part of the premises were burnt out in the fire raids at the end of

December 1940. On the morning of December 30 the manager and staff arrived to find the banking hall running with water from fire-hoses, basement strongrooms flooded to a depth of six inches, fire still smouldering in the upper floors and many records in indescribable confusion. No electricity or gas was available, and, as daylight was excluded by the boarded-up windows and light dome, the interior gloom could be relieved only by candles. . . . No fires could be lighted, and the central heating was not operating, for although water swilled around floors and safes, none came through the taps. Accounting machines were out of operation in the absence of electricity; and even had power been available, three out of a battery of five were water-damaged, and several typewriters were no longer serviceable. Just then the bank was particularly busy making up accounts for the half-yearly balance, and the loss of mechanical aids was a severe blow.

In a night the branch had moved back to working conditions worse than those of a century earlier. All entries were made by hand in candlelight, the branch counter with flickering wicks reflected in the pools of water scattered over the banking hall presenting a sorry spectacle. Letters were handwritten, and as far as possible, (hand) delivered; no telephones were working, essential messages being sent in the form of brief notes, while the office itself was damp and cold and wretchedly unhealthy. The staff, delayed by transport difficulties, arrived slowly, but well before noon all had reached their posts. Those arriving early helped to deal with the smouldering fire in the upper part of the premises, a task completed after an hour or so, when all helped to clean up the branch and sort out the day's work. Few customers called, for most office premises in the district were in similar straits, but those who came received attention more or less as usual. At mid-day a large jug of coffee was obtained by a messenger sent foraging far outside the area affected, in which no restaurants or cafés were open, bringing cheer to the desolate scene. At a conference of the staff it was decided to carry on in the branch . . . this representing a lesser evil than seeking and setting up in fresh premises. Somehow the volume of work was mastered and final figures for the half year produced. Within a week temporary repairs had been made, working conditions were more or less normal, and the customers of the branch suffered scarcely any inconvenience. Indeed, some had cause to be grateful for the prompt assistance given by the bank as they sought to restore business premises and office equipment destroyed by air damage.   JOHN WADSWORTH

1941

She volunteered,

She volunteered to be a Land Girl!

Ten bob a week,

Nothing much to eat,

Great big boots,

And blisters on her feet.

If it wasn't for the war,

She'd be where she was before.

Land Girl – You're barmy!

Song of the Women's Land Army

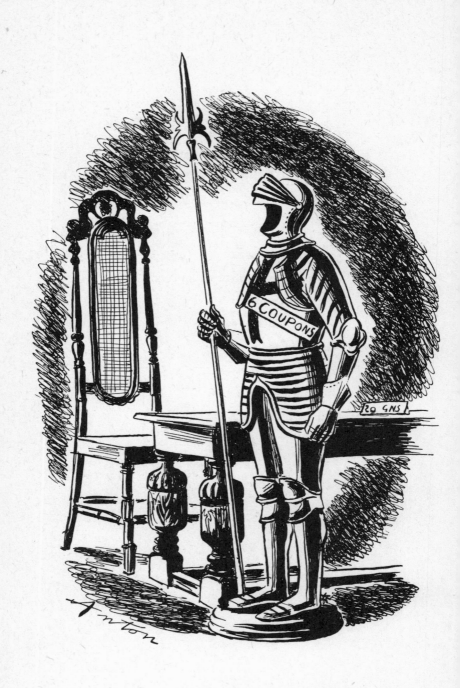

1941 was the most miserable year of the war. It began in gloom and ended in disaster. Although at sea the Navy still held open the Atlantic life-line, the U-boats were far from beaten. In the air, the night fighters were at last beginning to master the enemy bombers, and Bomber Command to hit back hard at Germany; but the Blitz reached a new peak of ferocity in April and May, and sporadic raids continued for the rest of the year. On land the record was one of unrelieved defeat, with retreat in the desert, in Greece, in Crete, often ending in evacuation, and at the end of the year the familiar pattern was already beginning to repeat itself on a larger scale than ever in the Far East.

For the ordinary civilian the unwilling entry of Russia into the war, in June, and of the United States, in December, failed as yet to raise spirits, especially as both these new campaigns opened with defeats. At home it was a year of increasing shortages and restrictions, of compulsory fire-watching and conscription to the Home Guard, of the call-up of women for both the Forces and war work, of the start of clothes rationing, the threat of fuel rationing, and the 'Is your journey really necessary?' campaign. Jam was rationed, the cheese ration reached its lowest point ever – one ounce a week – and tinned food went on points. Goods of every kind became scarcer and scarcer, from saucepans to matches. The theme of the year was work, with no let-up in sight and victory a distant dream.

Friday 3rd January 1941   Found old suitcase in attic. Packed our shelter things . . . Mother bought pig's foot from Parrs. Made pea soup from it; quite a banquet. Sirens at 7.40. Down we went, I carrying suitcase which was very heavy, Harold with Denise in her drawer. . . . All clear, about 9 pm. Came back hoping for soup supper, but Wailing Winnie again at 9.40. So back. Returned at 10.30 to find our supper eaten by mother and father, who had not heard the sirens. Felt extremely disgruntled. Bread and cheese after all. Denise needed a feed, during which Jerry floating dismally overhead. Sirens again. Out into the snow once more. Returned at 1 am and slept like hell. . . .

10th January   Mother dropped the pudding mixture (treacle, made by me). Insisted on wasting-not, wanting-not, and scooped it up, despite protests from me about broken basin. I made another for H. and me. True enough, mother found a lump of pot in her pud and none of them enjoyed it. . . . Managed to scrounge extra bird seed for Mickey [a budgie] by wrongfully declaring that we had two birds. . . .

26th January Brought home nice big basinful of beef dripping from Clarice's in exchange for the sausage we took there to cover our meat ration for dinner. Letter has arrived for H. from Children's Hospital telling him he is for fire-watching duty on Monday night. . . .

28th January Morning shopping in town. Knitting wool; 1 lb pork. Go to Food Office and wait in queue to change retailer. Get tired of waiting, so decide not to change retailer. Milkman tells me he needs another milk coupon for first quarter. I've forgotten it. Go again to Food Office to obtain form. . . . Go to every fruit shop in town searching for oranges for Denise. Draw blank . . . I fill in milk form. H. and I go out to post it and we call at corner house with their fowl bits. Fish and chip shop open. We get some for supper. Cold, dark night. No sirens. . . .

4th February Leave Denise with Edna and mother and go off to pictures to see *South Riding* and *Dark Rapture* . . . Called at milk office with form. To my horror, it's still inaccurate, not signed by a 'responsible person'. Remedy this, when Denise in shelter, by going off to Peggy Hind's flat. . . .

8th February Ran to Parrs at 9 and procured prize of pork pie. But no eggs. Went later for eggs. None, but got 1 lb sausage, but pretty foul it tastes. . . .

10th February Went to Guildhall and had name put down for allotment.

14th February Managed some excellent purchases, including half dozen eggs and two large oranges. . . .

2nd March Try to make one egg do for two cakes. . . .

4th March Take Denise for usual walk to Arboretum. All railings are being taken up for war effort. . . .

14th March Jam, marmalade and syrup are to be rationed. Probably means we shall get more than we're able to get now.

18th March I go to enquire about a play-pen advertised for sale. But it's been sold. Radio announcement that cheese and milk are to be rationed during summer. . . .

5th April More sausage meat, but concoct it into quite a decent spread, made into savoury cakes, with potato and onion . . . H. is furious because he has no cigarettes.

17th April   Worst raid of war on London last night. Worried about Edith [a sister living at Uxbridge]. Mother queues for 1 hour to get one quarter of tongue.

19th April   Edith is coming. H. kindly offers to go the round of shops for food. He returns empty-handed, saying the queues are awfully long. Mother and I smile indulgently and let him off. . . .

13th May   Lucky day, manage to get some nice sausage. Also chocolate and sweets and some cakes. Bacon was hidden from view, under the counter, and I, pretending to be naive, grizzled about that on show, until the other was produced and it is fresh and delicious.

28th May   Lord Woolton announces that eggs and fish are to be rationed [In fact fish, though very scarce, was never rationed]. News from Crete is awful.

30th May   Get into interesting discussion in food queue about the merits, or non-, of possible communal feeding. We both agree that by next winter it will probably become a fact. . . . I see advert for a baby's crib and walk three miles to discover that it isn't worth buying.

1st June   Clothes rationing [introduced].

8th June   Cycle to Attenborough to see old man who is making Denise an osier basket to size, with four handles, two at either end, long-ways, two at either side, to accommodate either two, or one, carrier. Pleasant evening, in the osier marshes, watching the old man weaving the willows in and out. We feed his fowls on dried beans – they are ravenous. We return home with one and a half dozen eggs.

10th June   Mother brings liver and kidney . . . Get six packet cigarettes from Co-op, in exchange for ten milk tokens. . . .

25th July   Walk grandly into S. and R.'s and ask for half pound of gooseberries which are miraculously on show. 'Four shillings a pound, Madam', the assistant so superciliously says. I have 1s 6d in my purse. . . . How humiliating to have to buy only a quarter pound. . . .

26th July   In need of onions. None to be had since price control. Return with a bottle of onion essence.

31st July   H. queues for fish and chips for supper, afterwards tries all the pubs for beer, without success. . . .

6th August   Go round town trying to buy petrol lighter for Jack's birthday, without success.

12th August   Lots of time wasted scouring the city shops for baby bricks for D's first birthday present. Disgusted!) . . .

20th September   Make three winter vests for D. out of my old ones bought pre-war and save lots of clothing coupons.

6th December   Spent four precious points on tongue to use as meat for dinner.

7th December   Nine o'clock news pretty disquieting. Japanese have bombed American base (Pearl Harbour). We stay up late, discussing how soon U.S.A. will come into the war.

12th December   To Food Office for permit for free blackcurrant purée and cod liver oil, but have brought the wrong ration book, so have to return empty-handed. DORIS BREWIN

Following the great Fire-Raid on the City at the end of 1940, the government introduced compulsory fire-watching for both business and domestic premises.

When a fire-fighting party had to be formed for what remained of Shawfield Street, it consisted of a widow with two young boys of sixteen and seven, an elderly couple with a boy of sixteen, and an elderly invalid chef with an invalid daughter. These were the remaining residents. When, one night, incendiaries fell, this fire party, helped by an unknown lady from Radnor Walk, found a fire bomb blazing in the annexe of an unoccupied house. They climbed over the garden wall with buckets and equipment and attacked the bomb, which had fallen on a dining-room table with the remains of the family's breakfast still on it. They put it out most effectively and turned to attack a second bomb which they had located in the ruins and found it had been extinguished. They were so indignant that they sent a deputation of formal complaint to Post K that the Town Hall be asked to do something 'about people from another street without even badges, and without invitation, coming and extinguishing bomb No. 2 which they themselves had been perfectly capable of dealing with'.

A lady living in the same street . . . lamented bitterly that she had missed the Fire Blitz. She had heard the people laughing and talking in the street and thought it was those girls with the Canadians; and subsequently discovered that it was the people with their bombs.

On this night Richard and I had a wonderful time. He belonged to a fire-fighting party for our part of the street and incendiaries were falling everywhere. They were small and pretty, like fireflies coming down, and the sky looked fantastically beautiful. They were easy to extinguish with sand or a stirrup pump provided they were tackled immediately. We put out quite a number and were joined by Anne and Cecil, who enjoyed it as thoroughly as we did. In Tite Street a fire had started in an unoccupied house. We could see through the windows that the front room was blazing and the furniture and carpet alight. There was no time to find the warden who might have the keys to the house, so Richard picked up a brick from the gutter and hurled it through a window of the room. I followed suit with another, smashing the glass, so that it was possible to climb in from the area steps. It was such a relief to hurl those bricks, it released some of the anger which we all felt against against the murderous raids. . . .

The incendiaries fell in a peculiar way – it was impossible to see whence they had come. Suddenly they were all there. They were quite small – about eighteen inches long – and weighed very little, but the height from which they were dropped gave them sufficient momentum to penetrate roofs and slates and they ignited on impact. They fell with little plops, rather as insects fell in India when coming in contact with the lamps. . . . They were quite easy to extinguish with sand or smother with anything as one did an ordinary fire. Mrs Freeth picked them up with a pair of coal tongs and dropped them triumphantly into the coal bucket where they burned themselves out. In the road and on the pavements they burned harmlessly. A plane could carry thousands of them – and apparently did. FRANCES FAVIELL

Although 'looting' was heavily punished often it involved no more than finding a use for scarce articles being ruined by the weather.

For a low rent we were offered a pleasant family house in St. John's Wood, with a good garden. Some bomb damage had just been repaired, and the owner was not anxious to have the house requisitioned with its new windows and clean paint and walls. . . .

Only one other house in the road was inhabited. Behind us a long crescent of over a hundred huge empty villas was slowly disintegrating, with the aid of the weather and former bombing. It was an eerie street to go along, with some of its ornate houses lying flat in their own gardens. Rotting laths and powdered plaster mingled with the mud along the untended roadway.

The furniture we took out of store was enough only for a small flat, and now we had a four-storied ten-roomed house to fill. But in the deserted gardens of the crescent I had seen broken chairs and tables and bedsteads. If the shops were empty, I knew where to get what we needed.

The Blitz had played some queer tricks with its victims. Into our garden had been blown a broken lawn-sprinkler, which we converted into a standard-lamp for our drawing-room. Beside it lay a linen-basket which we bent back into shape and painted a nice shade of crimson and cream. From other gardens, sometimes digging a little to unearth them, I collected curtain-rods and rings and coat-hooks and other things needed, but impossible to buy then, for moving into a new house. . . .

A nursery fire-guard was something impossible to find in any shop. The day I stepped out of a bombed site with one in my arms, I walked straight into a policeman. I thought instantly of the notices saying that looters might be shot. The policeman shook his head in a disappointed way, as though he expected better of me.

'I know,' I said. 'I'm ready. You can shoot me.'

'It's not that, miss,' he said. 'I've had my eye on it to take home after dark for my own toddler.'

'Take it,' I said, holding it out to him. . . .

'No, miss,' he said sadly. 'You got it first.' And he continued on his beat.   VERILY ANDERSON

At the start of the war domestic shelters had consisted of strengthened cellars, small brick-built buildings with concrete roofs on the surface, and the famous 'Anderson', which resembled a small corrugated iron bicycle-shed half-sunk in earth in one's back garden. This often suffered from damp and in March 1941 distribution began of the equally famous 'Morrison', a steel table designed to be erected in a downstairs living-room and strong enough to bear the weight of the ruins of a small two-storey house.

One of my outstanding memories was the erection of our Morrison Shelter. We had no man to assist us. It was 1941.

The shelter was delivered by council men, dumped in the front garden in pieces, and left with a pamphlet on how to assemble it. At that time I was taking a government course in engineering at the local technical college. This was a scheme to train women and girls in a skilled trade, prior to call-up, so they would be capable of taking over from skilled men in factories. I was progressing very well in this course, making my own tools from raw steel, learning to read and draw blue-prints, soldering, riveting etc. and anxious to pass out as a 'semi-skilled fitter', – or as I was prone to say, a 'semi-filled skitter'. I had chosen to do this in preference to being drafted into the women's forces, as I did not want to leave my mother alone. It was certainly a change from hairdressing, and I took to it like a duck to water.

Mother and I decided we'd put the shelter in the bedroom, which was the front downstairs room. We employed the assistance of my married sister who lived in a nearby town. Firstly we dismantled the beds, and stacked them in the hall. My engineering training had given me considerable experience in the use of a wrench and spanner, which I found invaluable during this escapade. Studying the assembling instructions, it all looked comparatively simple, and we soon erected the frame. This consisted of four steel stanchions, joined top and bottom by four lengths of steel, bolted in what seemed to be masses of places, and riveted, forming an oblong box shape, roughly five feet by eight feet.

The base consisted of a wire-type mattress, secured all round the edge to the framework by lightly coiled springs spaced one foot apart. This proved to be a man-sized job which three muscle-less women found almost impossible. One end of the spring hooked into a hole in the framework and the other end had to be stretched to hook into the wire mattress. Hooking in one side was comparatively easy, but when it came to the other side, and the springs had to be forced open to make them rebound, making the mattress taut, it was a somewhat different story. The three of us lay flat on the floor, hanging on to these wretched springs for grim death. We yanked and pulled until every muscle ached and throbbed, and just when we almost had the hook in the hole the spring would rebound with a loud 'DOING', dragging us three struggling females with it.

Between fits of utter hysteria, when we'd be rolling around on the floor helpless with laughter, and as a result feeling much weaker and sapped of all energy, we finally managed to secure the last of these endless springs into position. We laughed so much and so long, and mother would suddenly cough, put on a solemn expression and say 'Come now! That's enough hilarity! Think positive girls! It *has* to be done!' – So with laughter bubbling up inside, we'd again throw (and I mean throw) ourselves into the battle. It must have taken three hours, and, typically English, we stopped for a cup of tea – and then with the battle cry, 'Once more into the breach!', we recommenced battle.

The roof of the shelter consisted of a solid sheet of steel roughly five feet by eight feet, and to manipulate this massive heavy object, from the front garden, along the hall and into the front room was indeed a work of art. The three of us surveyed it, attempted to lift it, and went into deep thought. The obvious solution was to move it on wheels, or something similar. Ah! The rolling pin! 'The very article!' my mother exclaimed triumphantly.

This operation in itself was a masterpiece of planning. We managed to stand the sheet of steel upright, and levered the end up with two chisels on to the rolling pin. We were then able to roll the sheet along the ground, and when the rolling pin reached the other end, we repeated the process. Manipulating the thing up the front steps, we placed a board to form a ramp, and ran it up easily into the hall. Turning into the doorway of the front room proved troublesome, but with a little 'heave-hoing', we actually managed it. Then we rolled it into position beside the frame and allowed it to fall over on to it. The resounding 'crash' it made sounded like a 'direct hit', and then we managed to manoeuvre it into position and bolt it down. Battered and bruised we congratulated ourselves. . . .

Making up the bed in it proved awkward and the wire-netting sides amused us. It resembled a cage, but throughout the rest of the war, it proved a trusty friend . . . mother and I had faith in its protection. Many is the time one of us would crack our head on its roof through sitting up in bed suddenly, and we'd often lie there listening to bombs falling . . . laughing and joking with each other.

ROSEMARY MOONEN

Now that we are apparently to have a return of the four-poster in the shape of a substantial table placed over our beds, may I suggest that the ancient accompanying nightcap should reappear in the form of a large, well-stuffed tea-cosy? It is obvious that some special protection for the heads of sub-table sleepers is urgently needed, for we have been told that a gentleman who had slept under his dining table was so overjoyed on waking to find himself unbombed that he sprang up and knocked his head against the table with such violence that he was insensible for hours.   Letter in THE TIMES

When the first savagery of the night attacks faded we left the cupboard under the stairs and moved into a Morrison shelter.

This was a large metal cage a little higher than a dinner table. It had a hefty iron frame with a sheet steel ceiling screwed together with chunky nuts and bolts. Underneath was a crude wire mattress. It was massive and angular and filled the dining-room except for a space in front of the fire. It became part of the house, a foundation almost; we slept in it and on it, we ate from it, we played in it.

When the siren sounded we were supposed to dive inside and put up steel mesh around the sides. Thus, according to the theorists, we were protected from falling masonry by the frame and steel ceiling and from flying rubble by the mesh cage.

When the Germans resumed the destruction of such military targets as schools, shops, houses and sleeping cows we spent all night in the shelter. And it was my father with a reputation for quiet efficiency who took command of the nightly operation of retiring into the rusting four-poster.

I crawled in first into the farthest corner and my father caged me in with three walls of mesh. The volume of the radio was lowered, voices were muted and it was presumed erroneously that I was asleep beneath the blankets on the twanging wires. . . .

Somewhere near the stars an aircraft droned monotonously. At 10.30 my father swung into his drill. While my mother undressed in the kitchen, he wound the clocks, checked the doors, brought out the remaining side of the cage, inspected the millet-starved budgerigar. Then my mother crawled stealthily into one side of the shelter so that our bodies formed a sort of T-junction.

'Shush,' said my mother to herself. 'Mustn't wake him.'

The wire mattress sang and the aircraft throbbed. . . .

Outside the cage my father was working up to his nightly crescendo of controlled rage. Out went the light, down came the blackout. The sirens had decided that the aircraft was one of theirs and were opening their lungs to warn us.

My father blundering blindly around the room knocked over a

potted fern which had been in the family for twenty years. The budgerigar fluttered his wings and grumbled wearily.

'What are you doing, Will?' my mother whispered.

'Just checking up,' said my father.

Far away a bomb exploded with a gentle crump. And without warning the gun on the Downs loosed off as loud and sharp as if it were in the back garden. An upstairs door sprang open; somewhere down the road a window broke.

'Come in, Will,' my mother said urgently.

We waited for him to crack his shin against the corner of the shelter. He cracked it and said: 'Damn.'

'Will,' said my mother reproachfully. The mildest of oaths was forbidden. . . .

I moved further into the corner making a right angle with my mother while my father burrowed into the triangle of bedclothes between us. With a lot of heavy breathing and exclamations accompanied by murmurs of reproach from my mother he put up the last mesh barricade.

As the bombs stirred the ground and the shrapnel clattered down the road we fought a quiet battle of cunning for the bedclothes. Feet touched faces, arms swung across chests, elbows elbowed; snores bubbled and spluttered to be silenced by ostensibly accidental blows; fragments of wild dream-talk escaped from the depths of our private lives. Enmity was closer to the surface during those caged nights than at any other time in our well-mannered lives.

The system collapsed after a few weeks. White-faced, shadow-eyed, we decided that for the sake of health and happiness two of us would have to evacuate the shelter. For the next few months my parents slept on top of it while I rolled and stretched and crawled and sometimes slept beneath. When the next lull in the bombing came we crept back to our beds.   DEREK LAMBERT

After a lull, the Blitz on London came to an end with three devastating raids, 'the Wednesday', 'the Saturday' and another 'Saturday' on 10 May.

It was Wednesday, April 16th, and a lovely warm day – so warm that it seemed that summer had arrived without any proper spring. . . .

Vicki had been trying to get out all day to Peer Gynt [another dog], who . . . was sitting hopefully in the middle of the Royal Hospital Road watching our windows and our front door . . . At lunchtime a policeman had rung the bell and asked if it were my dog in the road as it was obstructing the traffic which had to go all round it. I explained about Vicki being the object of his attentions and we chased him off. . . .

Richard suggested that we went out for dinner. We would go and see Madame Caletta, who had been carrying on the restaurant very successfully since her husband's death. [He had been drowned in the *Arandora Star,* torpedoed while carrying interned enemy aliens to Canada.] We talked with Madame Caletta about the sunshine, the quieter nights, the war, and everything in general and we had a very enjoyable dinner. It had been quite light when we entered the restaurant, but when we came out it was quite dark. As we walked home enjoying the warm air to our astonishment the sirens went . . . It was five minutes past nine.

Almost immediately there was the sickening roar of a great drove of planes which increased and increased so that we knew that there must be hundreds of them. The guns opened up at once – a terrific barrage, so loud that it was difficult to speak, and huge flares – different from any which we had seen – were being dropped. . . .

The raid became heavier and heavier after we reached home. And sitting in the road, oblivious to the noise of guns, was the faithful Peer Gynt. I tried unsuccessfully to send him home. . . . We left the studio and went downstairs to the dining-room in which we still slept when the raid became even more heavy. As it intensified and more and more planes came over I telephoned Kathleen and asked her if she were not going to take shelter over the road in the basement of her little shop. She said she was tired and felt like sleeping in her own bed. Her bedroom, like Anne's and Cecil's, was right under the roof. I don't know why I begged her so strongly to come downstairs, offering her a bed in the hall, which we considered the safest place as it had one wall of ferro-concrete and the others were very thick. Richard added his arguments to mine in vain. I asked about Anne and Cecil. 'What d'you expect?' she said. 'They've gone to bed.'

Anne came to the telephone herself; she sounded as if she were in a dilemma. It was quite clear that she did not like the raid – the noise must have been even more deafening up there and with the terrific barrage it would have been quite possible for shell-caps to penetrate the roof. Cecil settled the matter. He quite obviously took the receiver from her, speaking to me himself. 'Have a heart,' he said laughingly.

'It's still our honeymoon – we've got two more days.' 'You can have our bed,' I said, 'if you'll only come down. Richard says it's a terribly heavy raid and that there are droves of German planes. *Do* come down – anyhow for a while.' 'Sure we'll come down,' he said jokingly. 'Don't worry. *We'll come down with the rubble.*'

We had never experienced such a night – bombs seemed to *rain* down – and in the intervals of their explosions which tonight were the loudest and longest we could remember we could hear the guns in the planes as the fighters chased them. The sky was alight with flares, searchlights, and exploding shells – it was a magnificent but appalling sight. The fires which we could see were terrifying – the largest, in the direction of Victoria, was enormous and appeared to be increasing. Behind us, much nearer, there was a terrible blaze in the direction of Burton Court. Wardens kept running by and we heard the revving up of engines from the auxiliary fire-station a few doors down at No. 21. . . . About twenty past eleven we decided to settle down and read for a time. Neither of us felt like going to bed – it was far too noisy and exciting. A warden raced by shouting, and suddenly we heard a shout of 'Lights, lights' from the street. Richard wondered if the recent near explosions had caused the blackout curtains to shift in the studio and he said, 'I'll run up and have a look.'

He had scarcely gone when the lights all went out. There was a strange quiet – a dead hush, and prickles of terror went up my spine as a rustling, crackling, endless sound as of ripping, tearing paper began. I did not know what it was, and I screamed to Richard, '*Come down, come down!*' Before I could hear whether or not he was coming down the stairs, things began to drop – great masses fell – great crashes sounded all round me. I had flung myself down by the bed hiding Vicki [the dog] under my stomach, trying thus to save her and the coming baby from harm. I buried my face in the eiderdown of the bed as the rain of debris went on falling for what seemed ages . . . ages. . . . The bed was covered and so was I – I could scarcely breathe – things fell all round my head – some of it almost choked me as the stuff, whatever it was, reached my neck and my mouth.

At last there was a comparative silence and with great difficulty I raised my head and shook it free of heavy, choking, dusty stuff. An arm had fallen round my neck – a warm, living arm, and for one moment I thought that Richard had entered in the darkness and was holding me, but when very, very cautiously I raised my hand to it, I found that it was a woman's bare arm with two rings on the third finger and it stopped short in a sticky mess. I shook myself free of it. Vicki, who had behaved absolutely perfectly, keeping so still that she could have been dead, became excited now as she smelt the blood. I screamed again, '*Richard, Richard*', and to my astonishment he answered quite near me. 'Where are you?' I cried – more things had begun falling. 'At the bottom of the stairs,' he said.

'Keep there. Keep still – there are more things falling,' I cried, and buried my head again as more debris fell all round me. At last it appeared to have stopped. I raised my head again – I could see the sky and the searchlights and I knew that the whole of the three upper storeys of the house had gone. 'We've been hit,' I said . . . and the only feeling I was conscious of was furious anger.

It was pitch dark – too dangerous to move without some idea of what the position was. I had had my torch in my hand but the blast had thrown it from me. 'Light a match,' I said. 'What about gas?' asked Richard. 'Can't smell any yet – be quick,' I said. He lit several matches, standing, as I saw by their light, in the entrance to the room. There were no ceilings, nothing above me as I crouched there. The front of the room had blown out – but the wall nearest to the one where I was crouching, the ferro-concrete one, was still there, as was the one to the hall. By the light of the matches I saw something more terrifying than the arm which was now partially covered with debris – the light laths from the ceiling had all fallen down across me – so that their weight had not hurt me at all – but balanced on them were huge blocks and lumps of masonry. If I moved they might all crash down. 'Don't come any nearer,' I shouted to Richard. He said, 'Keep still – I'm going to try and get out – the front door is twisted and jammed.'

I had seen where my best exit passage lay when Richard had lit the matches for me and while he was trying to shift the broken door I began wriggling very, very carefully and cautiously, along the floor. It was not easy – for I was not as slim as normally, and I had Vicki. It was so perilous that I thought of loosing her and letting her find her own way out. Had she not behaved so wonderfully I would have been obliged to leave her – for the thought uppermost of anything else in my mind was to save my baby. The baby, hitherto a nebulous dream of the future, now became urgently real and my only thought was of it. I shouted again and again – for if only the heavy rescue would come, as they had always promised me they would if I were buried, I would not

have to face this perilous crawl – but no sound came from the streets.
. . .

There were constant terrific explosions and things fell each time there was a fresh thud. If I did not get out soon some of those huge blocks were bound to fall on me. I shouted again, 'Help, help,' and so did Richard. The sounds echoed in the darkness and then far away I heard a woman's voice calling . . . 'They're coming . . . they'll come . . .' and it died away and we didn't know if it was to us they would come, because from the thuds and whooshes and violent explosions all round they must have been pretty busy.

'I've got the door open enough to squeeze through,' Richard called. 'Don't light any more matches, I can smell gas,' I warned him. I could not see him – nor he me. 'I'm going to try and crawl through this space to the door,' I said, and I began doing it immediately. I remembered what Tapper [a rescue party man] told me, *Test it first, tap it gently,*' and his warning, 'Don't go scrabbling at anything in case it all comes down on you.' Very slowly and cautiously I squeezed my way along the tiny tunnel under the hanging lathes, on which were balanced the concrete blocks which I had only caught sight of for a split second in the light of the matches. It seemed a life-time. There were two awful moments when my shoulders brushed something and there was a fall of stuff again – and then I was at the door and Richard had caught me and pulled me carefully up. We stood there for a minute clinging together . . .

We now had to squeeze through the jammed door, which he had managed to shift a little. I begged him not to put his weight on it again in case there was another collapse of what was left standing. It was almost impossible to get out because of the piled-up glass in the entrance to the flats under the archway. I had to climb and even so I could feel the glass cutting my legs. At the back of the archway there was a solid mass of debris – and above it nothing remained of the Marshmans' flat – just this great pile of rubble. I rushed at it crying frantically, 'Kathleen, Kathleen! Cecil! Cecil!' but there wasn't a sound.

Above the garage the flat where the landlord's chauffeur lived looked pretty badly damaged. I shouted for him – and he answered from the shelter, the entrance to which was blocked by another great mound of debris. 'We can't get at you,' I screamed. 'We'll tell them to come – the house has gone.' But there was no answer to this, and none to my further halloos. We climbed out finally over the broken glass to the Royal Hospital Road. A great fire was blazing in the direction of the Elms Garage behind Paradise Walk and the whole street was piled several feet high with glass and rubble. In the sky the light from fires was brilliant, it looked like Blake's pictures of Hell. . . .

On a pile of glass in the middle of the road sat Peer Gynt, who had been courting Vicki all day. He was in the very spot where he had been when the policeman had complained that all the traffic had to go round him.

When he saw me come out carrying her, he leaped from his pile of glass and saluted her with joyous barks and whines. He had sat there through all that appalling Blitz, and would not leave her now.

The Ferebees were, we knew, in the basement under the shop, but the whole shop was wrecked and we ran to the entrance and shouted again and again. The fire behind their premises was appalling. We shouted and banged on the ruined door to try to get some reply from them. . . . Fires blazed on every side, great masses of brickwork and masonry kept falling and falling, crashing into the already huge mounds, and the smell was like Guy Fawkes night.

There was not a warden, not a soul about – it looked like a dead place – not a sign of life from anywhere and yet we knew that in many of the houses people were down in their basements unconscious of the horrors above them. I looked down at my legs – they felt cold – and saw that I had no dress below the thighs. It, and my slip, had vanished; the top of the black dress was quite whole – but the skirt was gone. The whole of it felt wet and sticky – and I knew it was the blood from Anne's arm.

I went back resolutely under the archway in spite of Richard's protests and shouted again and again but there wasn't a sound. In the mass of glass under the archway I saw something which looked like a garment – white – and I thought I could wrap it round my bare thighs, but it was caught firmly and I could not get it. 'Come along – the whole place is going to collapse,' cried Richard as another tremendous thud shook the road, and I had barely got back under the archway before another avalanche of what had once been No. 31 fell on to the remains of No. 33. . . . It was horrible!) . . .

In the telephone box at the top of Tite Street a badly wounded warden was trying to get through. 'God, what a night!' he gasped. He was bleeding profusely but would not let me help him in the street.

'Let's go to the F.A.P.,' I said to Richard. 'It's only a second from here.'

'Go there,' shouted the warden. 'They'll be glad of help.'

We were just turning down Tite Street when we saw two parachutes floating down in the direction of the river. 'Lie down! lie down!' screamed the warden. We flung ourselves down – but it was not pleasant to lie on glass. After what seemed a lifetime there followed two long dull roars and then an appalling explosion. The fires in Burton Court were mounting high in the sky and against them Blossom the balloon stood out in brilliant relief, and at the bottom of Paradise Walk there was a tremendous red glare. . . .

I did not want to go to the F.A.P. *Anne, Anne,* I kept thinking. Could one live with one's arm ripped off at the shoulder? *Was she alive, and Kathleen? What of her?* . . .

Richard pulled me firmly by the arm now. 'There's nothing you can do – only the heavy rescue can get through those piles of masonry and bricks,' and he steered me firmly into the heavily sand-bagged F.A.P. . . . There had been a bomb so near that it had severed the water mains and damaged the place itself, and they had no means of sterilising. The roof, which had been damaged on a previous occasion, had a sort of canvas overhead. Stretchers lay all over the floor awaiting ambulances and casualties were everywhere, humped on benches, huddled on chairs, lying on the floor. We walked in and I bumped into Peggy [a fellow first-aid worker]. She stared at me obviously without recognition. 'Peggy,' I said, 'our house has gone – I think everyone else is dead.' And then she knew me. She put down her tray and took me upstairs. She found me an overall and a cloak.

'The A.F.S. Station has been hit – that's only a few doors from you,' she said. 'It's one hell of a night. There are people trapped everywhere and we're full of homeless as well as casualties.'

'We're homeless,' I said. 'The whole of our piece of the Royal Hospital Road has gone.'

'Are you hurt?' she asked, still looking at me as if I were a ghost. I said I was all right and we went downstairs to the surgery where the casualties were being attended to. Suddenly my legs gave way, and I sat down on a bench next to an old woman wearing a straw hat. Waves of terror came over me – each resounding crash of the bombs which were raining down sent fresh waves of awful sickening fear over me. I was *terrified* now, and I knew that this was really craven fear – such as I had never known. I wanted the ground to open and swallow me up – to hide me from this fearful terror from the skies – it was a disgusting, degrading, nauseating feeling . . . – my body was still wet with Anne's blood – I was literally petrified with terror. . . . Peggy brought me a glass and told me to drink. It was brandy – hot and fiery as I swallowed it. What I wanted was water – my throat and mouth were full of dust and filth, but the brandy pulled me together. I went to a table on which was a bowl for scrubbing up and washed the filth from my hands. All over the floor were casualties and stretchers, for every ambulance was out. Lots of the Canadians who were billeted over the garage behind were in with cuts and wounds from glass – some had burns. Sister-in-charge said, 'Come along, you can start here,' and I took my place with the other V.A.D.s who were flooded out with waiting casualties and more and more arriving. . . .

For one moment I felt I couldn't do it. How could I dress wounds, pick out glass, bandage and clean up when Kathleen, Cecil, and perhaps even Anne were still alive lying under that weight of debris?

We worked at the lines of grey-faced, patient, huddled people. We made tea for them under great difficulties, we boiled our precious store of water for some kind of sterilisation, although the casualties, like me, were filthy. At about two o'clock there was a brief lull and we thought for one glorious moment that the raid was over. . . . But almost immediately there was a fresh wave of planes and a new rain of bombs and the guns opened up again in a deafening barrage. I found myself about to deal with the old woman in the straw hat who had been next to me on the bench. 'Where are you hurt?' I asked her. She put both hands up to the straw hat and clutched it firmly. 'It's me 'ead,' she said. 'It's got a bit of something on it – it's cut and I found me 'at so I jammed it on quick.' And then I saw that there were bloodstains all down her neck.

'Take off your hat,' I said very gently. But she would not. She seemed afraid to uncover her head. Very gently I lifted it when at last she allowed me to do so. Part of the top of her scalp was gone – and for one second the whole room spun round again. She was talking quite rationally. I took a large dressing and laid it gently over the top of her head and took her over to Dr Lendal Tweed. She examined her briefly and Sister put on a dressing, then they nodded in the direction of the stretcher-cases for hospital. The old woman put the hat firmly on top of the dressing. She was very cold, she told me. I fetched a blanket and wrapped it round her. Dr Lendal Tweed called me back. 'I heard you've been bombed?' she said, looking at my curious attire. 'Come here. Are you all right?' 'The baby's jumping,' I said. 'It's frightening – a most queer feeling.' She felt my pulse and said, 'You're fine. What d'you expect it to do? It's time it jumped – it's quite normal.' . . . I went occasionally to see Vicki, who was being nursed in turn by the casualties. She seemed to give them some comfort. The stretcher-bearers told me at intervals that her suitor was still outside the F.A.P. and that no amount of bombs or guns had any effect on his ardour!

That it was our worst night yet was on everybody's lips – and when news came in that the Old Church had gone it seemed the climax to the mounting horrors. . . . 'It's a pile of dust,' one of the stretcher-bearers said. 'The whole of that bit – all Petyt Place seems to have disappeared – and the fire-watchers with it.'

Soon after we digested this it was quiet – and at long last the welcome distant sirens sounded far away – then nearer – and then loudly our own from the Albert Bridge proclaimed that the raid was over.   FRANCES FAVIELL

Suddenly somebody called out: 'There's another one coming!' and I remember looking up and seeing what I thought was another parachute mine coming down. It was absolutely terrifying. You couldn't look away from the thing and there you were, just trying to make yourself as small as possible in the debris, and I suddenly realised it wasn't a mine, it was a man, it was an airman on the end of this parachute, and he dropped down quite fast over the roadway and down on to the foreshore of the river, on the [Chelsea] Embankment. A number of us rushed across there and then we looked rather cautiously over the wall. We had ideas about paratroop invasions. I remember a couple of firemen training a hose and I was clutching my axe and I expect everybody else was wondering what we could do if the man turned a gun on us, but someone went down the steps which are just a little way along the Embankment there, and got hold of him. My recollection is that it was one of our wardens . . . but anyway, he brought him up, and he was a youngster I should think in his early twenties. I remember he was wearing a green flying suit and he was pretty well the same colour himself. He was very correct in his behaviour – he didn't say anything, he didn't do anything, he just stood more or less at attention. I remember feeling his arm quite rigid when I got hold of him, and then something rather surprising happened. . . . Somebody rushed and kicked him in the seat, very hard. I suppose it was somebody who'd had someone killed or was just overcome by the strain of events, but anyway he, the man who kicked him, then rushed round to the front of him and succeeded in getting a pistol out of the pocket in front of his flying suit, and anyway, somebody else took the pistol from the little man, I don't know what he'd have done if he hadn't had it wrested away from him. Then a War Reserve policeman came along at that point, and shortly afterwards another one, and I remember seeing them marching this German airman off along the embankment just as if he'd been drunk and disorderly on a Saturday night.   POST WARDEN MATTHEWS, Quoted by Constantine Fitzgibbon

When dawn broke and crept through our rafters, showing itself between the plasterless laths of the ceilings, we shook ourselves, stretched cramped limbs and took stock of the situation.

It was not a new one to us. Our first land-mine had uprooted us from a house of long standing and even now, six months after, cast a long shadow of difficulties and problems over our lives.

And here was another visitation by another of the same kind – but this time not only had we suffered less damage but we were mentally better prepared for it. . . . The time was 5.30 am. . . .

We concentrated our own forces on the dining-room–sitting-room first, and then worked solidly through the house togther. . . .

First we picked up the larger bits of ceiling and glass and threw them through the window. Everything went through the window whether debris, to be swept into heaps later, or rugs to be beaten. We were working in a large way, which has its own exhilaration.

Vacuum cleaners should not, ideally, be used for getting up glass. So I ran the sweeper quickly over the carpet and then went down on hands and knees with a pan and stiff brush.

I performed mopping up operations on the surround with the pan and a soft brush, going well under the carpet. I left the underneaths of the heavy furniture to another day.

Then I rough dusted, in the course of which I remembered that instead of window-sills we now had ridges of jagged brickwork. By the time I had swept these of fragments, part of the floor needed doing again. I didn't make the mistake twice.

It was now 7.30 am and except for a certain draughtiness, one room had become liveable again. The kitchen seemed to be next in line. It was an indescribable mess.

Even in the cupboards the uncovered food was full of glass-splinters, the sink was full of wet grime, the table and floor thick with debris. Even the covered food, on inspection, too often revealed those bright specks. . . .

We rolled up mats and threw them out and swept the entire floor, as well as everything else that would sweep, including tops of cupboards.

Where things were scrubbable we scrubbed. The steam from the hot water tap rose like a blessing on our labours. There was plenty of fresh air, and we began to sing.

The lawn outside was full of mats, the air beyond full of bangs and clashings of glass as neighbours toiled with their own blasted properties. They, and a host of workmen, walked freely in and out, demanding milk, hot water, and a wash-and-brush-up. . . .

Incidentally we realised how very difficult it is to safeguard food. Locked cupboards fly open, tops fly off, tins are riven through, heavy boxes smash open. On the other hand fragile things often escape. Our pan of last year's preserved eggs survived their second land-mine successfully.

Meanwhile we had started on the bedrooms. By the lunchtime break we had done two, using the same methods as for downstairs, but putting everything possible under the already dirty bedspreads to save them from further mess.

Books we swept quickly of the larger lumps of ceiling, but otherwise left alone. . . .

The handyman of the house we made O.C. Repairs . . . though of course his handiwork was all of a purely temporary nature.

Where practically the whole window was out, for instance, he boarded it up. Luckily there is never any lack of timber after a Blitz. Planks and doors litter the place, and there is firewood for weeks.

In this case it was fragments of the party fence that came to hand. But the handyman's special problem was, that this being a modern rough-cast house, with steel frames, there was nothing to which to nail the planks.

He solved the problem by sawing the wood so that it would just knock tightly between the tops and bottoms of the stonework. This helped with blackout, too. . . .

We worked ferociously through the house all that morning till the early afternoon. By four o'clock we could sit down in the midst of our labours and say they were good. . . .

Shocks bring a temporary upsurge of reactionary energy. You have to cash in on that at once before it goes on the ebb. If you can do this you can handle a major catastrophe (or what would have seemed like one once) in terms of routine. *HOUSEWIFE* August 1941

Throughout the war, the great event of the day, linking families together, as well as keeping the nation informed of the events, was the Nine O'clock News.

The actual reading of the news carried a very great responsibility. It was up to us to instil a spirit of courage and hope into millions of listeners even in the very darkest days and there were times when the content of the bulletins made this very difficult.

'Our troops have retired to previously prepared positions.'

'Fifteen of our aircraft are missing.'

'The German communiqué reports a considerable advance on the Russian front.'

'Enemy aircraft were over this country during the night. Damage and casualties have been reported.'

For weeks at a time these and similar phrases were repeated constantly, with little on the credit side to lighten our darkness.

Throughout the war the Home Service bulletins stuck strictly to the facts, or to such as might be stated without giving information to the enemy. On several occasions, when our fortunes were at their lowest ebb, I have begged to be allowed to include some more cheerful little item which had come into the news-room over the tape. The editor was adamant; if it had not been double-checked for accuracy, it must not be inserted. This was undoubtedly the right policy. It was almost unheard of for us to have to contradict anything we had put out, so that listeners all over the world came to rely absolutely on the B.B.C. Home News as the real truth about what was happening. . . .

Frequently, the bulletin was not ready when the newsreader left the news-room for the studio. We often started to read with nothing but the headlines and hope. The rest arrived page by page and we just sailed on through the uncharted seas, praying that no typist's error had escaped the eagle eye of the senior sub-editor on duty. At times there loomed ahead some fearful Russian snag such as Malojaroslavetz or Dniepropetrovsk – rocks on which the most confident ship might founder if encountered without warning. . . .

It is astonishing how keenly some people seem to feel about correct pronunciations. Sarawak and Perak, for instance – in both of which we sounded the final consonant for the sake of clarity – provoked many an indignant retired planter to ring up or write, insisting that these intrusive 'K's' should remain silent. One persistent caller was only slightly mollified when I suggested that Perak without its 'k' might be confused with Para and so spread alarm and despondency by giving the impression that the Japanese had invaded Brazil.

Whenever the war news allowed enough time, we used to read out the football results after the six o'clock bulletin on Saturday evenings. I had finished this operation and was groping my way across the road for a breath of fresh air and a glass of beer, when I was pursued by one of the commissionaires with a message that I was urgently required on an important trunk call from Scotland. I hurried back, but at least fifteen minutes must have elapsed from the time the call was put through, and I assumed therefore that the matter must be extremely critical if a trunk line could be occupied for so long. Rather anxiously I picked up the receiver:

'Hullo – this is Belfrage here – who is that?'

'Never you mind who it is – are you the ignorant bastard who has just read the news?'

'Well, I . . .'

'Do ye no ken that the football team from this city is the Glasgow Seltic?'

'Oh, is it? I always thought C-E-L-T-I-C was pronounced Keltic.'

'Well, all I can say is that if that's all the education you have, you have no business to hold your job down.'

'I am very sorry you feel so upset about it, but I . . .'

'Upset? It's a disgrace – no wonder the country is in a mess – you'll hear more of this, I'm telling you.' And the receiver went back with a crash.

As he was speaking, the nightly ration of bombs had begun to fall.
BRUCE BELFRAGE

On Whit Sunday, 1 June 1941, the nations took another step towards total war with the introduction of clothes rationing, for which responsibility rested on the President of the Board of Trade.

It was soon clear to Arnold Overton [Permanent Secretary to the Board of Trade] and me that more could and should be squeezed out of civilian consumption, and that more production and distributive services could be released for the war. He tentatively suggested that we should ration clothes. To which I replied, 'Let me know what it would save in men and materials, and if it is substantial, ration clothes we certainly will.'

'But don't you think it would be politically very difficult? Can you ever hope to get it through the Cabinet?'

'I don't know,' said I, 'but if it is a sound measure, I expect we can'. . . .

The scheme was perfected and polished by Watkinson, the head of the Clothing Department, and was ready for its first trial run. This meant that it had to be sponsored by me before the Lord President's Committee, the most formidable and powerful body on home affairs, and presided over by Sir John Anderson.

For two long sessions of several hours he and his colleagues frisked the scheme, took it apart, fitted it together again and asked every sort of question. In the end they only made one or two minor improvements and pronounced it sound and workable. . . .

Winston, however, would have none of it: the war, he said, would be won by the civilian population whose morale held out the longest. Poor people, in rags and tatters on the bureaucratic orders of a new Minister! . . . I replied that the scheme saved 450,000 workers, either for the armed forces or for the munition factories, and that ever since Dunkirk the public were eager to make sacrifices . . . 'Who are you,' he said, 'to tell me what the public want? Why, I only picked you up out of some bucket shop in the City a few weeks ago, and what can you know about politics and public opinion? . . . Clothing rationing! What next? Office has gone to your head. Please, please go back and look after trade, and don't try and strip the poor people to the buff.'

However, I had by now powerful allies in the Lord President and Kingsley Wood, the Chancellor of the Exchequer. Even they could not move him.

The day when I wanted to launch the scheme was not far off when the hunt for the *Bismarck* began. Anderson and Kingsley Wood were waiting to see Winston on my business, and eventually got into his room at Church House. It was covered with charts, duty officers from the Admiralty were handing him reports, and he was in close touch with the First Sea Lord.

'Clothing rationing?' he rasped to these two senior Ministers. 'Can't you see I'm busy? Do what you like, but please don't worry me now.' John Anderson came out and said, 'You can go ahead,' so I rushed back to the Board of Trade and pressed the button.

When the *Bismarck* was caught and sunk, Winston wanted to return to the attack on clothes rationing, but was told that it was now too late, the machinery had begun to turn. He was not pleased, but could hardly be very angry with me: he had to round on John Anderson and the Chancellor. . . .

About a week after I had launched the scheme [1 June 1941] I was asked to Ditchley [Churchill's weekend retreat in Oxfordshire]. I came down to dinner a little late and found a party of about a dozen, including the Prime Minister, gathered in the drawing-room. 'Ah,' said the Prime Minister, with unconcealed satisfaction, 'here's Oliver, who knows nothing of politics, who rejects the Prime Minister's views on public opinion about clothes rationing, and turns out to be right. . . . We will have an extra glass of champagne to celebrate.'
OLIVER LYTTELTON, VISCOUNT CHANDOS

Although the immediate danger of invasion had passed, Home Guard training was continuing and becoming more ambitious.

One absorbing question was whether the Home Guard would be called upon to deal with tanks, and if so how could they do so? No very decided lead was forthcoming from the Higher Command until the County Defence Officer staged a demonstration . . . to show how a tank-trap could be constructed in any village, provided the main street had sufficient curve to prevent an uninterrupted view from end to end.

According to information then available, German tanks were accustomed to move on the road, through enclosed country, with sixty to eighty yards distance between each. . . . If a tank met sudden opposition it would normally stop at once and . . . the tanks behind would follow suit as each one saw that the tank immediately preceding it had halted. . . .

Now it is clear that, if a careful recce was previously carried out, the exact spot on the road where the leading tank, after rounding the bend, would suddenly sight the road-block in position could be definitely determined and also, working backwards, the exact spot could also be definitely fixed at which each of the other tanks, having seen that the one preceding had stopped, would themselves come to a halt.

These spots thus definitely located and suitably marked, the position for each Home Guard ambush party could then be chosen and they, concealed behind the garden wall . . . merely had to plaster their own particular tank with Molotov cocktails, sticky or anti-tank bombs and flame-throwers, and then shoot up the crews when they emerged from the tanks, as they grew too hot to hold them.

It could, therefore, readily be seen that, provided the Hun played the game and stuck to the rules, the destruction of all the tanks in the trap was . . . 'a piece of cake'. . . .

Several platoons, in villages where the necessary curves in the main street existed, worked out their tank-traps and demonstrated them in action, with the remainder of the platoon as spectators. Tanks, as a rule, were represented by private cars, Molotov cocktails and sticky bombs by small bags of soot or chalk (which burst on impact with devastating results), anti-tank bombs by thunderflashes or home-made bombs, and flamethrowers by stirrup pumps.

One such demonstration . . . was held at the village of Loudwater on Whit Sunday 1941, and as part of the trap crossed the main London–Oxford road it was timed to start at 07.30 hours in order not to hold up traffic. . . .

The Company Commander attended the demonstration. . . .

'I reached,' he said, 'the Loudwater road junction just before 07.30 hours. It was a beautiful spring morning. . . . Shortly afterwards the first tank came round the bend and obediently halted on seeing the obstruction. A shower of Molotov cocktails, hurled from behind the bushes of the nearest garden, immediately struck it with unerring precision and we then waited for the anti-tank bomb which was to finally disable it. There occurred instead, however, almost directly behind me, a terrific disturbance, a noise like that of a big rocket at a firework display.

'On turning round, I saw the most extraordinary sight; two figures standing amid the bushes of a cottage garden enveloped in a thick cloud of black smoke. One of them seemed to have lost both eyebrows and the entire half of what had been a fine crop of auburn hair, while the other had all the appearance of a jet-black nigger. . . . It soon became clear that a home-made anti-tank bomb had not been entirely successful. First-aid was quickly rendered at platoon H.Q. . . . For some days, two of Loudwater's . . . most intrepid anti-tank fighters were most definitely out of the war.

'A move was now made to the second tank, which was waiting patiently for treatment at a spot where the right-angle turn in the road had enabled it to observe that the first tank had stopped ahead of it.

'This happened to be immediately in front of and a few yards distant from the churchyard gate, and the platoon commander informed us that the attack would be made with Molotov cocktails and a flamethrower, concealed behind the brick wall of the Vicarage garden, at right angles to the church. On the signal being given the tank was quickly covered with a glorious coating of soot and chalk, followed by a vigorous jet of water from the stirrup pump deputising for the flamethrower. There was a plentiful supply of water and the jet was striking the windscreen and cascading along and over the roof of the car in fine style. . . . If it had been the intention to synchronise this deluge of water with the opening of the church door to let the congregation out at the end of the early service, the timing could not have been more perfect and exact. I saw a group of people at the door of the church wiping the water from their clothes, and I heard them angrily declaiming that it was simply disgraceful for the Home Guard to wash their dirty cars outside the church door on Sunday mornings.'
L.W. KENTISH

Nothing did more to damage Home Guard morale, or make the organisation a source of jokes, than the issue of pikes, which consisted of a sharpened metal rod attached to a long handle; to most of the recipients they seemed about as useful in modern warfare as a bow and arrow. Some Home Guards resigned rather than carry them and the wisest units left them unissued in their stores. Only one commander succeeded in finding a use for pikes.

Sports Galas were held every year from 1941. . . . Everything except the hiring of a few side shows was organised, made or printed and erected by the platoon. In each we incorporated a special free spectacle for the interest and amusement of the public. In 1941 this took the form of a frontal attack on a machine-gun post by riflemen and bombers. This, I admit, fell rather flat from a spectacular point of view. The attackers, during most of the time, were either crawling or lying prone. In the long grass they were for the most part invisible.

The racing and sideshows were, however, very popular. A point worthy of mention is the clearing up of the ground next day. The amount of litter left by a crowd of about 2,000 people has to be seen to be believed. We cleared the ground in half an hour by the simple process of arming each man with a pike and sandbag – the only occasion the pikes were ever used in this platoon – forming the men into line in open order and giving the order to advance. As each man went forward he impaled all pieces of paper, etc, on his pike, and transferred them to his sandbag. By the time the line had been up the field and back no vestige of litter remained.   H.E. FLIGHT

One important social reform brought about by the war was the provision for the first time of proper maternity services for all expectant mothers.

The authorities at the ante-natal clinic told me that they liked their expectant mothers to prepare themselves for their ordeal with a month away from air raids. The mothers were accommodated in a large house at Woking. This plan also cut down last-minute rushes to the evacuated hospital. . . .

Together we went to Woking. It was easy to identify my destination. Women of all sizes and colours, but only one shape, were dragging themselves up a steep incline to a large modern mansion labelled, incongruously, *The Barrens*.

It was a fine house with flowering bulbs bordering the drive, which wound steeply up to its front door, leaving its inmates breathless and exhausted long before they reached it. . . . We *mothers*, as we were in many cases prematurely called, slept in large dormitories and ate our meals at long trestle tables. . . .

Like some religious ritual, each mother as she came down to breakfast glanced quickly round the table in search of empty places. The names of the happily delivered, if any, would soon be supplied, together with full details of the ordeal and such less interesting information as the baby's weight and sex.

A delivery was always stimulating. The turnover was quite noticeable, with an average of forty mothers there at a time. But it was erratic. For a while one or two left daily, then, by some trick of nature, none would leave for a week. At such times every occupant of *The Barrens*, right down to the man who made up the boiler, wore the pent-up expression of people waiting for something to blow up.

Suddenly ten would leave in a night, like hens inciting each other to lay eggs after a thunderstorm. The ambulances would be jostling each other in the drive, for we supplied other hospitals besides the evacuated Westminster at the village of Ripley. . . .

At midnight I went down to the kitchen and made some tea. It was the custom at *The Barrens* for those in labour to do this, usually taking a friend in order to leave someone behind to report details. . . .

There the warden found me, gave me one look, and rushed to the telephone.

'There's plenty of time,' I said when she came back, trying to comfort her.

'You never know,' she said. 'It's five miles to the hospital, and in the blackout. . . .'

She was interrupted by the barking of guns not far from the house. A distant siren piped thinly and was followed by a nearer one. Three bombs dropped in quick succession.

The warden went upstairs to fetch my suitcase.

Presently two very young-looking A.R.P. girls clattered in from the blackout.

'What a night!' said one.

'Where's the patient?' said the other.

'Here,' I said, 'but there's no special hurry.'

'Come along,' said one, picking up my suitcase and going out into the dark again. The other took my arm as though I was blind as well as pregnant. The warden said good-bye with an anxious look.

In the back of a car the two girls heaped cushions and hot-water-bottles around me, as though piling sandbags around a public statue. The guns grumbled and yapped; and I became almost hysterical with pleasure that so much seemed to have been laid on for me to remember. It was a brisk moonlit night with just a touch of frost, although it was already May. The girl sitting beside the driver kept turning round to look at me, obviously afraid that I might not last the journey. When the driver lost her way among the confusing little lanes round Ripley, the other started to fumble behind her for a book on first aid. Although it seemed funny at the time, it was really commendable that those girls were not only happy to drive about in the night to the clatter of gunfire and thump of exploding bombs, but were also prepared to deliver a baby, for their country, by moonlight in a country lane, with no guidance except from a book which they had lost. . . .

They left me alone on the operating-table. I recited the names and ages of my brothers and sisters, the Lord's Prayer, and then the names on the boxes in those wicked-looking glass instrument cases . . . I had no idea how long this would go on. In spite of the table-talk at *The Barrens*, I had no idea of what to expect beyond a liberal share of Churchill's blood, toil, tears, and sweat. . . .

As the pace grew fiercer, outside interference was added to the drama by the crash of gunfire and drone of aircraft overhead.

'Ours,' said one student with confidence, and was immediately contradicted by a bomb dropping a few fields away. By now I had ceased to care, and would have welcomed a whole bread-basket of bombs on the top of us. . . . Then came a small, high, furious wail above it all; and I was suddenly fully conscious and able to feel something soft and wriggling against my knees.

With absurd appropriateness a far-off air raid siren sounded the all clear.

'It's a girl,' somebody said.   VERILY ANDERSON

The outstanding feature of this period of the war was the mobilisation of all women without small children for war work, either to replace a man or to enable a younger, 'mobile' woman to be sent away from home to a factory.

For several months I trained to be an engineer, and passed out as a 'semi-skilled fitter', reasonably competent in welding, soldering, tool-making, drilling, riveting, drawing and reading blue-prints. My instructor was an R.A.F. man, released specifically for the job of training women and girls. He made the work interesting, amusing, and things were never dull. Being such a good instructor, he was forever saddened to see the girls he turned out as good semi-skilled engineers end up doing their war work as laundresses, telephonists, railway porters etc. Through no fault of their own these girls were directed into these jobs by the Ministry of Labour, because suitable jobs weren't available at the time their course had terminated. Such was the case with me. I had expected to be sent to 'Fords', but instead of working with metal as I had been trained to do, I was directed to a 'Wood' factory, which made assault barges and aeroplane wings. It all seemed such a waste of effort on both trainee and instructor's part.

My initiation into factory life was shattering. Being a hairdresser in a high-class salon situated in a select area of the town, I was a somewhat genteel, reserved type of girl. To be plunged abruptly into a world of coarse, ill-bred men and women, where language was foul and bluer than the bluest sky, was an experience so harsh and unreal, that had God not endowed me with a true, strong sense of humour, I fear I should have floundered and stayed wretchedly unhappy for the rest of the war years.

The factory was vast, and I was told to report for the night shift. Although quite a few of the girls had been recruited from other walks of life, like me, most of them were real rough-tough die-hards, heads swathed in turbans, sporting curlers beneath, cigarette dangling, loud-voiced and hard-faced. They eyed all new-comers suspiciously, and were most unfriendly until one's face was an everyday thing, which eventually blurred into the pattern. I was sent with a group of die-hards to report to a certain foreman. He surveyed us all, grimly gave each one a job to do, with the exception of yours truly. No doubt I looked nervous and scared. He ignored me, and as he turned to walk away I said 'What shall *I* do?' He turned toward me, sneered 'Oh yes! We've forgotten Sunshine here! What shall *you* do? – Here! Take this!', indicating a broom 'And sod around!' – With that he threw the broom at me and walked off. I was stung to humiliation before the rest of the girls. One of them said 'He's just showing off and trying to be funny. Don't do that, kid!' He returned thirty minutes later to find me sitting on a box doing nothing. Furiously he demanded 'What the blankety blank I thought I was doing?' Summoning all my courage I retorted that until he had the decency to show me the job I had to do, presuming it *was* to help the war effort, I intended staying where I was. Somewhat taken aback he treated me to a stream of foul language calling me some of the filthiest names imaginable. I was so angry and disgusted by this time, that I brought up my hand and slapped him hard across the cheek. The scene was electric, and girls had ceased working to watch. He raised his hand as if to strike me, and I counter-attacked with 'Take me to the office! I wish to report you.' Perhaps he hadn't encountered anything like this before, but it had a becalming effect upon him. He apologised grudgingly, and took me to a machine, and demonstrated the pedals, handbrakes and rollers for me to operate. During the night he came over and asked my name. I curtly gave him my surname, and he troubled me no more. At the end of that shift I went home and wept bitterly. How was I ever going to stand the atmosphere?

The following night, he came up to me smiling broadly and whist-ling 'Rose-Marie, I love you' – it seems he'd taken the trouble to check on my Christian name at the gate. From then on he was very friendly, and although I didn't like him terribly, he would have lengthy discus-sions with me, and tell me I was a 'smasher'.

The day foreman were much nicer and more polite, and as time went on I found my niche. As they discovered I could work a certain machine and get good results, I was transferred to another depart-ment. The girls by now accepted me and I was no longer treated with suspicion. Many of the men with whom I worked tried to 'date' me, but as most of them were married, their wives and children evacuated, I declined all the offers and invitations. Even the foul language began to flow over my head, and the coarse dirty jokes which prevail in factory life, I ignored. More new girls arrived on war-work. Models, secretaries, housewives, shop-assistants and even a solicitor's wife, and a doctor's daughter. I made many friends, and there was a solid camaraderie between us all, and we shared moments of gladness and moments of sorrow.

Some of the men had bets on how soon I would be swearing with the best of them. But they lost their money. After five years when I left, several congratulated me on my strength of will-power.

ROSEMARY MOONEN

In peacetime I had been a ballet dancer and then an usherette . . . When I first volunteered for work at Creeds of East Croydon, during the second year of the war, I was given a short test of ability. My mathematics were not good and I was introduced into the Press Shop to work a hand press, throwing around sideways, from right to left, a heavy handle which brought down a heavy hammer to flatten out metal. Later I was transferred to a machine driven by electric power, which one worked with a foot, feeding metal into it with the hands. After about a week of this I was asked to report at the drilling machines. Then the fun commenced. Most of the drills were about the thickness of a stout darning needle. These I managed to break, one after another, until in desperation my 'setter' sent me to the store for a rubber drill. Guessing there was no such drill, I walked around . . . and reported back that the store keeper was very sorry to be 'out' of rubber drills but was expecting some in the following week.

The next morning I was given a lesson in 'tapping' holes instead of drilling them. This I found much easier to do, but sitting at one machine was very boring, so when a girl dressed in men's overalls, with a peaked cap on, and carrying a ladder and an oil-can, came to my machine, I was at once interested, asking her as she oiled my machine if any more oilers were needed. I was told 'Yes, on night work. Would I do it?' Only men had been allowed on night work until then . . . I volunteered the next day but about a month passed before I actually started doing my rounds as an oiler and greaser. . . . Later I learned that during this month when I was still working on drilling and tapping machines (and, incidentally, had now got the knack of it) most of the maintenance men had come either to look me over from a distance or they had a few words with me. I was pleased to learn that the Chief Fitter, who was our boss on the night shift, had pronounced me to be 'Just right for the job'.

At first I found the ladder heavy to carry but managed it, and enjoyed running along the tops of walls, filling the grease caps on the wheels of the overhead belting system which drove a row of machines making teleprinter parts. This greasing was done when the girl machine operators were having their dinner from 1 am until 2 am. I had my meal earlier. . . . On my oiling rounds on the shop floor, while machines were working, I carried two grease guns, and a handsome red oil can. If these machines needed oiling the operators would stop them and have a little chat with me as I oiled or greased. For the larger machines, I soon learned the knack of tipping over the large oil drums to fill up gallon tins. There were times when not many machines needed oil on the night shift, then, when my work was done, I would become 'mate' to whoever was the most busy maintenance man. I learned to mend machine belts, also to pull wires through pipes in the wall for the electrician. I went seriously about my work and enjoyed it very much.   VERNA [VIK] KAY

Factory workers often thought the women in the office had a soft time. This was certainly not true, however, of at least one secretary, working for the Managing Director of an aircraft factory in Gloucestershire.

I had two days holiday that Christmas [1940], my first in nine months. Looking back now on the year which followed I cannot remember anything but work, work, work. Getting up at 6.30 am I would make my way to the bathroom with closed eyes, staggering with tiredness.

At 7.30 am I would go down the front steps, with the aid of a torch, in the blackout. I was fortunate in knowing someone who would give me a lift to the office, where I would work all day with the light on.

Girls in the works, protected by their unions, were allowed fifteen minutes break in the morning for a hot drink. They had an hour for lunch and another break for tea. At 7 pm they finished promptly, and buses waited in the car park to take them to their homes. I was not protected and did not have a break. Frequently at lunch times R.H.C. would decide to 'work through'. How I dreaded those words. Sandwiches were sent over from the canteen and I would eat mine while I was taking down shorthand. Later, R.H.C. would eat his in peace, while I was typing. 'Tea-time' meant drinking a cup of tea while I typed. Many times I had just poured it out when R.H.C. rang for me, and it would be stone cold when I got back. I tried asking for permission to drink it while it was hot but it made him so bad tempered I eventually preferred to let it get cold.

I would hear the buses pulling out at 7 pm and gradually the building would empty, but still I would be working. Eight o'clock, nine o'clock, ten o'clock, sometimes later, R.H.C. would announce, 'Well, I'm going', and then I would put his papers away and go down the road to the bus stop, hoping I would be seen in the blackout by the driver, and less afraid of the gunfire than I was of the soldiers stationed nearby.

When I arrived late at the Guest House supper was 'keeping hot'. Prepared at 7 pm it was almost uneatable. Sausage and mash was the cook's favourite dish. How I came to loathe it, dried hard and stuck to the plate. I would tumble into bed, too tired to sleep, and going through my brain would be the work of the coming day, and the names of the engines like a refrain, 'Hercules, Pegasus, Merlin; Cheetah, Sabre and Taurus'. For the first time in my life I could not read. I tried but I always fell asleep.

One night I got home 'early', in time for the nine o'clock news, and was told that Lord Beaverbrook was broadcasting a speech. I sat down on my bed to listen, still wearing my coat and with my handbag in my hand. Next thing I knew someone was shaking me and telling me it was 11.30 pm and I ought to be in bed.

I did not go to London so frequently that year, but my firm now had dispersal factories all over the country, which I visited with R.H.C. in rapid succession. Sometimes at eight o'clock at night he would announce that we would go to Manchester and I would rush home and throw a few things into a case. He would always dictate in the car as long as the light lasted, sometimes sitting next to me, but at other times shouting over his shoulder from the front seat. Occasionally he would take the wheel himself, and dictate as he drove at high speed along the highways.

By autumn I could not keep awake if I was not working. In the car, in buses or trains, or even sitting on the side of my bed removing my shoes, I would fall asleep. R.H.C. was furious if I nodded between notes, but I could not control the desire for sleep and started having strange pains in my head.

All kinds of welfare facilities were being introduced at the Factory. Welfare Officers, up-to-date First Aid Rooms, a Post Office, and even a hairdresser's shop. Still, no one was ever supposed to have a tooth which needed filling, or an appendix which should come out. Occasionally I would see newspaper headings 'Absenteeism grows in Factories' and I was indignant. Of course there was absenteeism, when no time was allowed to take a pair of shoes to be repaired or to buy necessities. The absenteeism was greater among the women now employed in the works than among those on the staff, but that was understandable as the former were largely married women with home ties. Eventually married women were allowed Saturday mornings off for shopping, but the rest of us managed the best way we could, with the help of relatives and friends.

By November 1941 I was beginning to feel really ill, and knowing I would not be granted time off, without a display of R.H.C.'s temper, I simply stayed out one morning and went to see my doctor. I asked for a tonic and brought his wrath down on my head. He lectured me and ordered a complete rest. I went to the office later in the day and told R.H.C. what had happened, but he insisted he could not get along without me that week, owing to a big press dinner being given by the firm in London. I could appreciate his point and agreed to work until the week-end, whereupon he became very good-humoured and invited me to the dinner.

I had about three weeks away from the office. I had thought it would be just wonderful to laze and do nothing, but found it impossible. I did not want to visit shops; I could not read; I was restless and irritable. Being unable to read worried me considerably, but I felt as if a dull weight descended on my head whenever I tried to look at a page.

After about ten days I was persuaded to visit a relative in a remote village in the Cotswolds, and quite suddenly one morning there I wanted to go for a walk with the dog. From then on I began to get better and I shall never forget the delight of realising I could enjoy a book again.

For some time I had toyed with the idea of leaving my job and joining one of the Women's Services, and had actually obtained details regarding the W.R.N.S. I had tried to persuade myself that I would be doing more to help the war effort, but inwardly I knew I was looking for a way to escape with an easy conscience. It was not always easy to cope with an accumulation of work and R.H.C.'s mercurial temperament. If someone, or something, upset him, he was liable to arrive at the office in a towering rage which might not subside for days. Some of his staff had transferred from the north with him and worked in such fear that they would flinch when he rang for them. I was determined not to get to that stage and decided if ever I should become afraid of R.H.C. I would leave.

Journeys with R.H.C., particularly in bad weather, were frequently a nightmare, with his continual back-seat driving. He would shout, 'Go on, man, you can get through there'; 'You —— fool'; 'You this'; 'You that'. Sometimes he would not cease the whole way, and I have seen chauffeurs mop their brows in the middle of winter. Why none of them ever stopped the car and told him to do his own driving I never could understand. He insisted on driving on the right-hand side of the road too, and once yelled at a driver, 'Drive smoothly, I want to read', but when the speedometer slowed down to 50 mph he was furious and roared, 'I didn't tell you to stop'. I used to take letters and reports down, interspersed with his bellowings and I often wondered what his reaction would have been to a verbatim account. . . .
FLORENCE JACKSON

It was the end of the day; all the innumberable evacuees and visitors had gone to bed and I was sleepily tidying up downstairs before going up myself. Someone had left a paper on the table in the hall; it was folded back at a picture showing a girl, standing on top of a barge with a boat-hook in her hand, in a kind of 'Come to the Broads' attitude. I love boats, so it caught my eye. . . .

The photograph was published at the instigation of the Ministry of War Transport, who were doing one of their periodic recruiting campaigns for the Women's Training Scheme. Women were being trained to work as canal boatwomen (or 'bargees' as most people mistakenly call them) in order to release men for the Armed Forces. . . .

Both the children would be going off to boarding school in a week or so's time and I should then be free to do some real war work. . . . I knew a bit about boats, having had many holidays on the Broads before I was married. . . .

I discovered, first, that the things I was hoping to learn to manage were not barges but BOATS; that these long-boats, monkey-boats or narrow-boats (whichever you like so long as you don't call them 'barges') are seventy feet long and seven feet wide; that they work in pairs, one with a heavy-oil engine towing the other which is called the 'butty-boat'; that three women made up a crew, working the boats entirely from the moment when they set off down to Limehouse to load with cargo, to the time when, having emptied in Birmingham and picked up a second cargo of coal in Coventry, they empty again somewhere in the London area and come back to the depot for fresh orders. I was told that this whole round trip took something like a fortnight, that the crews lived entirely on the boats and were responsible for their own feeding arrangements, and that I should be entitled to a short leave after every two trips.

Further, the boats were capable of a speed of about 5 mph empty but only 3–3½ mph loaded; that there are 152 locks between London and Birmingham, all of which we worked ourselves. 'I received this piece of news quite calmly, without the faintest idea of its magnitude). . . .

They evidently thought I might be worth a trial because they arranged for me to go down to Southall . . . to the offices of the Grand Union Canal Carrying Company, who were co-operating with the Ministry in the Women's Scheme. . . .

Rain is about the worst thing that can happen to you on the boats. If it is a really heavy downpour you have to shut the sliding hatch-cover to keep the cabin dry, and steering becomes very difficult; rather than bother, one usually tries to compromise and the cabin floor becomes a shambles. We had to keep running in and out in our wet things, too, and every single bit of us was wet at the end of a few minutes. Hands wet from the paddles and climbing up lock sides, mackintoshes wet from the same cause, boots (if you were lucky enough to have them) soaking from the puddles, sou'wester dripping down the back of your neck, bottoms of your trousers clinging damply round your ankles . . . altogether horribly uncomfortable and only one small range and the line above it to dry two people's wet clothes on. They never did get really dry till the weather changed, and each morning presented the problem: Which are my least wet things? . . .

I had the most awful mackintosh on my first trip. It was too big and too loose and it wasn't really waterproof. It kept catching in the windlass and the balance beams of the gates, flapping and getting generally in the way; but it was a poem compared with that sported by [a fellow trainee] . . . who appeared later in the day draped in her husband's Home Guard rubber cape, which was never intended for the job, and was tastefully embellished with camouflaging. I can well remember the poor thing getting caught up at every turn and getting thoroughly wet into the bargain because her 'cape' fitted nowhere. At intervals she would become inflated like a child's balloon as the wind got under her floating draperies and blew her up. It was a fascinating sight.

By about this stage of my first trip my hands had become agonisingly painful. It was pretty well hopeless to try to wear gloves while working because our hands were constantly getting wet with the ropes; in despair one shed them and worked with bare hands, which was much easier. At the same time the wind blew, and the rain rained, and the frost froze, all on top of one's defenceless wet skin which didn't like it a bit, and retaliated by developing such chaps as I did not know existed. We dried them when we could but it was not easy to dry the towel that dried the hands that stopped the chaps that saved the skin, etc., etc., the net result being that by this time my hands were swollen, cracked and sometimes even bleeding. To bend my finger round a pen and write a letter in the evening was nearly impossible; if I did try I used to find my tongue sticking out with the effort, like a five-year-old doing pot-hooks.

Darning I had given up completely; if I had caught a thread on my cheese-grater hands there would be a ladder, and to try to slip my hand inside a sock to look for holes was like trying to insert a hedgehog. This turned out to be only a temporary inconvenience; on my next trip my skin got harder and I suffered a good deal less and, later on still, I used always to sleep with my hands smothered in grease and gloves on; several people did that, and it made a lot of difference, though it took the first big clothes-wash on leave to get our hands clean. The dirt and oil got into all the cracks and chaps, so that it really would not come out, however hard you scrubbed; anyway, scrubbing sore hands is not one of life's pleasanter experiences.

While we were on a trip and had occasion to go into any public place . . . we used to keep our hands in our pockets, we were so ashamed of them. I remember Kit [a crew-mate] saying once: 'Do you notice, when you go on leave, how clean all the *men's* hands are?' That just about sums it up.   SUSAN WOOLFITT

The need to increase food production had led to the mobilisation in September 1939 of the Women's Land Army, consisting largely of girls and women from the towns with no experience of farm work.

The Land Army Song

Back to the Land, we must all lend a hand.
To the farms and the fields we must go.

There's a job to be done,
Though we can't fire a gun
We can still do our bit with the hoe . . .

Back to the Land, with its clay and its sand
Its granite and gravel and grit.
You grow barley and wheat
And potatoes to eat
To make sure that the nation keeps fit . . .

We will tell you once more
You can help win the war
If you come with us – back to the Land

Quoted by W.E. SHEWELL-COOPER

If you want to go to heaven when you die,
Wear a pair of khaki breeches and a tie.
Wear an old felt bonnet, with W.L.A. on it,
If you want to go to heaven when you die.

Quoted by SHIRLEY JOSEPH

Newspaper stories about the Land Army were usually illustrated with pictures of spotlessly clean and tidily dressed girls giving bottles to lambs or posing elegantly besides sheaves of corn. The reality was different.

As soon as enough drills are ready, the muck-carting begins. The muck (farmyard manure, that is) is carted from the midden on horse-drawn, two-wheeled carts. We use farmyard manure at the rate of twenty tons to the acre, and consequently muck-carting is, to say the least of it, quite a big job.

The muck is dropped in forkfuls at frequent intervals down the furrows. It is another of those jobs that looks as easy as falling off a ladder, until you try to do it yourself. The horsemen seem to be serenely unaware of the tiltings and jerkings of the cart, and how they not only keep their balance standing on top of a load of muck, but manage to throw it off steadily in neat little piles, is beyond my comprehension. . . .

The men laugh at me and tell me how very simple it really is. Many times they have tried to persuade me to attempt it myself. As the loss of balance for one moment would mean immersion in the wholesome but not exactly palatable load, it is an experiment I have always avoided.

Behind the muck-carters come the muck-knockers, armed with forks. The muck-knockers are everybody who doesn't happen to be doing anything else – the Irishman, the 'bloody wenches', and very often the boss.

Of all the jobs that we do, I think that knocking muck is the most gruelling. The neat little piles that the carters have left down the furrows have to be knocked with forks, so that the muck lies level in the bottom of the furrow. The knocker walks crabwise on the ridge and bends nearly double to hit the muck with his fork in the furrow. Sometimes the muck is light, dusty stuff, mostly sawdust, and one wallop with the fork sends it flying to the next pile in a most encouraging way. This sort of muck, beloved by the knockers and cursed by the boss because its value as manure is negligible, is very rare. It is usually heavy, sodden and rich, and has to be shaken and persuaded and bullied into going in the right direction.

I often wonder if I shall ever forget the searing ache that knocking muck produces in the small of the back, and all the nagging muscles that it discovers in the wrists and shoulders. I know I shall never forget the day when Marjorie [a fellow landgirl] was first introduced to the business.

It was a very warm day in April. We had started knocking at seven o'clock in the morning and had been at it steadily until four in the afternoon. For the last few hours Marjorie had been finding it heavy going. Her chin was jutting out and her teeth were clenched with determination. Her face was streaked with earth and sweat. Suddenly she stuck her fork into the drill and slowly, with an agonised grimace, she straightened her back. She bent weary, dejected eyes upon me, and said dramatically:

'Rachie, I think I'm going to die!'

Remembering my own struggles of two years before, I tried to find a few comforting words of sympathy. Marjorie cut short all such banalities by adding:

'Not that I mind much if I do.'

Knocking muck is not a job that is over and done with in half an hour; it goes on for weeks and weeks and weeks.

RACHEL KNAPPETT

The rottenest job I ever had was re-stooking corn. . . . When corn stooks fell down due to wind and rain, an attempt was made to save the situation by going round and standing them up again. It's no use waiting till the sun has been on them for a couple of days, this must be done while they are still damp. Since you have to grasp them against your body to carry them, you get wet in the process. Also, having been down, and battered out of shape, they never set up well again, and you kick and shove them with all your strength, only to see them topple again, as you turn away. I never decided whether or not it was a good idea to wear a mackintosh for this job. If you wore one, you stayed dry and got hot. If you didn't, you got sodden and chilled. It was a job you could do alone – very suitable for a landgirl! – and it was boring, lonely and frustrating.

There was a combine-harvester on the next farm doing most of the work in one process. Combines were very unusual in those days and our harvesting was still picturesque and long hard toil. The end results were pretty ricks, neatly thatched, standing in groups in the corners of the fields. Very nice if you are an artist.

KATHLEEN DICKER

1941

Bread

Be gentle when you touch bread,
Let it not lie uncared for, unwanted,
Too often bread is taken for granted.
There is such beauty in bread,
Beauty of sun and soil,
Beauty of patient toil,
Wind and rain have caressed it,
Christ often blessed it.
Be gentle when you touch bread.

Poem in WOMEN'S LAND ARMY CHRISTMAS CARD, 1941, quoted by V. Sackville-West.

By late 1941 the shortage of coal was endangering war production and domestic supplies had been heavily cut.

1. Prevent dust forming by keeping coal out of the rain and by breaking lumps along and not across the grain.
2. Sprinkle each scuttleful with water containing salt and washing soda at the rate of a handful of each to a bucket. This makes it burn more slowly without soot and smoke.
3. Use up dust by making briquettes. Here are some recipes. (a) Mix ten parts of coal dust with one part of clay into a stiff paste with cold water. Make orange-sized balls of the paste, keep them moist by covering with a moist cloth, and place on the fire still moist. (b) Mix sawdust, coal dust and a little paraffin. (c) Pour one part tar and two parts water on to a heap of three parts coal dust and one part sawdust. Mix thoroughly and make small tennis balls. Leave to dry.
4. Reduce the size of your grate by means of firebricks. These get red hot and give out heat.
5. Make balls of fireclay and water. Dry in an oven. These when placed on the fire become red hot and give out much heat.
6. To keep a fire in, wrap tea leaves, coffee grounds and broken egg shells in newspaper. Lay this as a flat pad on top of a red fire and cover with damp small coal. *HOUSEWIFE*

A Christmas sparkle is easy to give to sprigs of holly or evergreen for use on Christmas cakes . . . Dip your greenery in a strong solution of Epsom salts. When dry it will be beautifully frosted.

'I'll miss my gay bowl of fruit on the Christmas table.'

Not if you have a bowl of salad in its place. Vegetables have such jolly colours – the cheerful glow of carrots, the rich crimson of beetroot, the emerald of parsley. And for health's sake you should have a winter salad with, or for, one meal a day. Here is a suggestion; it looks as delightful as it tastes.

Salad slices. Cut a thick round of wheatmeal bread for each person and spread with margarine. Arrange a slice of tomato in the centre of each slice and, if liked, put a sardine on top. Surround with circles of chopped celery, grated raw carrot, finely chopped parsley or spinach and grated raw beetroot on the edge. Sprinkle with a little grated cheese. MINISTRY OF FOOD ADVERTISEMENT: *LET'S TALK ABOUT XMAS FOOD*, December 1941.

Christmas [at Trinity College, Cambridge] passed off quietly and was shorn of some of its usual ritual, for the side-table, which should groan from Christmas to Epiphany with boar's head, game pies, and the like, for the Fellows' lunches, and the sideboard, which should hold a display of College plate, were both bare – the latter because, owing to shortage of staff in the plate-room, we have put most of our silver away. Still, we had a tolerable Christmas dinner, enlivened as last year by the Fire-Party, which included three Siamese . . . a German, a Russian and a Lithuanian. They might have included also two Estonians, a Hungarian, a Rumanian, a Chinese, an Indian, and perhaps a Malay, but these went off to heathenish celebrations elsewhere.
A.S.M. GOW

As 1941 drew to a close, some enthusiastic Home Guard commanders issued seasonal greetings to their men.

Every day that passes brings nearer the time when the enemy will attempt invasion, and when that time comes, as come it surely will before our final victory, we must be prepared to give a good account of ourselves.

The enemy may or may not already have had his Moscow. We cannot tell yet. But at any rate we must see to it that by our own efficiency we shall take our proper share in presenting him with his Waterloo.

This efficiency, for which we must all strive, has two objects:

(a) To qualify ourselves to give Jerry a perfectly appalling time should he have the temerity to land in this country.

(b) To free the Field Army to go abroad and defeat the enemy armies.

I give you as your motto for the coming year: 'Continue in the same.'

Special Order of the Day, 31 December 1941, by Lt Col D.C. Crombie, commanding 5th Battalion (Bideford) Devon Home Guard

1942

In war a strong defence is the springboard
from which an offensive action can be launched . . .
'Lag your hot water system now!'
Ministry of Fuel advertisement, September 1942

'I say – WHAT a persuasive man.'

1942 began calamitously with the fall of Singapore, the worst disaster ever to befall a British army, and with a humiliating rebuff for the Navy and R.A.F. with the escape down-Channel of the Scharnhorst *and* Gneisenau. *But at last the tide was about to turn. In the autumn came the American landing in North Africa and the great British victory at El Alamein, after which the Allied armies began the long advance which was ultimately to carry them into Germany. In the air it was more Germany which was 'taking it', with the first Thousand Bomber Raid. With German forces at full stretch in Russia, the invasion seemed to be off for good, and apart from one series of raids, to be mentioned later, the air attacks on British cities at night were, by the standards of the Blitz, on a small scale, although there were scattered daylight raids by fighter-bombers.*

For the housewife shortages of all kinds were now a far greater worry than bombs. The crisis in the mines led first to threats of fuel rationing, then to an immense publicity campaign for voluntary savings through the 'fuel target' scheme. The few remaining railings were largely removed, and the appeals for salvage and war savings reached their peak; but the dominant themes of the year were how to keep the family warm and fed.

6th January 1942.   Make Denise an eiderdown out of Gran's old quilted dressing gown and five yards figured nursery material (ten coupons).

12th January.   Buy No. 3 of John Lehmann's *New Writing.* Spend evening trying to melt bits of lipstick to make a new one. We spill it all into fire.

7th February.   Nothing at O's (fishmonger) except a most attractive array of tiny shells, cockles and winkles. Dye new dress I've made for D. with red ink. It comes two shades of pink.

14th March.   Take D. to Beeston to have her new baby Mickey-Mouse gas mask. Wardens' Post unbearably hot, with two electric fires on. D. struggles and screams when they try to get her into her new gas mask. . . .

8th May.   H. gets his 'papers'.   DORIS BREWIN

By now the Home Guard, with adequate weapons at last, was beginning to suffer from an excess of paper.

In April (1942) company commanders were somewhat surprised to receive the following letter from Battalion H.Q.: 'Full instructions have been received re burial of Mohammedans. If any company commander has a live Mohammedan on the strength these instructions will be sent for use when necessary.' LT.-COL. L.W. KENTISH

In April 1942 the cast of ITMA were invited to give a special performance at Windsor Castle to celebrate Princess Elizabeth's sixteenth birthday.

Afterwards we were all presented to the Royal Family, and it was clear from their conversation with us that they were all keen followers of the show. . . .

One of the Gentlemen of the Royal Household told me: 'There's a saying amongst the Household that if the war ends between 8.30 and 9 on a Thursday, we shan't dare tell the King until after "ITMA" finishes!' JACK TRAIN

So far the German airmen had aimed mainly at military objectives, although much civilian property had also suffered. From April to June 1942, as a reprisal for the destruction by the R.A.F. of Lubeck, Hitler launched what he described as a series of 'terror attacks' on British towns selected for their historic and artistic value. They became known, after the famous German guide book, as the Baedeker Raids.

When the raid [on Bath] began on Saturday night, we went into the tiny coal cellar with Mr and Mrs A., their daughter Wyn and schoolboy son Ron. Besides my mother and myself there were two people from opposite, one of whom was in her eighties, and the oldest present, so we all knew we had to be at least as brave as she was. . . . Mr A. had lost his right arm in a railway accident. . . . As I sat by him on a wooden form, I could feel the little stump of his poor, lost arm flutter against my own. Ron sat on a stool and rested his head on his father's knee. Two things remain particularly in my mind as terrifying. One was the gradually approaching thuds of a stick of bombs, so that one wondered if the next thud would be on the house. The other terrible thing was the spraying hail of machine gun bullets as they accompanied the bombs. It seemed as if there could be no escape from one or the other.

The Sunday raids were worst, partly because there were two of them. Bath had no defences at all, and I think every bomb dropped found a target – usually a church. At the bottom of our road a shelter was hit, killing many people, including a bride whose bouquet was placed on the top of the shelter.

By Monday morning there was no running water in most houses near us, so everyone went to the one house with a tap still working and perfect strangers calmly walked through the house to the kitchen and out again, with a pail of water. Carts came round with drinking water. There was a platinum dust on everything, but mercifully the weather was fine and furniture from damaged houses was neatly stacked on the pavement outside, ready to be put in a municipal store. Notes were fastened to doors and walls, telling relatives where the occupants had gone to stay.

Everybody thought there would be another raid on the Monday night, and as a colleague had promised a bed for my mother and me outside Bath, if we could get there, I spent Monday morning hunting for a taxi. I found they were all commandeered, as the bus station had been bombed. I was so anxious to get out of our lodgings because all that family were going to sleep elsewhere and I did not fancy the prospect of being there on my own. Just at lunch time, as I was coming home, I saw a farm cart loading furniture from a house and asked the driver if he were going in the direction I wanted. He said we could go part of the way and use two of the chairs for seats. My relief was so great that I started to run up the hill to our lodgings, and who should I see coming towards me but my brother from Harpenden. He had been told outside Bath that our road no longer existed, but had been allowed at last to come through and enquire.

My school had been destroyed, so I asked permission to go back for one night and settle my mother in Harpenden. This I did . . . and returned to work the next day. I promised the family that I would not sleep in the empty house in Bath and in fact left the train at Calne in Wiltshire, intending to stop the night. No one could accommodate me – they also were short of water, every room was taken by refugees from Bath of one sort or another, and after hours of search, beginning at the hotel in the main street and ending up at cottages by the station, I had to admit I was beaten. I took a bus to Bath and ended up there at about 10 pm. A policeman was on duty near the city centre, so I told him I did not want to sleep in my empty lodgings and he suggested spending the night in the public shelter under the Pump Room. The vestibule was blacked out, but I was able to make my way over to the entrance to the underground shelter. The warmth of the spa water in pipes round the room, and the smell of terror that was in the air, put me off going in, and I turned back to the chairs in the vestibule. Behind me came a married couple, and when they saw me hesitating in the half dark, they asked if I would care to go back and spend the night nearby in their flat. They explained that their mother had been on a visit and had decided to settle in the shelter for the night as she could not walk quickly, and if the alert sounded, these two had promised to race back and stay with her in the shelter. Meanwhile I was welcome to use her camp bed.

They were living just near the main station, on the ground floor. The front room was used as an office and they had the back room. Before we went in to this room, they asked if I would first like to use the W.C. further along the corridor. I went along and opened the door, sat on the seat and then realised that most of the rest of the place was missing and I was looking over the garden. Back in their room I found a door had been placed on a table to black out the missing window space. However there was a cosy fire, we had tea and something to eat and before I knew where I was, we were deep in a discussion on nudism. They were very serious, earnest believers in the benefits of nudism and, after going into the philosophy of the thing, we said goodnight and had some sort of rest and slept till morning – with no alert to disturb us. . . .

When I reported for work, I found that all the teachers of art subjects were being used at the Guildhall to do various jobs, including the lettering of many public notices. I was asked to go with one of the men teachers to a bombed out shop in Bath, where we were to salvage every scrap of artists' materials to replace all that was lost in the demolished school. My rendezvous with the other teacher was at the smaller station in Bath, from where, looking across a small patch of green, I could see the row of small basement houses, two of which had been the school. Firemen were still playing hoses on the facades and the water went up over the top and then cascaded down on the other side of the brickwork – there was nothing left, just the fronts of each house. As I watched, a woman arrived at the end of the road, and evidently realised that the destruction meant either the end of a cherished home or perhaps the death of someone dear to her. She stared at the tall brick fronts and then fell into the arms of one of the firemen and he comforted her. While this was going on, from another direction came two rescue workers assisting a man whom they had evidently just dug out of some rubble. He was going along in jerks, just like a monkey on a stick and with no idea where he was walking.

When my colleague's train came in, we went to a nearby builder's yard and borrowed a truck which we then pushed to the bombed-out shop. We loaded all the paint, etc, that was easy to reach, on to the truck and then pushed it through the city centre and up Lansdowne Hill, to the headmaster's house. Some of the students and relatives had been made homeless and they were staying with the headmaster and his wife. . . . After a very few days, school started again in other premises. MAY HICKMAN

I was in my studio, in St. Giles [Norwich], loading my camera, when the Hippodrome next door was hit [on 29 April]. The stage managers and the owners of a troupe of performing sea-lions were in the indoor shelter of a one-storey building near the stage door. The bomb killed the stage manager and the sea-lions' trainer, blew the two house managers down the steps without hurting them, ripped the back out of my studio, and lifted the stage of the theatre into the air. The stage supports fell, but the stage remained four inches above its normal level. From inside the theatre came a terrible sound – a wailing worse than the whistle of a bomb. It was from one of the sea-lions which the bomb had released. I shall never forget the noise it made, flapping its ungainly way through the dark, emptying theatre, crying for its master. GEORGE SWAIN

I was called from bed at 3.45 am on June 1st by the ringing of my telephone. The message (it came from the Regional Commissioner) was brief but portentous. Our emergency personnel and equipment [from the Ministry of Information's Regional Headquarters] were to be ready to leave Tunbridge Wells by daybreak. Hurrying to the office, I learned that a severe attack had been made on Canterbury . . . I think none of us will ever forget our sensations as we fortified ourselves for the journey with biscuits and hot tea and checked our equipment into the cars. Now, for the first time, the organisation which we had so painstakingly rehearsed in all its details was to be put to the acid test of 'the real thing'.

One after another, in quick succession, the cars were given the 'O.K.' and set forth in the first dim light of dawn. I drove the leading vehicle, accompanied by Tremayne, one of our assistant officers. Tremayne, an artist in peacetime, loved the mellow architectural glories and history-laden atmosphere of Canterbury as deeply as I, and as we passed eastward through the trim Kentish countryside, swathed in ground vapour and sparkling with dew, we speculated with fear in our hearts. . . . Already the horizon was a vast black smudge – the smoke pall overhanging the pyre. . . . I could not think of one ancient building in Canterbury the destruction of which would not constitute a calamity, not merely for Britain but for the world. Canterbury belonged to all mankind.

Soon we were at the West Gate, and here we had to make a diversion, because heaps of debris and a maze of fire-hoses blocked the direct route to the centre of the city. But a few minutes later we were installed at the offices of our chief local representative, Mr Harold Young. Then off I went to report our arrival and discover how we could best make ourselves useful. Meanwhile Mrs Young, by some incredible miracle of housekeeping, had produced an excellent breakfast for us all. As we hastily gulped it down, planning the morning's work between bites, so to speak, Harold himself came in, begrimed and red-eyed for want of sleep. He had been up all night fighting the incendiaries, and following that, from crack of dawn onwards, he had patrolled the streets with announcements about accommodation for the homeless and communal feeding arrangements. . . .

There was much work ready to hand for us; and as each emergency service of the Local Authority or of some Regional Government Department settled down into its stride, fresh tasks were added. Our loudspeaker vehicles toured all areas of the city from morning to night, ceaselessly repeating announcements or instructions which a large proportion of the townsfolk were still too dazed to take in save through this process of reiteration. The public had to be familiarised with the new addresses of organisations whose regular premises had been destroyed overnight – organisations to which they must turn for first-aid repairs to buildings, for replacement of lost food or clothing coupons, or for monetary assistance; they had to be made acquainted with emergency transport arrangements; they had to be given important instructions in regard to sanitation and other health precautions. . . . The spoken word had to be supplemented and reinforced by the written, which meant that posters must be printed and put up within a matter of two or three hours if they were to serve their purpose. . . . Our Assistant Press Officer and I visited printing works after printing works, but only to find each standing in ruins. At last we succeeded in locating a firm still able to accept and execute orders, however, and by the afternoon the posters were up.

1 Air raid practice in a North London factory. Employees of the Standard
Telephones and Cables Co., New Southgate, rehearse taking shelter, July 1939.

2 Evacuation. School children en route to a station in South-East London.

3 Children practising wearing gas masks.

4 Entering the Anderson shelter. September 1939.

5 Table-tennis on the Morrison. The first Morrison shelters were not distributed until March 1941 and were not in use for most of the Blitz.

6 The Home Guard on a route march. All now have uniforms and rifles, though there is a mixture of steel helmets and forage caps.

7 A housewife collecting her rations, January 1940, shortly after the introduction of bacon, ham, butter, margarine and sugar rationing.

8 Lord Woolton, formerly Minister of Food, at a Forces Club, December 1943.

9 A collection of saucepans and other kitchen-ware following Lord Beaverbrook's appeal for aluminium for aircraft manufacture in July 1940.

10 Landgirls, 1939. Work of this kind was far more typical than the pastoral scenes which appeared in the propaganda pictures.

11 Machinist in armaments factory, 1940. The mass call-up of women for war-work came later, in 1941 and 1942, followed by the 'grannies' call-up' in 1943.

12 A street scene in Balham, South-East London, 17 October 1940.

13 Holborn underground station, October 1940. The use of the tube as a shelter was at first banned, but the government rapidly gave in to public pressure. Later bunks and other amenities were installed.

14 Making soup in the streets of Coventry after the city's second
major raid in April 1941.

15 G.I.s outside a village pub, with small girl. Their love of children was famous,
and reciprocated.

16 VE-Day. A street party in Nottingham. The car has lost its headlamp masks but there is still a serviceman in uniform in the background.

It was during this search tour that we had our first opportunity of gaining a general impression of the extent of the damage. . . . The Cathedral still stood four-square, though vast craters gaped in its green Precincts and the walls and windows bore grievous scars. . . . But the eastern half of the High Street was in a condition only comparable to that of Ypres during the last war. It presented an almost unbroken vista of desolation, and among the buildings battered into shapeless rubble heaps or irreparably damaged were many hallowed by antiquity. The birthplace of Christopher Marlowe, the Elizabethan dramatist, had been obliterated. St. George's Church, in which he had been baptized, was left a burn-out shell, and the Church of St. Mary Bredin was in a like state. . . . The Cathedral Library had been demolished, together with the residences of two Canons in the Precincts. St. Martin's, the earliest Christian Church in all England, had suffered damage from blast. Uriah Heep's reputed ''umble 'ome' was in ruins, and 'The House of Agnes' in St. Dunstan's Street, likewise immortalized by Charles Dickens in *David Copperfield*, though still standing, had suffered injury. King's School, England's most ancient existing educational foundation, had received damage in a block of buildings once used as the brew- and bake-house of the old monastery. A gateway at St. Augustine's College, dating back to the year 1284, had been badly scarred by a heavy bomb. The Royal Fountain Hotel, said to be the oldest hostelry in the country and known to have been visited by Queen Elizabeth, had been burnt to the ground. . . . During the days that we worked in Canterbury I saw tears on only one occasion. . . . Behind the Union Jacks, the slogans and the brave bearing, however, lurked many a tragedy. . . . A Ramsgate family of seven, who had evacuated to Canterbury after the raids on their home town, were wiped out in one block of demolished houses. Beside one mound of wreckage that had been a home I saw a girl in A.T.S. uniform. Her father and mother lay buried somewhere in that debris – they had been there since 5 am. At one stage of the afternoon the A.R.P. workers discovered six live rabbits in the ruins. They had belonged to the girl's parents, and her hopes were raised accordingly. But as the afternoon dragged on into evening it became increasingly obvious that all hope of finding the victims alive must be abandoned. . . .

One very noticeable effect of the raid was the well-nigh universal manifestation of kindness and consideration for others which followed in its train. The 'good neighbour' spirit was predominant. People gave shelter to the homeless, both in Canterbury itself and out in the surrounding country. A general meeting of traders was called, and as a result every shopkeeper who had been 'bombed out' was found accommodation in premises that had escaped – sometimes those of his erstwhile bitterest competitor! The same excellent principle was observed by rival banks and newspapers, the offices of the *Kent Messenger* being put at the disposal of the 'blitzed' local papers to enable them to continue publication. . . .

Through that first day and the days which followed, Canterbury presented a picture which seemed fantastically unreal to anyone familiar with its normal aspect. Along its streets lay miles and miles of snaky hose-pipe. The gutters were full of sweepings of broken glass and other debris. Over great mountains of wreckage climbed swarms of human figures, dimly to be seen through a curtain of fine dust and ash. At frequent intervals stood the Y.M.C.A. mobile canteens, supplying endless cups of tea to emergency workers and the dispossessed. From morning to night the air was filled with the stroke of pick and shovel, the nerve-racking clatter of pneumatic drills, the thudding of fire-pumps, men's shoutings, and every now and again the roar of collapsing masonry. Everywhere was the smell of burning.
HUBERT S. BANNER

Even when the Luftwaffe was inactive the U-boat war continued, placing a continuing burden upon Lord Woolton, the Minister of Food, an outstandingly successfully member of the Government.

The outstanding problem in feeding the nation became that of finding the necessary shipping space. The country never realised how nearly we were brought to disaster by the submarine peril. . . .

During the course of two hours one Friday afternoon, I received five separate signals from the Admiralty reporting that food ships had been sunk on the Atlantic route. By some extraordinary misfortune, these five ships were largely stocked with bacon. . . . We were determined that we would not fail in the pledge given to the public that the ration would always be honoured, so all existing stocks of bacon in the warehouses within easy reach of Liverpool – which were going to be used to honour the ration in Lancashire for a few weeks ahead – were at once reallocated and sent off to other parts of the country, and as the one solitary ship that had bacon on board came in to the port of Liverpool, a special squad of men was charged to bring off the bacon with all speed, load it into lorries and send it straight off into distribution. We honoured the ration, but it was a near thing.

Some amusing incidents enlivened our somewhat strained lives! The problem of soap rationing was very difficult because soaps were not sold by weight, and . . . involved a file of papers containing the arguments and instructions on the subject passing through many departments and many grades of staff. For security reasons we could not label the papers 'Soap Rationing', so we gave the file the code name of 'Nutmegs'. Nobody was particularly interested or curious about nutmegs and there was no sign of any leakage of information on this subject until the Saturday afternoon before I was going to make the announcement on the Sunday. Then, somehow or other, the story leaked that nutmegs were to be rationed; reports came in to the headquarters of the Ministry that there had been a sudden rush in the shops on nutmegs. I wonder what happened to all the nutmegs that the credulous people who cleaned up the market purchased on that Saturday afternoon.

I fear that my name had become a sort of bogey in the nurseries of the country, where children were told that they must finish unpalatable food, otherwise Lord Woolton would be annoyed! One day I was staying overnight at the Lygon Arms Hotel in Broadway; I used to break my journey there when I travelled from London to Colwyn Bay, where the major part of the Ministry was accommodated. A lady came to ask me if I would speak to her small girl before I left in the morning, as she was suffering from a certain amount of religious confusion which I might solve. She had been told that I was coming to the hotel and that night, whilst she was saying the Lord's Prayer, she stopped after saying 'Give us this day our daily bread' and, looking up at her mother, said, 'Mummy, why do we have to have both God and Lord Woolton?' The next morning I convinced the child that one part of her troubles was just an ordinary human being: beyond that I could not answer her question.   LORD WOOLTON

Much of Lord Woolton's success was due to the brilliant publicity staff he employed. Among the devices used to make the public aware of the need not to waste food were new versions of nursery rhymes.

Because of the pail, the scraps were saved,
Because of the scraps, the pigs were saved,
Because of the pigs, the rations were saved,
Because of the rations, the ships were saved,
Because of the ships, the island was saved,
Because of the island, the Empire was saved,
And all because of a housewife's pail.

MINISTRY OF FOOD ADVERTISEMENT, quoted by Lord Woolton

For many people, especially those engaged for the first time in hard manual labour, getting enough to eat was a constant preoccupation.

Food was our obsession. . . . In my first digs [as a landgirl] the landlady never cooked a second vegetable, except on a Sunday; we had cold meat on Monday, and sausage for the rest of the week. Sometimes she cooked potatoes with the sausage, but often she left us a slice of bread each. The two sausages on a large, cold, green glass plate greeted us on our return from a day on leeks or sprouts, and a three mile cycle ride each way. My friend combated the gloom with a small bottle of whisky which had been given to her, and which she hid behind the curtain until dire need arose. A neighbour once brought round a sack of carrots, which he said were for the rabbit, but we benefited from this act of kindness. . . . At the hostel, we had dried egg once a week for breakfast, but the good lady in charge liked to cook it overnight, so it resembled, and tasted like, sawdust on toast. We had fish paste on toast, too, some mornings, which brought forth rude remarks. . . .

Once a week a van toured the countryside with fish and chips and we were lucky on occasions to buy them when still hot. Otherwise, they were sold warm or cold and heated up for the next meal. The Americans used to drive into Evesham from Broadway Hill, about six miles, to buy chips, petrol rationing notwithstanding. . . .

We never went home without taking something in the food line, generally whatever crops we were working on, and odd bits of our rations saved up over the week. This, plus firewood, and our washing, saw us off home at weekends looking like camels. . . . One Christmas we were allowed to buy a chicken to take home. My bird was so old and tough that we could hardly chew through it, although we cooked it for hours longer than should have been necessary. My father asked if we hadn't better use it for shoe-mending. . . . JOAN IERSTON

Of all the female callers that we had [in the Press Office at the Ministry of Agriculture] I remember best a large, red-faced woman who burst into our room one Saturday morning. . . . She blew right up to my colleague's desk and thrust beneath his nose a bottle containing fish. The fish, she said, was bad; in fact it was damned bad. She had bought it at a local grocer's shop and had come to us with the following alternative suggestions: (a) we could change it for a bottle of good fish, (b) we could give her her money back plus her return fare from the suburbs, or (c) we could all go to hell and take the fish with us. My colleague's counter-suggestion that the matter was more likely to be one for the Ministry of Food was vehemently repudiated on the ground that the board outside our front entrance stated that this was the Ministry of Agriculture *and Fisheries*. . . . Between us we got rid of her at last. She blew out as noisily as she had blown in, telling the world that this, like all Government offices, was run by —— fools. We never saw her again. . . . I have often wondered what she did with the fish. . . . There is no doubt that it was bad. F. HOWARD LANCUM

Twice only have I got aggressive over food. Once was when waiting to be served with cheese, which my girl [eight months old in 1939] loved. I noticed the well-dressed lady in front having a piece of cheese weighed. It went over 1lb and I saw she had handed in only one book and that only one coupon was cut out. I said nothing until the assistant said, on taking my two books, 'Four ounces of cheese love', throwing it on the scales.

'No,' I said quickly, 'I will have a piece the same weight as the previous customer.' There was a great to-do, but I stood my ground, I'd seen the car outside the shop and gathered the shopper was a somebody. 'Fair shares!', I said, other shoppers took up the call, and the shopper was called back and the cheese coupons adjusted. I wasn't being mean, but one saw so much of the greed of some able to pay extra, and the serviceman's family scraping along, and making do.

My second row was over milk. Living now with an aunt, after bombing, I worked in a confectionery shop, and the eye-openers I had there! – but they didn't affect me, so I didn't bother. But one day my aunt said the roundsman had not left the kiddy's milk as he was short.

Fair enough, she could have mine, but on returning to work after lunch I noticed the same roundsman leaving more than the permitted amount at the flat above the shop. I waited, then I stopped him. I was shocked – we had had the same milkman for years. 'Right,' I said, 'I want my baby's milk and you're not to leave extra there again if it means others go short, or I'm reporting you.' My aunt told me the man said he never thought I was such a firebrand, but all mums that I knew fought for their dues where there were kids.   ROSE DILLY

The meat situation became so impossible that we decided to become vegetarians. To do this we had to get certificates signed by a doctor and a minister. We were entitled to twelve to sixteen ounces of cheese a week each, as well as dried bananas, fruit bars and nuts. I was very popular at Christmas when I was able to take a small bag of almonds to each of our neighbours. When I was asked to give a small prize for a Lexicon Drive at the local church I offered two pounds of mixed shelled nuts and this was the most popular prize on the table.
EVA WHITE

A bachelor friend once brought me a birthday present of an un-opened, unlabelled, rusty tin. It had come from salvaged stock and was thought to contain gooseberries. Tinned fruit vanished during 1940, the last being 'pineapple', which was allegedly turnip. My precious tin sat on the shelf until my husband's next leave, when I managed to buy a small piece of suet, so we could have a gooseberry suet pudding. The donor was invited to share the feast. He came early, to share also the excitement of opening the tin.
The paraffin stove (the only cooking facility I then had) was alight, with the steamer ready on top. The pastry was made and the basin lined. All three of us stood looking as we opened the tin – to discover it full of butter beans! We still had our feast, though, for some scraps of meat and a little gravy were added to the butter beans in the suet pudding, and it became the meat course.   MEGAN RYAN

A major event, though one only enjoyed by a minority of people, was the arrival of a food parcel from the United States or the Dominions.

A girl friend rang me one morning in great excitement: could I come at once and spend the weekend, as the postman had brought a food parcel from Australia and she wanted to share the thrill of opening it and deciding what to do with the goodies it contained? We had a very happy weekend, which included making delicious jam from the luxury of dried apricots. Every scrap of that parcel was used to the limit, even the paper wrappings. My friend's elderly widower uncle came to Saturday tea and stared in astonishment at the sight of the dining-room table, laid with the best cloth and china, with a large paper bow in the centre, flanked on one side with a jelly and on the other by a plate of freshly-made pastries filled with Australian grape jam. My friend's R.A.F. husband used some of his precious petrol to drive the few miles home for Sunday lunch, and with another grass-widow friend we had a feast of kangaroo-tail soup, tinned ham, served with fresh vegetables from the garden, finishing with tinned peaches. The packets of dried fruit and the dark, rich fruit cake were put away with the remains of the white flour to be used for the following Christmas. MEGAN RYAN

My 21st birthday cake was a 'wow'! It was 1942, and we had difficulty in saving our points for both dried fruit, *and* tinned meat for the 'party'. So we compromised and used soaked prunes, and a few sultanas. The result was somewhat 'heavy' – but filling. Icing sugar was scarce and eggs even scarcer, so we made a type of chocolate frosting with cocoa, icing sugar, one egg white and water. We found some candles, but had no icing sugar or forcing bag rosette nozzle, to write on or decorate the cake. So I had a brain-wave. I cut the end off an empty toothpaste tube, and filled it with condensed milk! With this I adorned the cake – 'Happy 21st Birthday', and to my relief it didn't run too much! However, with our meagre points to provide sand-wiches, and our 'Prune and Condensed Milk Cake', we managed to feed around thirty guests, and have a wonderful party. The cake was demolished with relish! ROSEMARY MOONEN

Every morning on the radio Freddie Grisewood (affectionately nick-named 'Ricepud' by younger listeners) introduced a programme of hints and recipes, The Kitchen Front. *He became in great demand as a public speaker.*

In my travels I met practically every mayor in existence, as it fell to their lot to introduce me – indeed, in many a town which I visited frequently, I became, as one mayor put it, an old friend of the family. Those mayoral introductions were ordeals which I had to suffer. For the most part they consisted of a dreary recital of my past, read most unconvincingly from a piece of paper, and I used to heave a sigh of relief when they were safely over. There was one brilliant exception to this routine, which happened 'somewhere up North'. The mayor in question had started on his usual course of reading about me from a large sheaf of notes which were blatantly displayed, when he stopped abruptly, and as if communing with himself said: 'Freddy Grisewood. Why, good Lord! He's the chap who told me what to do with frozen cod at eight-fifteen in the morning. I could have told him what to do with it, if he'd asked me!'

That was the perfect introduction, and I could have hugged that mayor from sheer relief. One other was not quite so happy, but inadvertently had a magical effect on the audience. I had to go to Worcester to open a 'Food Advice Service' there. We had an enormous audience which caused the local police some consternation, as it overflowed on to the pavement and the road outside, causing chaos among the traffic. The mayor was a very old but charming man, who began his introduction of me by calling me 'Mr Greensward'. 'He is the man,' he continued, 'that you hear in that programme at half-past eight every morning.' (By that time the 'Kitchen Front' programme was well over, as its time was 8.15 am) 'Mr Greensward has another claim to fame, as he used to play cricket for Gloucestershire.' (It was Worcestershire, to be strictly accurate.) 'And now,' he continued, 'I have much pleasure in introducing to you Mr Greensward himself.' Whereupon he turned to the local Food Officer, who was sitting on his left, bowed slightly to him and gave him a beaming smile. The audience up to this point had behaved splendidly, an occasional titter or so, no more, but this was too much for them, and gusts of laughter came not only from the room itself, but from the street outside.

FREDDIE GRISEWOOD

Despite the universal admiration for its namesake, one of the least successful of wartime recipes was Woolton Pie.

1½ lb cooked, mixed vegetables; 2 tablespoons chopped parsley; ½ pint stock or water. *Pastry*: 2 oz. oatmeal; 2 oz. mashed potato; 2 oz. cheese; Salt; 4 oz. flour; 1 oz. fat; Water to mix.

Place cooked vegetables in pie-dish and sprinkle with coarsely chopped parsley. Add vegetable water and seasoning. To make the pastry cream fat and potato together. Mix grated cheese, oatmeal, flour and salt and stir into it the creamed fat and potato. Mix to a stiff dough with water. Roll out the pastry, cover the pie and bake in a moderate oven for 30 minutes. Serve with baked jacket potatoes and greens.   MINISTRY OF FOOD LEAFLET NO. 12: *CHEESE*

Mock Lemon curd
For 4: 2 oz. custard powder or cornflour; 1½ gills water; 1 pinch bicarb. soda; Lemon substitute to flavour; 2 tablets saccharin; ½ oz. margarine

Blend the cornflour with a little water, boil up the rest of the liquid, and pour over the blended cornflour. Return to the pan. Boil and cook for 2–3 minutes. Crush the saccharin tablets and stir in until dissolved. Add the flavourings and margarine and bicarb. Beat well and use when cold.   MINISTRY OF FOOD LEAFLET NO. 6: *CARRIED MEALS, SNACKS AND SANDWICHES*

Carrot Croquettes

12 oz. finely grated carrot, raw; 6 oz. finely grated potato, raw; 4 oz. grated cheese; 1½ teaspoonfuls salt; pepper; ¼ teaspoonful dry mustard; 3 oz. oatmeal.

Mix finely grated vegetables and cheese. Season, add the oatmeal to form a fairly stiff mixture. Form into croquettes and fry in hot fat.
MINISTRY OF FOOD WAR COOKERY LEAFLET NO. 4

It was a mother's war on the Home Front. And my mother answered the call of the nation with zeal, application, ingenuity and worry so acute that she might have suffered a nervous breakdown had she not realised the harmful effect this would have on her family. . . .

She worried about my father fire-watching and shovelling incendiary bombs into buckets of sand; she worried about me dodging shrapnel as I cycled to school; she worried about ration books, gas-masks, Food Flashes, air raids, collecting cardboard and punctured saucepans for salvage, rents in the blackout material, feeding the budgerigars, starving Russians and sailors on convoys.

Mostly she fretted about food. But here the worry was eased by the enthusiasm with which she answered the pleas of the Ministry of Food to improvise; and the privations were dwarfed by jungle-cunning victories over adversity. . . .

The core of the crisis in the kitchen was rationing with all its complexities. There were green ration books for babies, blue books for children, buff for adults; different coloured books had coupons with different values; tinned foods and biscuits were rationed by points instead of coupons; and the meat ration swelled and shrank according to the season, the convoys and the temper of the butcher.

My attitude to all the culinary skills and sacrifices involved was one of indifference. I devoured my weekly pat of national butter – scarcely enough for a round of hot toast – and sliced into my mother's ration while she scraped my greaseproof paper clean and applied margarine to her own off-white national bread. I crunched up bacon and my second egg of the week while my mother ate diluted porridge. I knew that she was going without on my behalf: I accepted the gesture as my birthright.

In the kitchen she assiduously collected the Ministry of Food's hints. In one of these . . . she found a recipe for carrot marmalade. Dessert oranges were a rarity, Seville oranges non-existent.

From the garden where, in the chalk-diced earth, carrot flies were nurtured more readily than carrots, she gathered a withered harvest. The carrots were boiled and sweetened, the scum, thick with carrot fly corpses – removed and the residue sealed in jamjars.

One morning a jar was put on the breakfast table with supreme nonchalance. Only those accustomed to the prelude to one of my mother's war-time offerings would have recognised the symptons: stertorous breathing, high colour, an exaggerated indifference to our reactions.

My father, an undemonstrative man, spread the nectar on his bread and bit into it. He frowned and said: 'What was that?'

'Carrot marmalade,' said my mother.

With unusual deliberation – I have since pondered on the tyrannical undertones – he picked up the jar, took it into the garden and poured it on the compost heap.   DEREK LAMBERT

This country has not reached a stage when the wholesale destruction of household pets is necessary but every effort should be made to use for dogs and cats only such food as are: 1. Plentiful; 2. Grown here; 3. Not suitable for human beings.

The Waste of Food Order, 1940, does not forbid the feeding of animals with food that can be consumed by a human being. Many people have been concerned at inaccurate statements made on this point. . . .

Potatoes are plentiful and if you put in extra tubers when digging for victory you will not have it on your conscience that shipping space is being taken for food for your animals. Potatoes boiled in their jackets are not ordinarily recommended for dogs and cats, but the harmful effect is avoided if they are mixed with gravies made from bones. The bones can then be used for waste collection as their boiling does not interfere with their value for war purposes.

There are also patent powder and gravy extracts on the market or you can purchase stewing meat with your coupons and give the gravy from such meat to your animal – it would be a sacrifice that every owner would be prepared to make. . . . The Ministry of Food will not permit the use of cod liver oil for household pets.

RSPCA: *FEEDING DOGS AND CATS IN WARTIME*

Pets found little comfort in the shortages. At the outbreak of war we had two white mice, a tortoise, a goldfish and a budgerigar.

Bran and oats for the mice soon ran out and for a while they existed on a diet of bread, sawdust and newspaper; then the larger of the two found the answer to rationing and began to eat the smaller. . . . The diet ended one day in 1942 when the small mouse, tired of being eaten, lay down and died. Shortly afterwards the cannibal followed him.

The tortoise left us – a casualty of war – at about the same time. . . . One day he strayed into the garden next door, hid beneath some leaves and had his head chopped off by a spade digging for victory.

There was also a grave and inexplicable shortage of ants' eggs. From inside his bowl Charlie the goldfish made pop-eyed pleas for more food and sent up bubbled distress signals. I found white eggs on ant hills but Charlie ignored them. He ate fish food sold in packets from necessity but was plainly wasting away. He lasted, with fishy resilience, longer than the other pets; then one day he leaped from the bowl and disappeared down the kitchen sink and was never seen again. DEREK LAMBERT

The Spring brought a new hardship, more resented by most men than clothes rationing itself.

From May 1st all men's and youths' jackets, waistcoats and trousers will be subject to the following restrictions:
Jackets. No double-breasted jackets; not more than three pockets, no slits or buttons on cuffs; not more than three buttons on front; no patch pockets; no half belt, no fancy belts and no metal or leather buttons.
Waistcoats. Plain, single-breasted only, no collar; not more than two pockets; not more than five buttons; no back straps and no chain hole.
Trousers. Maximum width of trouser bottoms nineteen inches, plain bottoms – no permanent turn-ups; not more than three pockets; no side or back straps; no extension waist bands; no pleats; no elastic in waist bands.
General. No zip fasteners and no raised seams.
Quoted in *THE TIMES*, 19 March 1942

These were boom years for the cinema as people of all ages found a regular escape – often twice a week – from the drab reality of life by 'going to the pictures'.

Much of our limited understanding of war was learned in the cinema. And never have children enjoyed their films so much. The heroes were soldiers, sailors, airmen and resistance workers who outwitted the enemy – Jerries, Wops and later Japs – with the same regularity that cowboys had always outwitted Red Indians. But this was the stuff of life with which we could identify ourselves: fathers, brothers and uncles were fighting the Jerry and possibly one day we would be joining them.

One of Our Aircraft is Missing, Target for Tonight, Ships with Wings, A Yank in the R.A.F., The Day Will Dawn, Mrs Miniver, The Way to the Stars – these were some of the films we watched. . . .

In black and white and sometimes gory colour we watched the glory of war unfolded. Always our bombs dropped on target, always our planes limped home. The officers were all decent and the men who sometimes said 'bloody' or 'basket' were cheeky but gallant. German soldiers were all oafish – particularly sentries who never heard saboteurs until they were cracked on the skull – and German officers were monocled sadists who clicked their heels crisply in the presence of superior monocled sadists.

These main courses were often served up with sweets to soften an otherwise grim menu. Dishes like Dorothy Lamour who was often to be seen in those days, saronged and seductive, beside deep blue seas and placid lagoons. . . . Betty Grable, with bright blond hair and fishnet legs; Rita Hayworth, red-haired and aloof; Betty Hutton, raucous and suddenly demure as she shifted from the night club set to the studio of romance. . . .

The funny men, too, had a heyday. I saw *Good Morning, Boys* with Will Hay . . . and *Backroom Boy* with Arthur Askey. Bud Abbott and Lou Costello began their take-over from Laurel and Hardy, Bob Hope started his long sparring match with Bing Crosby, Charlie Chaplin ate his boot once more in a reissue of *The Gold Rush*, Tarzan fought another crocodile, Ray Milland took on a giant squid in *Reap the Wild Wind* – for which I queued for three hours – and Fred Astaire continued to dance towards his ever-retreating retirement.

After the first British war films came the American sagas of heroism and slaughter. Sweating G.I's divided their time between chopping down the Japs in their thousands, dating singers at camp concerts and popping up in London to court English roses who always wanted them to meet daddy. And Errol Flynn took on and defeated the Japanese single-handed.

How much more calm were the British movies of war as they fed us the brand image of island fortitude. In the CO class was Leslie Banks, paternal and monosyllabic; under him on bridge or tarmac, brave and always decent to his women, was John Mills; the gruff but golden-hearted sergeant was William Hartnell; and among the men you could usually find Gordon Jackson or Jimmy Hanley who had usually some sort of trouble at home; Jack Warner was the genial josser who kept up morale on the Home Front. The women generally pined bravely and drove ambulances, or joined up and pined bravely; hussies who had affairs with other men were polished off with a bomb.

The cinema also gave us *The Warsaw Concerto* played by Anton Walbrook as bombers ravaged Poland in a film called *Dangerous Moonlight*. . . . It seems to me to have been the theme music of the war. . . .

Whenever we went to the cinema my mother was a satisfactory companion.

'Swine,' she muttered as a German jackboot crushed the hand of a captured partisan.

'Go on, give it to them,' she exhorted a merchant seaman as he poured bullets from a bucking machine gun into the belly of a dive bomber.

We emerged into sandbagged, blacked-out Sutton or Epsom, damp-eyed and proud. Sitting on the double-decker bus going home I was drunk with patriotism and I would readily have died for my country, preferably in the arms of a nurse who looked like Ann Sheridan. DEREK LAMBERT

The audience in flea-pit cinemas was always quick to express anger or pleasure. It only needed Winston Churchill to appear in the newsreel and there would be loud clapping and cheering, whistles and stamping of feet. If Hitler was shown making a speech, or shaking hands at a meeting with Mussolini, they booed and hissed like a crowd of angry ganders. I recall one man blowing the loudest raspberry I have ever heard at the end of one of Hilter's rantings and ravings. The raspberry, vulgar though it may be, has no equal as an expression of contempt, and it cut old Schicklgruber down to size with perfect timing, and the audience howled with delighted laughter.
MAY BECKER

While British troops were at last beginning to advance almost everywhere, the real heroine of this stage of the war was the housewife.

I moved into my teens and became correspondingly hungrier, and my mother became more harassed as the food shortages became more acute. Every day was a fight to provide calories, vitamins, carbohydrates and warmth for my father and I; the results of these daily skirmishes were many victories, a few defeats like the early encounter with carrot marmalade and a broadening sense of family unity.

The hardships with which a mother had to contend can best be appreciated by considering a raw January day when the coal ration had dwindled to precious dust and the food ration had been cut to a minimum by a submarine attack on a convoy. . . .

We woke in our familiar rooms or in our Morrison shelter breathing jets of steam like racehorses after a gallop. My mother arose first, satisfied herself that husband and son were still alive, and went downstairs to cook breakfast from nothing. We snuggled in our beds under our patchwork blanket, dozing, dreading the frosted day that would melt before freezing again into crystalline hostility with diamonds glittering on the pavements. The smell of cooking fragments of bacon or steaming coffee climbing the stairs like a Bisto advertisement winkled us out. Feet on cold green linoleum, hands in hard water, a shirt as cold as the sheets the night before . . . every morning was Monday morning in those austere days.

The soap was a ball melted and moulded by my mother from scraps saved from the ration. My father used it as shaving soap, too, and stropped his razor blade twenty-four times on his hand because blades were nearly as scarce as soap.

In the kitchen my mother lit a black oil stove with a pattern of holes in the lid that threw tremulous stars on the ceiling in the uncertain dawn light. . . .

We ate in the kitchen because . . . there was not enough coal to light a fire so early in the day. There we shivered in unison and watched the frost patterns slide down the windows as sadly as wax faces melting.

Then my mother dispensed breakfast. Porridge made with water and sweetened with a pool of treacle – there was no golden syrup – that could be channelled into canals in the grey oatmeal fields, coffee, mostly chicory, sweetened with saccharine to save the sugar.

'Bacon for you, Will,' said my mother, giving him a wisp of streaky on his plate. 'And a slice of fried bread,' giving him a triangle of bread fried here and there in the dribble of bacon fat.

Or sometimes it was half a poached egg. Or reconstituted scrambled eggs perched like foam rubber on a piece of toasted national bread.

Off I rushed, and off rushed my father. . . . And my mother was left to fight and forage, to save and improvise; to cajole the butcher and berate the grocer; to sift the ashes of last night's fire for nuggets of coal; to study the latest Food Flash.

We were always happy to be back. To shut out the mean and smoky night, to cluster around the fire as it began to glow and the slate, making up the weight of the coal ration, exploded. My father read his evening paper – one folded sheet of rough newsprint full of death and defeats – and I watched tar oozing and flaring from the precious coals and tried to stem the juices with the poker. . . .

Out from the kitchen, flushed and determinedly gay, came my mother with tea, dinner and supper all in one on two tin trays. This was her finest hour, her triumph over adversity, the Germans, the men's war. Like ravenous animals – had we not reverted to hunting and scavenging? – we set about devouring the meal.

For the first course there was corned beef stew lapping dumpling islands made from soya bean flour. Or whale meat steaks which they said did not taste of fish (but only if you had one of those colds when everything tasted of nothing). Many families ate horse meat but my mother refused to buy it. . . . Accompanying the stew was a vegetable. Curly kale, perhaps, or home-grown spinach or artichokes that tasted of sweet earth. . . . Nettles were also tried as a vegetable. . . .

If there were sufficient points in our ration books then my mother sometimes bought a dented tin of South African or Australian fruit. But such luxuries were rare. Blackberries and apples bottled in the late summer were occasionally served; or a suet pudding made again with soya bean flour; or a cake baked with a little fat and no eggs and snippings of prunes to simulate currants and raisins. If all else failed there was always a slice of bread and peanut butter.

Then, contented and unappreciative of the fruits of the day's battle, my father and I went about our evening occupations. Homework for me; a cigarette and a crossword for my father; while from the kitchen came the comfy clatter of the plain white war-issue dishes being washed by my mother while she planned tomorrow's campaign.

After the entertainment I went up to the bathroom, as hostile as the frosted world outside. . . . I had only one bath a week and confined the depth of the water to five inches – as instructed by the Government. For this purpose my mother left a ruler in the bathroom.

Shivering and hating it all, I took my clothes off and watched the water steaming from the tap; plumbed the depths with the ruler marked LAMBERT in green ink and found there was still an inch to go. As the water climbed the ruler in tenths of an inch I climbed in, one grubby foot after the other. . . .

Then off to bed while my mother gazed at a desolated larder and planned next day's strategy on the Home Front.   DEREK LAMBERT

By now everything seemed to be in short supply. The citizen was urged on all sides to economise in the use of raw materials and to salvage, for recycling, everything that was worn out.

Rubber Shortage.
Drivers! Yours is a special responsibility.

90% of the world's natural rubber resources are in enemy hands. Care in the use of the tyres on your vehicle is absolutely essential in order to conserve the nation's rubber.

How good drivers save their tyres and serve their country.

Have your tyre pressure checked every week. . . . Drive slowly over rough roads. Never scrape or bump the kerb. Avoid driving a car over 40 miles per hour. Never corner at speed. . . .

All worn out tyres and tubes – lying discarded in your garage, shed, garden or elsewhere – are wanted at once. Take *yours* to a local garage for despatch to a government depot. MINISTRY OF SUPPLY ADVERTISEMENT, 22 July 1942

Everyone recognises the need for the removal of iron railings for scrap, but I feel that publicity should be given to the wasteful methods adopted by some of the authorities. . . .

In this village, the representatives of the Ministry of Works and Planning descended a few days ago and removed, among other items, and without any prior notification to the owners, (1) the collapsible sliding steel gates which form the front of the Memorial Hall and are used for locking it when not in use (2) the gate from the school porch and (3) iron hurdles which fence off my corn ricks. On my making a protest they agreed to restore the school gate and my hurdles but not the Memorial Hall gates, which were an essential part of the building and of considerable value and negligible weight. They informed me that the question of usefulness or weight was not 'germane to the issue' and that there was a war on. Meanwhile the lorry-load of scrap-iron which I had taken some trouble to collect from my farm about a year ago seems likely to stay here for the duration. Letter from a Warwickshire farmer in THE TIMES, 15 September 1942

The Battle for Fuel. Fuel Communiqué No. 6

In the last war the infantry used sometimes to feel that they were bearing the brunt of the battle. In the Battle for Fuel the infantry are the domestic fuel savers. They have been heard to ask, 'What about the government offices, hotels and large blocks of flats with central heating? What's being done about them?'

You will now know that an order has been issued prohibiting the use of central heating in such places until after October 31st, unless the Regional Fuel Controller orders otherwise. . . . It is hoped by this prohibition of central heating to save sufficient fuel to manufacture a thousand Spitfires.

Therefore until central heating is allowed in his district the resolute and determined fuel-saver will cooperate by:

1. Not lighting fires or stoves . . . just for heating rooms. He can thus save each week the fuel to make enough bullets or cannon shells to supply a fighter pilot for ten seconds – with this ammunition saved in the grate he may shoot down one Messerschmitt or night fighter.

2. Not using his hot water boiler more than two days a week. If everyone keeps this rule it will save 10,000 tons of fuel a week, enough to produce a hundred light tanks. MINISTRY OF FUEL ADVERTISEMENT, 8 October 1942

To children too small to remember peacetime, wartime life now seemed entirely normal.

I can't remember when I was first aware of the war [which started when the writer was two], but I clearly remember the installation of a heavy iron table shelter in our dining room. . . . During the blitz on Sheffield we used it. When the gas was 'off', I remember my mother's struggles with cooking on the dining room fire. As children we learned to listen to the sounds of the planes at night, and we could recognise from their tones whether they were carying loads of bombs or had dropped them. At the age of three this did not frighten me very much. What did frighten me was to hear the call sign from Beethoven's Fifth or Lord Haw-Haw's 'Germany calling'.

As children we didn't fully understand what war meant. We saw trams stranded because their power had been cut off, we saw bombed out buildings, we saw damaged houses. These touched us, but they were soon forgotten in collecting shrapnel, and hoping we could lay our hands on empty bullet cases.

I remember the days of the gas masks. First I had a Mickey Mouse style, but I grew out of it and had to have the adult type while all my friends still had the children's style. This didn't please me. When I first started school in 1942 . . . we took gas masks with us, but the practice didn't seem to last very long.

At school we were trained for air raids. There was anti-aircraft drill and we had to lie flat against a wall. Then we had drill for going to the air-raid shelters, which were cut into a hillside at the top of the school playground. Sometimes it was simply a matter of being marched there and back, but there were attempts to accustom us to being in the dark, damp shelters for longish periods. Then we sang. The favourite was, 'There'll always be an England'. . . . Often prayers were offered for two men teachers who had been at the school. For the one in the Navy we sang 'Eternal Father Strong to Save'. . . .

In Sheffield there were several brick, box-like air-raid shelters. If ever they were unlocked during the day we would like to investigate them. We wondered if anyone could bear to put them to their proper use as . . . people obviously used them instead of the public conveniences. . . .

As we had allotments at schools . . . we usually spent half a day a week gardening. . . . We liked thinking that we were part of the *Dig for Victory* campaign. . . .

Many of us looked forward to our fathers having leave – yet when they came we often misbehaved outrageously. Perhaps this was because we resented not having so much of our mothers' attention. . . .

Many of us were avid readers of advice by Mr Therm and The Squander Bug. I appointed myself 'electricity warden' at home and enjoyed keeping everyone up to the mark in economising with the electricity. . . .

Often we came home in the blackout and we enjoyed what we thought was the excitement of it. We used to speculate about who were German spies. These were usually either people we disliked, or more particularly people with strange or foreign-sounding surnames. One house where there had been a man in the First World War who had collaborated with the enemy (so our mother said) so alarmed us that we ran past, though no one connected with him was there then. . . .

Before Christmas we wrote to Father Christmas and put the letter up the chimney. I remember, that as I knew things were short, I used to write 'any little thing that you can spare'. This touched my mother, but at the time I couldn't see why. It just seemed logical. . . .

EILEEN NIXON

1943

There'll always be a dustbin,
To save for victory,
So treat it right, and let it fight
For home and liberty,
We'll win this war together,
How ever hard it be,
If dustbins mean as much to you
As dustbins mean to me.

Song of the Children's Salvage Corps

'*Are you ready to cut the cake, Madam?*'

Although 1943 was a grim year for the civilian, with food and fuel no more plentiful than in 1942, and new shortages – of crockery, bed linen, furniture and much else – making themselves felt every week, at last one could discern the hope of victory. The year began with the overwhelming defeat of the German army at Stalingrad, and in the summer British and American troops landed on the mainland of Europe and Italy surrendered. Already everyone's thoughts were on the promised Second Front across the Channel and, as proof that it was coming, and that Britain was no longer alone, the country seemed to be steadily filling up with G.I.s. Although the Germans made a number of small air raids both by day and night, on London, Plymouth, Southampton and other favourite targets, by the autumn almost the only enemy activity over the British Isles was by reconnaissance aircraft, seeking to photograph preparations for the coming invasion of Europe.

Every American soldier landing in Great Britain was issued with a booklet of advice on how to behave.

You are now in Great Britain as part of an Allied offensive – to meet Hitler and beat him on his own ground. For the time being you will be Britain's guest. The purpose of this guide is to start getting you acquainted with the British, their country, and their ways.

America and Britain are allies. Hitler knows that they are both powerful countries, tough and resourceful. He knows that they, with the other United Nations, mean his crushing defeat in the end.

So it is only common sense to understand that the first and major duty Hitler has given his propaganda chiefs is to separate Britain and America and spread distrust between them. If he can do that, his chance of winning *might* return. . . .

In their major ways of life the British and American people are much alike. . . . But each country has minor national characteristics which differ. . . . For instance: the British are often more reserved in conduct than we. On a small crowded island where forty-five million people live, each man learns to guard his privacy carefully – and is equally careful not to invade another man's privacy.

So if Britons sit in trains or buses without striking up conversation with you, it doesn't mean they are being haughty and unfriendly. Probably they are paying more attention to you than you think. But they don't speak to you because they don't want to appear intrusive or rude.

Another difference. The British have phrases and colloquialisms of their own that may sound funny to you. You can make just as many boners in their eyes. It isn't a good idea, for instance, to say 'bloody' in mixed company in Britain – it is one of their worst swear words. To say: 'I look like a bum' is offensive to their ears, for to the British this means that you look like your own backside; it isn't important – just a tip if you are trying to shine in polite society. . . .

When pay day comes it would be sound practice to learn to spend your money according to British standards. They consider you highly paid. . . . The British 'Tommy' is apt to be specially touchy about the difference between his wages and yours. . . .

Don't be misled by the British tendency to be soft-spoken and polite. If they need to be they can be plenty tough. The English language didn't spread across the oceans and over the mountains and jungles and swamps of the world because these people were panty-waists. . . . Britain may look a little shop-worn and grimy to you. The British people are anxious to have you know that you are not seeing their country at its best. The houses haven't been painted because factories are not making paint – they're making planes. The famous English gardens and parks are either unkempt because there are no men to take care of them, or they are being used to grow vegetables. British taxicabs look antique because Britain makes tanks for herself and Russia and hasn't time to make new cars. British trains are cold because power is needed for industry, not for heating. The trains are unwashed and grimy because men and women are needed for more important work than car-washing. The British people are anxious for you to know that in normal times Britain looks much prettier, cleaner, neater. . . .

The British of all classes are enthusiastic about sports. . . . Cricket will strike you as slow compared with American baseball, but it isn't easy to play well. . . . The big professional matches are often nothing but a private contest between the bowler (who corresponds to our pitcher) and the batsman (batter) and you have to know the fine points of the game to understand what is going on. . . .

You will find that English crowds at football or cricket matches are more orderly and polite to the players than American crowds. If a fielder misses a catch at cricket, the crowd will probably take a sympathetic attitude. They will shout 'good try' even if it looks to you like a bad fumble. In America the crowd would probably shout 'take him out'. . . . You must be careful in the excitement of an English game not to shout out remarks which everyone in America would understand, but which the British might think insulting. . . .

SOME IMPORTANT DO'S AND DONT'S

Be friendly but don't intrude anywhere it seems you are not wanted. You will find the British money system easier than you think. A little study beforehand will make it still easier. . . .

If you are invited to eat with a family don't eat too much. Otherwise you may eat up their weekly rations.

Don't make fun of British speech or accents. You sound just as funny to them but they are too polite to show it.

Avoid comments on the British Government or politics.

Don't try to tell the British that America won the last war or make wise-cracks about the war debts or about British defeats in this war.

Never criticise the King or Queen.

Don't criticise the food, beer, or cigarettes to the British. Remember they have been at war since 1939.

Use common sense on all occasions. By your conduct you have great power to bring about a better understanding between the two countries after the war is over. *A SHORT GUIDE TO GREAT BRITAIN FOR ALL MEMBERS OF THE ALLIED EXPEDITIONARY FORCES*

I suppose we were as jubilant as everyone else in the country when the Americans came into the war. In Bournemouth we had seen troops of almost every colour and nationality, but when those G.I.s hit town, commandeering our homes, and our countryside, we were captivated at once. With their smooth, beautifully tailored uniforms, one could hardly tell a private from a colonel. They swaggered, they boasted, and they threw their money about, bringing a shot in the arm to business, such as it was, and an enormous lift to the female population.

'Come on babe. How about you and me steppin' out, huh? Gee, you look cute, babe. No kiddin'. . . .'

How those gorgeous G.I.s could shoot a line, and how we loved it. Not only that, but they were equipped up to the eyebrows with scented soap, cigarettes, food, sweets and dozens of other things we had not seen for years. They were so generous to everybody, it was just like Christmas. . . .

Almost every night found me dancing on an excellent but crowded floor to one or another of America's top-line orchestras. Coca-Cola flowed as champagne, there was plenty to eat, it was like finding an oasis after a long trek through a burning desert.

American boys were the master of the jitter-bug craze, we English girls took to it like ducks to water. No more quick-quick-slow for us. This was really living.

But it was not just their dancing which took us by storm, but their charm and good manners. I found myself being waited on hand and foot, with every little whim gratified, they even put on one's dancing shoes on bended knee. I returned home each evening with enough soap, cigarettes and candy to stock a shop. . . .

Of course there were times when the after dance snogging session got out of hand, and the over-amorous had to be kept at bay. But when this happened it was easy to palm them off with promises and find another escort. . . .

I met a young sergeant whose parents had been Turkish. After the dance, we would walk hand in hand along the clifts to a spot amongst the barbed wire where we could see the sea. Here we stood in the moonlight, whilst he recited long passages from Omar Khayyám. I was enthralled.

At a Sunday afternoon tea dance I met an American sergeant who was of Italian descent, with swarthy good looks and a way of gesticulating with his hands which I found completely fascinating. He was my constant companion until the invasion. . . . We would become so absorbed in conversation whilst sitting in a restaurant, that tired waiters would be stacking up chairs around us and we did not notice. He was married, so our relationship held no long-term prospects. I took him home to meet my mother, who liked him at once. At teatime I gave him a treasured egg, which I had been hoarding for the occasion. . . .   BRENDA DEVEREUX

Three years in the Milestone Club in Kensington gave me ample opportunity to study the young American male. . . .

On the whole the 'boys' behaved well, when account is taken of the fact that they came to the Clubs on leave in a strange land with pockets well-lined, and with the thrill of being in a capital that was at once a fairy-tale and a legend. 'Gee, what d'you know – Piccadilly,' one would say ecstatically; 'never guessed I'd make it:' another would exclaim. 'Say could you direct me to where that guy Winston Churchill lives?'

It was not, however, to Downing Street, nor even to *Bucking-ham* Palace that most of them wished to go. It was to Madame Tussaud's – the Wax Museum, as they called it. When questioned about this preference the reply invariably given was, 'My buddy said, don't miss it.' 'But why?' I persevered.

'It's different.' With that I had to rest content. . . .

It was part of our duty at the Information Desk to arrange tours, suggest places of interest and so on. One day a particularly fed-up G.I. came to me and said 'Say, lady, I've seen everything in this town – old buildings, new buildings, everything. Shucks! You can see them any place. We have 'em all back home – what have you got that we ain't got?'

I thought a moment and said deliberately – 'We've got one thing you haven't got back home.'

'What's that, huh?'

'Bombs,' I replied.

He saw the point immediately and apologised quite handsomely.
MURIEL MILLER

Whilst American convoys were going through the village [in Wales to which Dulwich College preparatory school had been evacuated] we noticed that one of the tanks frequently checked for a short time by the front door, and then started off again. It was not until I chanced to be outside one day that I realised what was happening. One of the more ingenious boys, whose bedroom window was on a level with the tank turrets as they passed, had found it very convenient to hang out a pole with the notice, 'Any gum, chum?' and a kind of fishing net attached, and, until I had discovered it, was reaping a very rich reward from our gallant allies.   J.H. LEAKEY

Some of the very first American soldiers to land in Britain came to Halston Hall camp near Oswestry. Very well behaved they were, too, but there was one court martial I had to attend to give evidence. I was given a low stool to sit on and when my name was called I jumped up to attention. The President of the Court motioned with his hand and said to me 'Sit down, Sit down!'. I did so. Immediately he called my name again I rose and stood smartly to attention, thinking I had not been quick enough the first time. Again came the words, 'SIT DOWN, sergeant, SIT DOWN!' I did so. I am six feet and even in those days had a good 'corporation', but rising from a low stool in my tight uniform wasn't too easy. All the same when my name was called the third time, I thought 'I'll show them!' and no guardsman at Buckingham Palace stood to attention in a more soldierly manner.

Most of the twelve high-ranking American officers facing me broke into a smile. I just could not understand what I had done wrong. The President of the Court said to me, 'Will the witness please tell the Court why he is bobbing up and down?'

Me: 'I don't understand the question, sir.'

He repeated the question slowly and plainly, and then it dawned on him. He said to me: 'Will you accept the Court's apologies. We should have explained to you that in American courts of law, and in courts martial, too, all evidence is given sitting down.'

When the soldier was brought in for sentence – he had thrown a bottle of beer at me – I asked permission to speak, which was granted. I said:

'May I make an earnest appeal that a light sentence be imposed? I am a grocer as well as a police officer. Our stores, in common with all other shops in this country, have had no stocks of tinned meats, sardines, pilchards, tinned salmon, etc, for many months, but when the Lease Lend Act came in what a difference it has made! Within six weeks of the signing, very big supplies arrived from America, and if I may say so, this country will never be out of America's debt.'

The President of the Court said to me: 'Thank you, that is the best speech of welcome we have heard since we came to this country.'

As I was leaving the camp the soldier stopped me, shook my hand warmly, and said: 'That speech of yours got me off very lightly.'
MACLAREN FRANCIS

As London became fuller every month, every week, every day, as fresh waves of American troops reached the capital and young men fleeing from bondage arrived from the Occupied countries of Europe, Piccadilly from the Green Park to the Circus and Coventry Street from the Circus to Leicester Square became increasingly animated and picturesque. This straight line little more than half a mile in length became Allied Main Street. It was not only the favourite beat of the Londoner. War workers from the Provinces thronged the pavements seeking the glamour of London. . . .

I used to join in the procession on Sunday afternoon towards five
o'clock, when Shepherd Market was half asleep. . . . Traffic in Piccadilly was so light that a green dray-cart filled with American soldiers
and their girl-friends and drawn by two white shire horses clattered at
full speed past Hatchard's. The driver's whip was garlanded and
everybody was singing *Idaho*, the melancholy strains of which were
wafted away in the breeze. A notice outside St. James's, Piccadilly,
[destroyed in the Blitz] announced an open-air service in the churchyard for 6.30, and a middle-aged woman with a blue hat was putting
out the chairs on the cracked flagstones between which grew the
sturdy rosebay. . . . Two itinerant vendors were selling their wares
displayed on the sand-bags next to the Monseigneur – one was selling
tinted spectacles, the other roses made up into buttonholes. A tall
London bobby, wearing the peacetime helmet that by now had replaced the tin hat of two years earlier, was looking imperturbably at
the various Military Police parading in twos round the Circus, rather
like the animals that walked into the ark – two girl soldiers with red
caps and M.P. on their armlets, two American M.P.s, two French
gendarmes, and a couple of Dutch *schupos*. 'Go ahead,' he seemed to
say; 'you're only playing at being policemen!' . . .

Coventry Street was more crowded than Piccadilly. The slow-
moving waves outside Lyons' Corner House surged round the two
entrances, and against the long queue of patient folk waiting for
permission to enter the tea-room situated at the far end of the dim
foyer. Another queue had formed for the 1s.4d. cafeteria. There was
yet another in Rupert Street opposite the Prince of Wales's Theatre,
but this one had nothing to do with the Corner House or with the
theatre. People were waiting to buy cherries from a stall in the middle
of the street. There were similar scenes all along the route, queues for
plums, for apples, and even for peaches. Everything interested the
crowds. They stood in contemplation in front of Keith Prowse reading the titles of the popular music-hall scores: 'I see you everywhere',
'Some day we shall meet again', 'By the light of the silvery moon',
'Taking a chance on love', 'A fool with a dream'.

The Rialto, one of the West End's oldest picture-houses, was
giving its last performance of *We Dive at Dawn*. The shored-up
entrance of the Café de Paris bore a notice saying, 'Danger – Unsafe
Premises'. . . .

In the middle of the road an Australian flying officer was limping
along on crutches. . . .

On the other side of the road the Automobile Association building seemed strangely silent. . . . In one of its windows was displayed a picture of a country road in peace-time – lines of family cars being given the friendly salute by an A.A. scout. Over the picture one read, 'Until these days return!' . . . In the next window we saw two Tommies in the turret of a tank in the Libyan desert looking back at an A.A. scout disappearing in a cloud of sand. One Tommy was saying to the other, 'Trouble ahead, Bert. He didn't salute.' [The pre-war practice had been for an A.A. patrol-man to salute all cars bearing an A.A. badge unless there was a police 'speed-trap' or other hazard ahead]. Past these harmless little jokes surged the slowly trudging crowds eager to laugh at anything. They overflowed into every establishment open on Sunday afternoon. They refreshed themselves at Forte's Milk Bar, which stands between Dolcis and the Ritz Cinema, where *Gone with the Wind* had been running for four years. . . . Its patrons sat on high stools or congregated in groups (I have seen the sailors of five nations gesticulating together), while on the pavement the long queue waited to enter the Empire, where Joan Crawford was playing in *Above Suspicion*.

On either side of the Monseigneur News Cinema, whose main attraction consisted of pictures from Sicily, were the Queen's Brasserie and the Queen's Bar. In Leicester Place . . . was Chris's restaurant with two tables in the open air like in continental cities. . . . An R.A.F. officer and a girl were sitting at one of them eating spam and drinking Algerian wine.

Some of the crowd surged on past the Café de L'Europe and Warner's as far as the Hippodrome. . . . George Black was producing *Lisbon Story*. . . . The Hippodrome marked the end of the half-mile, and though some people wandered into Charing Cross Road, most retraced their steps into Leicester Square. . . .

On my way back I cut across the square where Shakespeare stood in the middle of the gardens. . . . There was shade in the gardens from the four big trees round the playwright and colour from the light-blue flowers planted at his feet. Some of the trees on the outer perimeter were destroyed in the raids. These were replaced by young trees to give shade to future generations. Many people sought the cool of the gardens. They rested on the benches. An R.A.F. mechanic and his girlfriend were reading the same book held up jointly. A sailor was fast asleep. An American soldier was sitting on a pedestal which had once served for a bust of Reynolds, but Reynolds was destroyed in an air raid. . . .

It was past eight o'clock and the scene along the half-mile was beginning to change. The pay-boxes of the cinemas were closed and the commissionaire of the Rialto stood on a ladder changing the title of the big film. *The Life and Death of Colonel Blimp* would to-morrow take the place of *We Dive at Dawn*, . . . the itinerant vendors were packing up their barrows from which mountains of cherries and plums had disappeared; the queue for tea at the Corner House had gone, and in its place there was another for supper. . . . A group of Americans standing in the centre of Coventry Street shouted lustily for a taxi.

From Shaftesbury Avenue came a tall policeman riding a very small bicycle. He carried over his shoulder a long rod that looked like a pike, and when he reached the first traffic lights of the Circus he jumped off his machine and with the help of the rod lowered the half-shutters that must dim the traffic lights before the blackout. . . . The police cycle round with their rods like the lamp-lighters of our youth. Only they dim the lights instead of putting them on. . . .

Mrs ROBERT HENREY

I had an unexpected invitation to spend a short holiday in a Cornish fishing resort, with a friend whose aunt and uncle were caretakers of the local Methodist Chapel and lived in a cottage adjoining it. My friend, as a sister in a large London hospital, had been experiencing tiring and grim days at a time of repeated raids and welcomed the chance of quietness for a while.

When we arrived we found the lovely little place [St. Mawes] almost entirely taken over by H.M. Forces. Only one or two shops were still open and these sparsely stocked. All the others were boarded and closed. For entertainment the small village hall advertised a film show one evening a week and the Methodist Chapel . . . ran a canteen service for the benefit of the troops. That was all the activity in this well known and pre-war busy place. Yet, looking back, those ten days spent there were full of an extraordinary calm and peace. . . .

We arrived on a Saturday and on the Sunday evening after service the little Methodist hall was crowded with men in uniform and very soon I was roped into playing the piano – mainly in response to many requests for favourite hymns from the men, and also to help in handing round thick sandwiches, with very little fillings . . . and cups of tea, ad lib. Everyone was so friendly – the men themselves were as anxious to help as we were, and insisted on taking over the kitchen to tackle the washing-up. They produced their family snapshots for our benefit and when it really did become necessary to insist on closing, reluctantly the men departed. What a happy start to our holiday!

During the week which followed the highlight was the film show. . . . We found we had to book our seats, so, very innocently, extravagantly chose the dearest, viz 9d. each – and when we arrived . . . found we were the only Rothschilds, and old Lloyd loom chairs had been placed in the front row for our use, and behind us rather awed looks prevailed from local inhabitants who sat on benches. The film was *Escape to Happiness*, with Ingrid Bergman in the main role, a real tear-jerker, and when the lights had to temporarily go up, many tear-stained faces were observed. Twice that evening the film broke, the screen was terribly poor, the sound track hopelessly raspy, but, oh the happiness that was prevalent . . . and the friendliness of the audience, once they realised we were very ordinary folk and not 'visiting royalty'.

Alas, one night we were awaked by a loud bang . . . and we later learned a bomb had fallen somewhere near but no harm had resulted. . . . Our rower was full of the night's incident and in a tone of great awe informed us that a 'real bomb had been dropped on the rocks but hadn't gone off proper-like'. My friend wisely refrained from comment when he continued thoughtfully, 'I doan't reckon as 'ow it could be worse in London, that noise. Did either of ye ever hear a bomb fall up there?' VERA WOODHOUSE

The Dig for Victory campaign launched at the start of the war reached its peak in 1943, with a record number of allotments under cultivation.

One of the most interesting aspects of our job [in the Ministry of Agriculture Press Office] was the large number of specimens brought to us for identification. Our collection reached its peak with the Colorado beetle scare of 1943. By poster, press notice and other means the public had been exhorted to turn in anything that might reasonably be suspected of being a Colorado beetle, but although that very noxious insect had been described in great detail, the public's notion of it was, to say the least of it, hazy. . . . We received specimens of most things that crawl or fly and not a few that swim. We had centipedes, millepedes, stag-beetles, cockchafers, ladybirds, crickets, woodlice, and once a live newt; but never a Colorado beetle. One man brought in a fine specimen of the elephant hawk moth and another the only mole-cricket that I saw during the war. . . . The flood abated just in time to prevent a revolt of office charladies, and we declined to our normal, everyday intake of specimens.

One morning in the spring of 1943 our door opened very slowly and there entered, branch by branch, what appeared to be an entire young apple tree in full blossom. It proved to be precisely that, and it was borne by a small, perspiring woman who until she let fall her burden was practically invisible to us. The tree had become badly affected by a fungoid disease and she had brought the whole thing up from a coastal town. I am glad to say that we were able to tell her what she wanted to know. Also we gave her a badly needed cup of tea, after which she departed, leaving the tree with us. We had the deuce . . . of a job in getting rid of it.   F. HOWARD LANCUM

The village of Buckland is situated in the Cotswolds. . . . I was married in the village church on 12th June 1943. . . . My husband is Danish by birth. He, with other foreign seamen whose boats had been sunk, had been sent to work for the Forestry Commission, who had a large depot near here. My brother, too, worked there – that is how we met. Everyone in the village helped to make our wedding an occasion. People gave me fat, sugar, fruit and eggs and the baker made us a wedding cake. Of course, icing wasn't allowed, but the cook at the Residential Nursery (where I was a helper) was able to get some fudge icing from her sister. This she put on the cake and decorated with a vase with real flowers in it, and it looked beautiful. Other food was given me and I had sandwiches and cake for the reception. We were able to get several bottles of sherry and port-type wine from different landlords. We also had a small barrel of cider, which everyone enjoyed. The rector's wife gave me some beautiful white roses and those we made into buttonholes. I wore a grey suit, white silk blouse and Navy blue hat and shoes, all new, and bought with coupons saved up for over one year. Several friends offered to lend me their wedding dresses and veils, but I preferred to wear my own clothes.

Nearly everyone in the village came to church and about eighty people came to our cottage for the reception. Luckily it was a fine day, so people could overflow into the garden. People lent glasses, china, etc., some people gave me flowers to decorate the church and house. It wasn't very easy to buy confetti so some people gathered real rose petals to throw at us as we came out of church. Two friends were able to get films for their cameras, so we had snapshots taken outside the church and then were able to get them enlarged later on.

We had a weird and wonderful collection of presents, including so many glasses of all shapes and sizes that I lost count how many there were. We also had ten tablecloths. The most original wedding present we received was a carrier bag containing one pound of tea and four pounds of granulated sugar, from two bachelor friends of my husband, who said they never drank tea anyway.

We went by bus to Woodford near Bristol for three days for our honeymoon. We continued to live with my father and brother, so didn't have any worries about finding a house to live in or furnishings. My wedding ring was a utility one made of nine carat gold and cost 30s. 9d. It was possible to get twenty-two carat gold rings on the black market at £10 each, but my ring has worn well and has never been off my finger. Mrs J. MIKKELSEN

As new goods became ever scarcer the drive for salvage intensified. Among the most enthusiastic collectors were scouts.

We entered on the collection of waste paper in a big way. The [Stafford] Borough Council gave us the use of a derelict cottage, due for demolition, and . . . the paper came in by the ton. Some works gave us a standing order to collect all their waste paper on two days each week and . . . people sent in requests for us to collect newspapers, magazines and paper of all sorts. One firm . . . had a lot of carbon paper amongst their contribution and this we had to extract . . . as I frequently put my hands on my thighs to rest my aching back I found my khaki shorts were gradually developing blue fronts – and the blue took a lot of eradicating. . . .

The paper arrived . . . in cars, trek-carts, rucksacks – and . . . a pony and float. . . . The cottage had two rooms upstairs and two down, and the scheme was to store the loose paper upstairs, bring it down and bale it, and store the bales downstairs ready for collection by a scrap-dealer, who paid us for them. This dealer lent us a baler, and we had another made. . . . The paper was compressed . . . into cubes about twenty inches each way, and then sisal cord was threaded through and the bales tied up. Instead of running bowlines, however, some lads tried to tie them with reef knots, which are difficult to get very tight, and very often when a bale was taken out it burst. . . . The rooms upstairs got fuller and fuller . . . to get into the second room a boy had to lie down on the paper and 'swim' under the lintel. . . .

There was no heating, but there was a hole in the roof through which the rain would come, so that in one part the paper became a stinking, sodden mess. We made quite a bit of money doing this job, but after a while it became apparent that it was too much for us, so we gave it up and asked the local council to take it over.

CLARENCE FINLOW

A great feature of all war savings drives was the provision of price lists for different items of military equipment, which enabled each group to choose a suitable target to aim at.

BOMBS   Weights and Prices

Weight in lbs.	Description	£	s.	d.
2,000	Armour Piercing	138	0	0
1,900	General Purpose	83	0	0
500	Semi-Armour Piercing	49	0	0
1,000	General Purpose	42	0	0
250	Semi-Armour Piercing	33	0	0
500	Anti-Submarine	25	0	0
500	General Purpose	20	0	0
250	Anti-Submarine	15	0	0
250	General Purpose	13	0	0
100	Anti-Submarine	10	0	0
30	Incendiary	3	0	0
40	General Purpose	2	10	0
	Anti-Tank	2	0	0
$11\frac{1}{2}$	Practice	0	15	0
4	Incendiary	0	15	0
4,000	General Purpose	100	0	0
8,000	General Purpose	250	0	0

WINGS FOR VICTORY LEAFLET

As the boys were acquiring a considerable number of war souvenirs during the holidays, they suggested that they should open a museum in the sun lounge, and charge the local populace to come to see it. This was duly arranged, and a colossal number of bomb fragments, parts of aeroplanes, etc., were exhibited, and a considerable amount of money acquired for the Red Cross. Whilst I was on a tour of inspection I noticed amongst the relics a battered old comb to which was attached the label, 'Comb found on the body of German pilot during the Battle of Britain'. Something vaguely familiar struck me about this comb, but as the exhibit was immensely popular I did not stop to look at it for long and passed on. It was not until the next day that I discovered that my own comb had gone.   J.H. LEAKEY

The Fire Guard scheme had been introduced in haste early in 1941 as a precaution against further fire raids such as the one which had devastated the City of London.

26 December 1943   Besides being peevish I am qualifying not slowly for the madhouse under the deluge of paper which descends on me in reference to the Fire Guard Plan. One of them lately said that when I detected a small unexploded anti-personnel bomb, among my numerous and immediate duties would be to inform the headmaster of any school in session and supply him with a picture or poster of the bomb. Another said I was to equip my Sector Point with 'table, chairs for Message Clerk and messengers, blackout, mobilising slate, chalk, log-sheets, spare N.F.S. message forms, Sector Point sign, Sector Diagram and some form of emergency lighting' (in the next paragraph it said the Sector Diagram must be kept in my personal possession). It also said 'Sector Point Messengers must be earmarked', and if any-body has a humane branding-iron . . . which he can lend me I am prepared to do my best. More seriously, however, this scheme, which in fundamental outline is quite sensible, seems to me in danger of foundering under the weight of detail loaded on it. . . . It has got to be operated in their spare time by men and women of average intelligence and . . . it may be . . . that the majority of Fire Guards more readily remember the distinctions between blocks, sectors, areas, wards, zones and regions that we can, but I doubt it. Meanwhile my tin hat has been taken away and painted with so chic a design in black and white that if it were less hideously uncomfortable, and in my duties did not as a rule tether me to the telephones in the Wardens' Post, I might sometimes even be tempted to wear it.   A.S.M. GOW

By Christmas 1943 almost the only toys to be found in the shops were highly priced secondhand ones. The W.V.S. provided its usual commonsense answer.

Rural Dorking's Christmas Toy Exchange was only one of the many in the country that went with a swing. On six memorable days 293 parents and children came along, full of hope about changing their old familiar books and toys for some novelty, and were not disappointed. Many more books than toys were brought in for exchange – over 700 in all – and pointing was done accordingly.

Several mothers agreed that they were getting far better value than they had anticipated. And indeed, where else these days, than in a W.V.S. Toy Exchange, could you expect to meet four rocking-horses, six forts, two tricycles, a doll's house, and a brand new doll's sewing machine, not to mention china tea services, jigsaw puzzles, a whole army of soft toys and dolls and thirty mechanical toys? In Newdigate, where special efforts have been made to remove traces of wear and tear and to produce keys for all the mechanical toys, 109 children went home happy in one day. As many toys had been given, each child in the Infants classes at Newdigate School had a token of six points to spend as he or she chose. Of course it took hours for all those bewildered infant minds to become finally made up.

When six weary helpers were coping with the final packing up on the last afternoon, a party of children arrived, wished them a Happy Christmas, thanked them for their toy and said they were looking forward to next year. *THE W.V.S. BULLETIN*, February 1944

1944

If we have had long to wait for good news, we have had it
in full measure in 1943. . . . Though the prospect of 1944 is . . .
not calculated to inspire cheerfulness, it is at least possible
for the first time . . . to look forward to a new year
with some confidence that the last siren
will sound before the Last Trump.
A.S.M. Gow, 13 December 1943

'Now in the next game we all go out for an hour and come back with lumps of coal.'

1944 was a year of hope deferred. Although the Germans were now everywhere in retreat, it was clear that they were not yet beaten and between January and April they launched the heaviest series of raids on London since 1941, which became known as the 'Little Blitz'. In June Allied troops had barely, at last, landed in France, when the flying-bombs began to rain down upon Southern England, while an optimistic official announcement in September that the Battle of London was over was immediately followed by the arrival of the first rockets. Everyone had hoped and expected that the war in Europe would end in 1944. Instead Christmas was overshadowed by a new German offensive. Rationing and scarcity remained the constant companions of the civilian and it began to seem as though victory would never be won.

I washed and ironed dresses to take the babies out to tea in. It gave me a bad conscience when there was so much essential housework to do. But Marian hardly ever went further than the shops and Rachel had never been out to tea.

When we got there, Marian discovered and consumed half a pound of chocolates, one person's sweet-ration for six weeks. I left embarrassed, with Marian unrepentant and Rachel whimpering with tiredness and the cold. Snow was falling and it was rush-hour and the buses were full. I stood on the edge of the pavement with Rachel in my arms and Marian walking maddeningly round me hanging on to the hem of my coat. We were no attraction to the few taxis that ambled past looking for American soldiers who would pay double fare and take them to the remunerative West End. We would not go out to tea again till after the war, I decided. . . .

At last a taxi took pity on us; but the sirens sounded just before we got home and the miserable driver made me pay double for exposing him to danger. There was no danger yet, but I could not keep the babies out in the snow to argue with him, so paid him and then regretted it.

Instead of putting the babies to bed in their cots, I put them on the shelves in the basement, and immediately this small damp room assumed a magical quality of safety for me. . . .

Donald came in exhausted, hoping for a comfortable period of recovery in his fireside chair, to find me refusing to allow any of us to leave my damp little dungeon. He sat on the edge of a mattress while I darted into the kitchen to warm up a meal for him. It was one of those long silent alerts. Marian, excited by the tea party and by the novelty of her shelf, could not or would not sleep. Donald felt too tired to undress.

'But you can't go to bed in your clothes,' I objected.

'You can't go to bed on a store-cupboard floor,' he countered, lying down on his mattress and shutting his eyes.

The all-clear sounded.

'Shall we go up?' I suggested.

'If you like.' It was midnight and none of us except Rachel had been to sleep yet. I started to gather up the babies and some of the bedding. Donald came slowly up behind us.

Halfway up the stairs the sirens began again.

'Shall we go down?' I asked.

'If you like.'

'We'd better,' I said.

'No!' said Marian, crossly. 'Want to go to bed. Want an apple. Want a potty.' Suddenly she was sick. I was so busy dealing with her that I hardly noticed the clangour of raiders and gunfire which broke out above and around us. . . .

I had to break my security drill and go upstairs to fetch clean clothes and bedding for Marian. On my way up I could see through an unblacked-out window that the garden was like a firework display. Incendiary bombs spluttered silver fire about the frozen grass. Up-stairs I could hear them bouncing off the roof.

I ran up to the attic to make sure none had penetrated the roof. So far we were lucky. I fetched the clothes and went back to the base-ment, where Marian was being sick again. I dealt with this and then cuddled her down. 'One, two, three, and a –', she said unhappily, as a bomb whistled down. 'Bang,' she almost whispered.

It was the noisiest night since the old Blitz days.

Once more Marian was sick, and I had to go up for another lot of clean clothes and bedding. Part of the garden fence was on fire but it was some way from the house. We should have to leave it. A bomb whistled down as I went back to the others . . . Marian had scrambled out of her cupboard to reach the asylum of Donald's knee before the bang. 'One, two, three, and a –' she was still shouting breathlessly. She refused to go back to her shelf. 'One, two, three, and a,' she said again, standing up and holding on to her pyjama-trousers with one hand, as we heard another bomb fall. And then, instead of her usual

'Bang' when it exploded, she opened her mouth and screamed. I felt my nerve snap too.

But trying to comfort Marian helped to blanket my desire to scream as well. I held her in my arms and she buried her face against mine with each crash. . . . I looked up to see that Donald had taken the baby out of the carry-cot and was holding her away from the window.

My barrier of furniture fell down as the house shuddered with the crump of a nearby bomb. The glass shattered inwards. We leant over the babies with our backs to the now open window as another bomb came down and another. We could hear a plane dive just above us. The guns clattered out, shaking the house again. Marian made no sound now. Further away, six bombs dropped one after another. Then everything was quiet.

Presently the all-clear sounded. VERILY ANDERSON

17 March 1944 Well – we've had our lull and they say a cure for boredom is action. I was, as always, a lump of terror as we listened to the droning, revving and fighting above us; but when things happened I forgot to be frightened. A mighty swishing sound, then a pause and then glass, bricks, wood began breaking everywhere. At the same time water began pouring about, especially over my front door where it came like a curtain and would not stop. Waited a few minutes then thought we'd better investigate. Outside the door we saw something that hissed and looked quite revolting so we got back quickly to the others and pushed them all in the living room under the grand piano. By this time wardens were appearing, so we all went upstairs to see if it was there! Not much left, but no fire, then someone shouted up that we had a phosphorus bomb in the coke shed – and there it was! A long, green, glowing thing that hissed and puffed and smelt awful. 'You've got to keep the blighter wet or it'll go up' they said, so that's what we had to do all night – through the curtain of water still pouring from a broken pipe we had to pass bucket after bucket of the stuff to the warden who poured it on the evil smelling thing. Warning and raids all night but we just kept at it, and by morning we were all hysterical with laughter; there we were, watering a noxious flower in our coke shed, while we plodded through mud clouting some twenty incendiaries which dropped in the garden, made tea for all, looked for the double lilac bush where there was just a gaping red hole and got soaked through all night. The old people were

wonderful; they just stayed under the piano all the time.
VIVIENNE HALL

During 1944 a new post-raid service came into its own, the Incident Enquiry Point, which provided information about people who had become casualties or been made homeless.

Our incident was an extensive one, and by early morning, when things had sorted themselves out a little, the District Warden asked for a W.V.S. Incident Enquiry Point, and selected a very battered house just within the barrier. We swept away the worst of the debris from the front basement room, and by nine o'clock we were installed and the I.E.P. was officially open with a lopsided notice spiked on the railing outside.

Enquiries began streaming in at once, and it was impossible to log every separate enquiry as we had planned, so we concentrated on keeping our incoming information as accurate as possible. Names of people in Rest Centres and lists of casualties in hospitals came through to us direct or via the Warden Post, and many callers brought in news as well. We had plenty of exercise-books and cards, and we started a separate card-index for casualties and an index-book for the homeless. Unconfirmed reports were entered in a separate book, for we verified any bad news and made sure it was perfectly official before breaking it to the anxious relatives and friends.

One duty was the sorting and careful listing of personal property brought in by Wardens or Rescue Parties, mainly such things as insurance policies, ration books, clothing-cards and handbags; the duplicate lists being taken to the Town Hall each evening.

We had started work in an icy room, with no windows and make-shift furniture, but before long we realised that our I.E.P. ought to be a sort of oasis of comfort, however primitive, in that area of devast-ation, and by the end of five days we were almost home from home, with a roaring brazier fire outside, oil stoves within, hot drinks on tap, a proper table and chairs, and blankets and hot water bottles for our guests.

One day we had an S.O.S. that an old lady had come to tidy up her wrecked home and had collapsed. A helper hurried to the rescue with a thermos flask, and found a valiant old soul very loath to leave her own particular ruins. However, a son arrived with a timely offer of shelter outside London, and we were able to send them by car to Clapham Junction. Pets were another side line of the I.E.P. and one lodger, a white cat, was a constant anxiety as he kept diving under the floorboards and disappearing from view. About four days after the incident we had a message from the Warden to say that a cockerel had been dug up still alive, whose was it? But I am afraid we never really answered that one. More serious was the news that there was an unclaimed baby at a hospital waiting to be discharged, and who was the next of kin? We found that the child's parents had been taken to one hospital and the baby to another, where it had been entered under a mistaken name, and many false clues were followed before that little family came together again. *THE W.V.S. BULLETIN*

By early 1944 much of Southern England had become an armed camp, in preparation for the D-Day invasion.

We were aware [in Dorchester] from February 1944 that preparations for the invasion were nearly finished. The noise of the Sherman tanks travelling up the steep hill was so great that it was impossible to speak. I arranged with the pupils that I would dictate until these tanks drew near, then they should study their notes while we endured the deafening sound outside. The most frightening scene was a truck carrying two Sherman tanks. It must have required tremendous skill, and a heavy engine, to drive this heavy load through our narrow streets. Our narrow country roads were unsuitable for Sherman tanks and other traffic. The Americans trained men and put them on point duty. The girls called them 'snowdrops' because they wore white helmets, white gloves, white cords attached to a pistol and white bands round their waists. The teenagers were annoyed when they discovered the streets had become one way. It meant having to cycle a longer way to their home. Employers were considerate and allowed them an extra quarter of an hour for dinner, but they protested so loudly that it was agreed they could use the old route provided they were off the roads when extra military traffic needed the roads.

The American despatch riders roared through our streets and roads and as they generally travelled in sixes the noise was deafening.

Among the preparations the Americans built a hospital for wounded prisoners, a factory was turned into a large naval hospital and a large Army hospital taken over for Army patients. In order to provide an extra road into Portland they bulldozed through rocks and made a wide road at the end of Bridport.

When our troops left Dorset Barracks their families had to vacate the married quarters. They were transferred to another camp some distance away. After enduring the noise of constant jeeps, tanks and other vehicles for days the streets suddenly became quiet. We heard that the troops were on manoeuvre. As we walked home one evening the stillness was broken by a terrible rumble and the earth shook under our feet. Two days later a police car travelled slowly down the road and through a loud speaker ordered all vehicles to be moved off the road. Heavy trucks came down in a slow procession. They were either towing burnt out transport planes or gliders or carried a large pile of charred ash. This sight made us feel sick and sad. How many men had been killed? The G.I.s returned to the town looking decidedly shaken. We all went about our business with set faces.

Several paths were closed and notices placed on the fields telling us we must keep to the path. When we reached the railway bridge one evening we found the 'snowdrops' on duty. The men were ordered to put out their cigarettes. On the railway siding was a row of petrol tankers. A pipe had been affixed and the petrol was being poured into cans. As each one was filled it was placed into a waiting lorry. The job was tackled at top speed and the men worked until 11 pm when by that time most of the petrol had been removed.

We heard the G.I.s had handed in their walking out uniform; a theatre had been built at the Barracks and their Army band gave concerts. The time had come for the men to be kept inside their quarters and their policemen were on duty with their guns at the ready. No one was allowed to leave camp.

On the Thursday before D-Day an aeroplane could be heard overhead going to and fro putting up a smoke screen over the town. It was very quiet outside with hardly any traffic on the roads. The whole atmosphere was one of tension. Then one afternoon the police again cleared the streets of traffic and slowly came a procession of trucks drawing low trailers. From our upstairs window we could see men lying flat inside and wearing wool caps on their heads. Barbed wire had been fixed round the sides. They remained in a secret camp until the word 'go' was heard.

We in the South were waiting anxiously for the day. Everyone appeared geared up and ready. . . . Feeling very restless I persuaded my husband to go for a walk on the Sunday. As we reached a cross roads we saw 'snowdrops' on duty at the end of each road. We decided it was wise to go home. Just as we were turning round we saw a car with General Eisenhower inside, alone and huddled down on the seat.

After we had gone to bed one night we heard the roar of planes and guessed the invasion had begun. The Wellingtons towing troop-carrying gliders passed over our houses. That night we prayed for the men who had gone, maybe, to their death. The procession of planes went to and fro all day long.   Mrs D. MEECH

When I am pegging out sheets on wash-day, I remember another wash-day. We knew there was something afoot, as all day and all night the sky had been full of planes, wing to wing, streaming towards the coast. We did not know that it was Invasion Day. So I pegged my threadbare sheets out on the line, chatting to my neighbour meanwhile. Presently I heard her call: 'The sheets! Look at the sheets!' There they hung, streaked all over with black oil, blown across from the smoke-screens. Soap was very short and the stains never did come out.   THEKLA RODD

After D-Day the build-up of troops in Normandy continued, with a steady flow of reinforcements across the Channel.

During the first three days [after D-Day] we could hear the sound of guns being fired and our windows shook while the Americans were pounding the defences at Cherbourg. The Americans moved their troops which had been waiting in camps in Dorset towards the coast for embarkation. Then their convoys started. As they reached one corner [in Dorchester] a priest stood there all day long with a lad holding a cross while he made the sign of the cross as each vehicle went by and the men bowed their heads. When he reached the crossroads we saw trucks and other vehicles passing alone. There was no question of crossing the road. We waited in a crowd until there was a lull, then we hurried over. The convoy was always led by their military police cars, one convoy going to Weymouth and the other to Portland. Our own troops used Southampton. . . .

After the first weeks convoys drove in during the evening and the trucks were stationed in the road to wait until they could go to the petrol depot. . . . They slept at the Barracks. . . . Once the men arrived just before 10 o'clock; they ran to the corner shop and demanded a drink. It is an off-licence so beer could only be sold in bottles. When these ran out, the neighbours found empty bottles and the men ran and had them filled with beer from barrels. On another occasion we thought they had gone as usual to the Barracks but discovered next morning they had refused to sleep there as coloured troops were in possession. They returned quietly to their trucks and slept there all night. . . .

I invited two men in, gave them tea and the small amount of cake I had left. They drank the tea with relish; then they had a wash and brush up before returning to their vehicles. . . . One neighbour made jugs of tea and sent them out with her husband until her rations were gone. . . . Late one Saturday night an anti-tank convoy drew up. . . . As they were still there at 12 o'clock my husband took out three pieces of apple tart. Being short of fat I expect they thought the tart dry. It was fun to see three men sitting on top of their tank opening a tiny tin of meat with a huge knife. The local baker made up loaves and they were able to buy beer. Then they ate my tart.

An hour later they came to the door. We invited them in, the sergeant gave my husband a packet of cigarettes. One man had a hand grenade in his cap which he evidently thought we should like to see. I was scared stiff as I had heard of men being blown to pieces by accident when one of them went off. I pressed him to take the beastly thing outside but he assured me it was all right. . . . All the same I eyed it with suspicion. . . .

A week later we paid another visit to Weymouth. As we sat in a shelter and enjoyed the sun shining on the promenade, trucks carrying G.I.s were unloading troops for embarkation. Their police tried to keep the men away from us, but too many had arrived and were standing around. . . . An American Red Cross supply van was there, pouring out music. Each man received a cup of coffee, a bun and a box of chocolates, a personal gift from their President. It was only a small box but the G.I.s were very proud of it. . . .

One man threw himself on the asphalt and emptied his pockets to see what he could give the old people. He handed a few cigarettes to the men and soap coupons to the women. One man picked up a little girl of three and held her in his arms and refused to fetch his coffee. He held her until it was time to move on. The loving way he looked at that child made us wonder if he had one of the same age back in the United States.   Mrs D. MEECH

In spite of the warnings which had been given about German secret weapons, the start of the flying-bomb offensive in mid-June, only a week after D-Day, came as an appalling shock to the civilian population, especially as the attacks continued in all weathers and at all times of the day or night.

16–19 June 1944   A grim and unpleasant weekend if ever there was one! Sleepless and subject to an almost endless series of alerts day and night as these robot-planes or buzz-bombs or what you like to call them are tearing across the sky with a sinister hum and then coming to a deadly stop before dropping onto some hapless spot. I thought the Blitzes frightening enough, but this horrible machine is worse: you are always listening, always waiting for the drone of the machinery which drives the pilotless plane nearer and nearer. . . . And the damage done by the blast from these things is very considerable. As I was trying to have my bath on Sunday at 10.15 a burst of gunfire and the drone of the engine proclaimed another passing over: but there was complete silence almost at once, and then a terrific explosion and the inevitable wrench of torn wood and bricks and windows tinkling to bits. I forgot about washing my back and threw on some clothes. A pall of dust lay over us and five more windows had gone. We could see smoke and flame coming from the Upper Richmond Road and knew that was where the hellish thing had fallen. A row of shops, a bus and a street of houses were the worst damaged, [there was] loss of life, many casualties from glass and for a tremendous area around houses and shops were windowless and doorless – just one little incident among the hundreds caused over South England by these latest secret toys of Hitler's backroom boys.   VIVIENNE HALL

14–21 July 1944   God what a week! And how many more of them are we to have? After a lull, when we had hours at a stretch without flying-bombs and we began to feel we had got the measure of them and that they were dying down, on Tuesday night we lay and listened to an almost continuous stream being poured over us – all night long the sky was filled with the drone of the approaching, passing, stopping engine of a flying-bomb; and so it has more or less gone on through the week. On Wednesday morning [19 July] I got to the Bank station and as I walked up Princes Street I heard the danger overhead warnings from the Bank. I didn't know there was an alert on even, but quickened my pace and arrived at the Northern [Insurance Company, where she worked] and was waiting for the lift when all hell was let loose about me. A deafening roar and a sickening thud, followed by our huge eight-foot windows crashing in, frame and all, plaster and glass careering down the lift shafts.

I crouched under a counter and waited for the ceilings to come down but after a few seconds things stopped falling and we who were in the department slowly got up to survey the damage. A thick cloud of dust obscured our view for a bit, but as this cleared we saw that the windows and doors and fittings were all over the place and the building opposite was a horrible sight. The bomb had struck there and the inner roof had collapsed. Almost immediately the Civil Defence services and police started getting out casualties, poor dirty bleeding people. I wondered if our top floors had gone and dashed to the first aid room to get to work there. By a miracle we had no bad casualties in the Northern – about twenty cases of cuts, not bad ones and a few cases of shock – that's all. Had it been after instead of just before 9.30 we should of course have had many more people in the office – but all morning we had a steady stream of girls and men wanting tea and attention for cuts, for our men and a number of younger girls set to at once and with every available weapon cleared the glass and broken wood from the departments and stairways, got up the carpets. All this despite the fact that alerts and danger overhead signals were going all morning! . . .   VIVIENNE HALL

Saturday, 29 July 1944   At four this morning a beautiful flying bomb, roaring over, stopped and with a horrible whistle landed in the roadway just beyond 21, and then things happened with an amazing rapidity – the house shook all its glass to bits, doors flew in in pieces, ceilings and wall cracked and in some cases broke and all hell seemed to be loose. I groped my way out of the room – (in terror, James [the dog] had crawled under the bed) – and upstairs to find the front door in pieces in the hall with glass everywhere. On to fetch the old girl out of her glass and plaster-strewn room – it took us twenty minutes of agony to get her downstairs – and then until daylight paddling about in glass trying to discover the damage. Dawn at last, and then to try to clear up a bit. The rooms were strewn with glass and soot and plaster from the ceilings, and the depressing dirt we had tried so hard to dispel after the last bombing was worse than it had ever been. Some furniture scratched and one or two ornaments broken but my best loved stuff was packed away and safe. The wardens and surveyors came and pronounced the house safe – till the next bomb – and so we set about clearing up. Four weary long days at this, trying to get up the bucketsful of soot and glass and carrying it out on the roadway, packing up the furniture to the sides of the rooms away from the broken plaster and sleeping in a friend's shelter – raids on and off and thoroughly sick of the last bomb damage and here we are again, just as bad!! Blast Hitler!!!   VIVIENNE HALL

Along with the major tragedies caused by the flying bombs — also known as V–1s or 'doodlebugs' – went a variety of minor personal losses. In this incident, in Harrow, two people were killed and 270 houses damaged, but it was the loss of her wild-flower collection, which she was about to enter for a school competition, which one of those affected remembered best.

It was late next day before I managed to investigate the damage in my bedroom, and, filling yet another bucket with rubble, unearthed the remnants of blotting paper used to dry the wild flowers, which reminded me instantly of what I had been so engrossed with before the bomb. Was it only yesterday? It seemed like an age away. With nervous fingers I searched carefully through the glass and plaster. Surely there must be a few unscathed pages of flowers left in my book? But after patiently sorting the debris from the remnants of things that had been on my desk, it became miserably apparent that there were only a few whole flowers to be salvaged. There was certainly not enough time to start another collection – they had to be handed in at school the following week, and I had been building up this collection since March.

It was then that the impact of the damage hit me with harsh reality. A little later, when I felt my eyes were no longer red, I ventured downstairs. Mum was in the kitchen hopefully searching for un-broken cups – crockery was almost impossible to buy then. The sitting room was empty. The rubble and torn wallpaper had been removed, but there had not been much time for trifling things like dusting. I went up to the mirror hanging over the fireplace. 'Hitler is mad,' I wrote in the white dust. 'The British will win the war,' and then, in tiny letters at the bottom, 'School competitions are stupid.'
LILY PEARL MILLARD

For the following weary weeks we continued to have good views of doodlebugs [from the River Thames]. All London's citizens think that they saw the one which was different from all the others; but that very night I really believe that we met, and avoided, the unique V–1. We went up by night, and about 0200, the flood finished, we tied up to some barge-roads a little upstream from Ford's factory at Dagenham, but on the other side of the river. Before the 'watch below' could turn in, one of the 'Things' came roaring and glowing up from Tilbury towards us, and we all waited on the bridge to see it go over. But, some way short of us, the monster's light went out and the engine stopped. 'Boys!' I remember yelling, 'it's a by-election!' [Although he had joined the Navy 'for the duration' as captain of his own motor-launch, A.P. Herbert was still a Member of Parliament, whose death would mean a by-election].

We all scrambled below and lay flat on our stomachs, expecting the worst. Nothing happened: and presently, incredulous, I heard the noise of an engine again. I clambered out on to the bridge, and there, astern of us now, was the 'Thing' in full flight again, light and all, as if it had taken a good look at the *Water Gipsy* and decided to go for bigger game. It roared away and came down about two miles off in the Barking area. . . .

After that, 'By-election!' was always the operative word for our stomach drill on the cabin deck. This was, no doubt, in our little wooden ship, a fairly futile rejoinder to all that explosive power. But the cabin deck was a few inches below water-level, and I thought that the outward and upward blast from a 'Thing' bursting on the water, not too near, might go over our bodies, whatever mess it made of the ship.

'By-election' drills were frequent in the next few weeks. Once or twice a week we used to patrol down the river at night and lie at Blackwall or Woolwich. . . . These voyages were quite exciting, but made one feel not futile only but foolish.

Under way on the river, we were unable, because of our eighteen clattering horses, to hear the things coming; so, unless you kept your head circulating like a hen's, you looked round suddenly and saw one coming straight at you from abeam or chasing you astern. I must say, we felt very silly on those occasions, alone on our bridge in the middle of the Pool or Woolwich Reach. There was no basement to dive into, and no nice gutter to lie in. But at first, at night especially, the illusion was that they were not approaching very fast, and that 'evasive action' was still possible. One night in Greenwich Reach we were persuaded that three of the wandering lights were converging on us with devilish intent: and I remember cunningly calculating that if I worked across to the Surrey side and inside the barges I might thwart them all. What a hope! We were going about five knots against the tide and they – was it 350? We were not half-way across the river when the first went over us. . . . We did two 'by-election' drills and came up cursing after each. It was a shame to make you feel foolish as well as afraid. . . . There we were, a Naval vessel . . . and all we could do was to watch and record an unimpeded procession of enemy missiles over our country's capital, knowing that nearly all of them were bound to kill or injure innocent people somewhere.

This enemy was bound to win. A.P. HERBERT

Because it exploded on the surface, every flying-bomb incident was marked by a tall column of dust, visible for miles.

Drove swiftly through the quiet Sunday streets. Sometimes at odd corners or through a breach in the skyline of tall buildings the huge buff plume showed itself, calm and clean as sand against a pale bluish sky. Then gradually, the immaculate polish showed a ruffling, stray scraps of paper suggested the passing of a crowd, a weed of splintered glass sprung up here and there on the pavements, another and invisible weed seemed to be thrusting the window frames from their sockets and ahead, as this tangle grew denser, the street hung fogged with yellow dust.

Our destination lay within the dust. Once inside it was easy to see, only the outer air had painted it opaque. But it was like driving from the streets of a town into sudden country; nothing metropolitan remained to these torn pavements, to the earthen mortar dust and the shattered brick returning to the clay. . . .

Ambulances already. Two or three people stood about, handkerchiefs to their red-splashed faces. But we were ordered round the debris to search the broken buildings on either side.

At the top of the first flight of stairs, dark and rickety, a light shone through a crack in the unhinged door. The door came off easily. A single shadeless electric bulb hung over a tailor's table, shone weakly and yellow against the large daylit window beyond. On the table lay a pair of trousers, an iron, slivers of glass and splashes of red blood, comet-shaped, like flickings from a pen. Every lightly fixed furnishing of the room had shifted – bales of cloth, doors, chairs, plaster mouldings, a tall cupboard – all these had moved closer and now leant huddled at strange, intimate angles. Plaster dust covered everything. . . . There was nobody in the room. The blood led in wide round drops to the door, the tailor must have been 'walking wounded'. Had he been one of those outside, fingering blindly for the ambulance doors? The yellow bulb on its single string burned on, the only life in this lonely Sunday workroom, the only relic of the tailor's shattered patience.

Then, under the steady burning of this bulb . . . other sounds began to whisper. . . . Creakings, a groan of wood, a light spatter of moving plaster, from somewhere the trickle of water from a broken pipe. The whole house rustled. A legion of invisible plaster mice seemed to be pattering up and down the walls. . . . The house, suddenly stretched by blast, was settling itself. It might settle down on to new and firm purchases, it might be racking itself further, slowly, slowly grinding apart before a sudden collapse. . . .

Down in the courtyard they were carrying a man out from the opposite block. We caught a glance of him through the twisted framework of an iron footbridge. They had laid him on a blanketed stretcher on the grey rubble. He lay still, bloodless, only his face showing, and that plastered with the same sick grey dust. It lay evenly on him, like a poisonous mask – he looked gassed with dust. Once he struggled, his head turned from side to side. He seemed to be trying to speak. It was as if his real face, clean and agonised, tried to be free and show its pain.   Quoted by WILLIAM SANSOM

During those first days of the 'buzz bombs' Londoners made for cover at the sound of one flying in their direction, but very soon came the realisation that as long as they could be heard, there was no danger, so people continued about their affairs without so much as an upward glance. . . . I was standing at the window [in Hampstead], looking down at the morning scene in the street, while a buzz-bomb's sound came towards us. Across the road, two women were coming out of the greengrocer's, scarves tied over their curlers, and with laden shopping-bags clutched to their stomachs, they were deep in gossip. The young blind girl who walked confidently down the street twice every day on her way to and from work was rattling her stick along the kerbside barrier around the hole from which a workman was emerging and a smartly-dressed young man had crossed the road and was about to step onto the pavement. At that moment the buzz-bomb cut out. The two women, still talking, stepped backwards into the greengrocer's; the workman slid back down the hole; the young man raised his trilby with one hand, and with the other, took the arm of the blind girl, pulling her with him into the nearest doorway. There was a 'swoosh' of air, an explosion in a nearby street, and everyone moved again. The two women, still talking, came from the shop; the workman reappeared; the blind girl inclined her head to the young man, who raised his hat, and they all continued on their way after the moment's interruption. No one had looked up or shown the slightest interest in the bomb.   MEGAN RYAN

Many flying bombs – and finally most – were intercepted on or near the coast. Inland, London's last line of defences was a massed balloon barrage in Kent and Surrey.

I remember with joy the summer Saturdays when I was off-duty [from the W.V.S. and Civil Defence]. We would pack our lunch, get out our bikes, and cycle out into the country towards a village called Eynsford. We would stop at the edge of a barley field and have our picnic. There was a splendid view, as we were on rising ground. We could see the little hamlets nestling in the valleys, and we could hear the larks singing. And we could look up and see the massive balloon barrage. If the sirens sounded, we could watch with a feeling of detachment as the 'buzz-bombs' roared over, seeming to thread their way through the balloons. Later on, we would cycle home, often to find the house blown inside out again, and fresh holes in the roof. But the escape to the quiet countryside helped us to carry on once more, although the neighbours thought us a little mad to risk leaving the house at all, even for a few hours.   THEKLA RODD

Another unforgettable day at the office was when the promenade [in Bournemouth] was opened again. The other girls and myself could not contain our excitement at the prospect of getting down to the seashore. During the lunch break, eating our sandwiches en route, we scrambled down the steps leading to the beach. Like children having

their first day at the seaside, we tucked our dresses into our pants and waded in shouting and screeching with joy and happiness. In no time at all we were wet to the armpits, no one cared about having to work for the rest of the afternoon in wet clothes. After four years of war, swim suits were obsolete. I had grown out of mine, anyway.
BRENDA DEVEREUX

In the autumn, as the flying-bomb attacks eased off, the rockets (known to the Germans as V-2s), began to arrive. To mislead the Germans no news about them was published at first and the mysterious explosions which occurred were explained away as exploding gas mains, though few Londoners were deceived.

Saturday, 21 to Friday, 27 October 1944   This has been a week of bangs again – are we never to be free of them? On Friday night I awoke to a hideous explosion, followed by a smaller one, the house shook and I lay waiting and wondering – but it was just 'another flying gas main' as we all call these mystery explosions that must not be spoken about outside the town and that are still non-existent officially. Their noise is terrific, a flat enormous crack and then echoing rumbles, and I understand they create a pretty big crater and are most destructive. You cannot have any warning of their approach of course, as they dive upon you faster than sound can travel, so there's nothing one can do about them. Horrible contraptions! News of one or two of these comes from some part of London or another each day but there is no set time for them, you just don't know what might drop about you and when it does I suppose you still don't know, so maybe they are better than doodles which frighten you by their ever approaching drone and sudden silence. . . . On Thursday morning quite a number of the staff didn't turn up until 10.30 as they had been held up by a 'flying gas main' which had burst on the line near New Cross, and so we have gone on. Each morning there are fresh stories of noises in one district or another. There's a sort of sinister joke about the mystery of these things that do so much damage, cause such trouble and yet officially, are not!   VIVIENNE HALL

The existence of the rocket was officially admitted on 10 November. Thereafter, people whose homes were destroyed were at least allowed to know what had hit them.

We arranged to move to [a new home in] Holborn on the Saturday and, having spent a couple of nights with friends, moved into the flat and began the strenuous job of cleaning the furniture, etc., to get the flat habitable.

On the following Saturday, 25th November 1944, my husband and I were just ready at about 11.30 am to go out to do some shopping. He said, 'Now have you got everything, money, coupons, ration books?' when without any warning whatsoever there was a direct hit by a V-2 and we were both buried in the rubble. I heard afterwards there were only two V-2s in Holborn and this one got us.

I found my first inclination was to shout long and loud. We were buried close together and could speak to each other while awaiting rescue. . . . My husband said 'Let's call out', and I said 'Not until we hear somebody. Save your strength till then.' We lay and waited, hardly daring to breathe in case more rubble came down on us. The air was getting very short and then after about half an hour I heard the rescue men call 'Anyone there?' I gathered what breath I could and called as loud as I could, 'Help', and the answer came back, 'O.K., we can hear you.' The relief was enormous, more so because, as I found afterwards, my husband had passed out and he neither called nor spoke. The rescue men kept coming nearer, saying 'Keep calling' and I did and then one man stood on the rubble directly over my head. I called: 'You're standing on my head,' and he said 'Good, now we know where you are.'

After that began the slow process of carefully moving rubble to free us, and gradually the weight became less and the air more plentiful and then they managed to lift my husband clear – he had been buried on top of me and his body had shielded my face and part of my body. The rescue men strapped him to a stretcher to lower him to the ground. I was still trapped by my legs and had a girder across my right shoulder. The rescue men came back and said, 'You may be here sometime yet. We have to shift this lot.' They got the girder off and put a dressing and sling on my right arm. On looking down I saw my legs were trapped in two small hollows under the top part of our sideboard, and I said to the men, 'If you can lift that up an inch or two I think I can pull my legs out.' They said, 'O.K., let's try,' and about five men heaved up the sideboard top about two inches with all the rubble on it and I managed to whip my legs out. They said, 'Well done – that's saved us about three hours' work.'

The firemen had put ladders up the side of the building and wanted to carry me down, but I said 'No, I'll walk,' and although it was very exhausting getting down those ladders I made it. One of the doctors at the incident gave me a shot of morphia and I passed out for a time. When I came to I found myself on a stretcher awaiting attention at the Hospital for Sick Children, Great Ormond Street. My husband had already been taken to the Operating Theatre. There had been so many injured that, as we were among the last to be rescued, Bart's Hospital was full and we were part of the overflow. . . . Three of my office friends had been killed and a young mother who lived in the flat below ours, but by some miracle her baby was rescued unharmed. . . . My own luck held out to some extent as the surgeon at the hospital intended to remove my right arm at the shoulder as it was badly injured, and he came to see me about midnight that Saturday and told me 'We were able to save your arm. What we had thought was fat was in fact muscle and we were able to pull on it to stitch you up. I've never seen so much muscle on a woman.' So my years of P.T. work and lifting stretchers in the Ambulance Service paid dividends. . . . On Sunday morning a nurse took me on my bed to the next ward to see my husband. He had both legs in plaster, both arms in splints and his head and neck were swathed in bandages. He had lost his teeth and his spectacles and looked rather a sorry mess. . . . He was upset when one of the nurses called him 'Grand-dad'.   Mrs 'GYM' GLOVER

(Mrs Glover acquired her nickname, later adopted by her family and friends, as a result of her constant attendance at physical training classes during the 'phoney war'.)

But at least one danger, that of invasion, had lifted. And in November the Home Guard was stood down.

Meanwhile in Colwyn Bay the 'Stand Down' parade assembled. . . . In a steady drizzle, the Ministry [of Food] Home Guard marched at attention on what they expected to be their last parade. At the saluting base, among others, were Colonel J.J. Llewellin, Minister of Food, [and] Colonel J.R. Shennan, Sector Commander. . . . Once past the saluting base, the 11th Denbighs, and the G.P.O. unit, parted company with the 1st Denbighs, and swung down the road into the grounds of Penrhos College. There, drawn up in a hollow square, Home Guards and Auxiliaries were called to attention by Maclean [the battalion commander] for the last time, to be addressed by Colonel

Llewellin and Colonel Shennan. It had been agreed the Minister should dismiss us.

We stood in our hollow square in the wind and rain and saw Colonel Shennan go through the motions of making a speech. We could not hear what he said but we knew what he was saying. Then Colonel Llewellin presented the battalion flag to Maclean. We cheered, as self-consciously and unconvincingly as Englishmen always cheer, except at a football match. Maclean said something; we could not hear what it was, but we knew from experience that he was giving the flag away. He always gave things away. We learned next day that he was giving it to the Imperial War Museum. . . .

The rain came down harder and harder and the wind rose in intensity. Colonel Llewellin loomed through the driving mist and sleet, becoming more indistinguishable from [the mountain of] Carreold Llewellyn every moment. He concluded his speech. Again we went through the motions of cheering. Colonel Llewellin gave the order, for the last time, 'Home Guards and Auxiliaries dismiss!' Symbolically, the regular rigid lines broke and dissolved into a horde of individuals seeking shelter from the storm. As we turned away, it was difficult to get any clear picture of what most of us were feeling. For four years now we had given up a very large proportion of the time not claimed by the Ministry to our military training. Now we could do in our spare time all the things we had wanted to do. Instead of lying behind hedges with rifles in the foothills, we could climb the mountains. Instead of reading War Office manuals, we could read real books, and establish again that contact with things of the mind and the spirit on which we had turned our backs for so long. Or could we? Was there not a barrier between us and our peacetime activities and interests, which would remain there all the time that our younger brothers-in-arms were laying down their lives on the battlefield? Would not the resumption of the peace-time habit of life constitute the re-erection of that barrier between them and us which had almost vanished during our years of service? We did not know. The show was over. It was still raining.   HENRY SMITH

The Allied advances on every front meant an influx of prisoners of war.

The Italian P.O.W.s were not very good workers. Occasionally you might get a good one, but the general run of 'Eyeties' was poor. They were the first to go and sit under a hedge if rain threatened, and I imagine farmers considered them as units of work equal to one very inferior landgirl. They were also liable to make amorous advances – I once had to defend myself with a pitchfork. He soon disappeared – it's a pretty murderous weapon.

The German P.O.W.s were excellent workers. And they were well-behaved – almost too good to be real. Anyway, they helped us a great deal – in fact [due to them] I was let off summer overtime in 1944. If I met a Jerry P.O.W. he would click his heels as he opened a gate for me, with extreme politeness. I was almost embarrassed.

KATHLEEN DICKER

Very few German prisoners ever attempted to escape while in captivity in Britain, and none got home to Germany.

The next excitement took place at the top of Bugby where we tied [the canal boat] up one night. The bike had sprung a puncture, so Kit took it to a local shop before supper and said she would call back later. . . .

She was a long time getting back and had a very odd story to tell. The man had finished the puncture and had left the bike leaning against the wall outside the shop for Kit to pick up. The next time he went outside he found to his horror it had gone; in its place was a brand new man's cycle, all chromium and gadgets *but with both tyres flat*. . . .

We lay in bed and cursed fate. There was a mass of locks ahead and to be without the bike at this juncture was disastrous. It meant that someone had had got to *run* ahead to lock-wheel, [to fill the lock ready for our boat] a very exhausting pastime which I frankly detested. . . .

We did not wait about to see what the day would produce, but let go at our normal time in the morning; we had only got as far as the Toll Office, just round the corner, when a phone message came through saying would we go back again and wait for the bike, which had been found and was being sent by lorry from Towcester? . . .

We couldn't wind [turn round], so had to go backwards to our night's tying-up place, and hung about there for some time before the bobby appeared on the path, triumphantly leading our lost treasure.

'This is yours, isn't it?' he called out and was answered by a concerted shout: 'YES! Where *did* you find it!'

But he was not to be hurried. Laying *Matilda* gently down, he accepted an invitation to come in; removing his helmet and mopping his forehead, he announced dramatically:

'You may like to know, madam, that your bicycle was found in Towcester this morning in the possession of a couple of Jerries, wot was using it to escape from Stafford gaol!'

If he wanted to create a sensation he certainly succeeded. We plied him with questions and finally got the whole story. It appears he had noticed that the chromium-plated bicycle had a wisp or two of straw caught in the spokes, which had suggested to his inquiring mind that the rider had hidden it at some time in a straw-stack. People who don't want to be seen can travel by night and hide up during the day; accordingly, our policeman had thought it worth while to circulate a description of the bike to the County Police, who had passed on the information over a wide radius.

So, when two sad and footsore Germans walked into Towcester, leading the very easily recognisable *Matilda* with her old frame, new seat and total absence of mudguards, and a lady's cycle into the bargain, it didn't take the constable on point duty a week to spot her . . . and them.

Our bobby added that he thought they were rather relieved to be caught again. Knowing the bike, I could well believe it.

We fed him on cocoa and compliments which I think he richly deserved, and further regaled him with a minute tour of the cabin which was the first he had ever been in. Just as he was going, he told us that the unhappy man who had been riding our bike rejoiced in the name of Otto Blink, which quite finished us; the bicycle was renamed from that moment. When we next rode her (or him?) we discovered that the seat had gone up at least four inches, a thing we'd never been able to do as it was rusted into the low position. Evidently the misery and despair of poor Otto had lent power to his arm; the vision thus conjured up positively made our hearts bleed for him.

SUSAN WOOLFITT

The large city hospital [in Yorkshire] admitted all kinds of civilian patients and also had wards reserved for military sick and wounded. By now the pinch of war was being felt. . . . The hospital was short of nursing and domestic staff and crucially short of doctors. Most of the medical staff had joined the armed forces. . . . A good deal of domestic duties and even porters' work had to be taken on by the nursing staff.

Food was now scarce and . . . our dinners were boosted by huge amounts of grated carrot. Jam was a Sunday tea-time treat and was by now a nondescript mixture containing little real fruit. We nurses were all issued weekly with our personal ration of 2 oz. butter. There was always margarine on the table to go with the darkish National bread loaf. . . . There were a number of Irish nurses which brings Bridget to mind. We worked together on night duty and from her holiday at home on a farm she brought back a string of delicious home-fed sausages and Rowntree's jellies (then a luxury). . . . What a feast we had!

In the operating theatres we had to patch and repatch the thin rubber gloves worn at operations. The gloves were in short supply. So were razor blades, and shaving a patient ready for surgery was difficult with only a well used, blunted blade. . . .

In the large, luxuriously furnished nurses' home one day we found our beds covered with gay patchwork quilts – a gift from America. What lovely pictures of colourful dresses they represented. We would hold mock fashion parades of our own, perhaps the showing off of a vest darned nearly all over. I felt like a princess for five minutes in a beautiful heavy silk pre-war bridesmaid's dress of the luxury class. One friend had a bottle of 4711 eau de Cologne which she would dispense generously to any of us who had a headache. Some of us discovered that a solution of potassium permanganate crystals would dye our legs to a tan to simulate stockings. There were plenty of black 'uniform stockings' to be bought, but for each pair we had to give two of our precious clothing coupons.

The hospital received convoys of wounded soldiers from the Far East and Italy. Their first thoughts were for a cup of tea.

It was soon after D-day that we were kept hectically busy. . . . As well as British servicemen, German casualties began to inundate the hospital. As they became less victorious, the Germans apparently neglected their wounded and we received large numbers of them with injuries encased in thick plaster of Paris which should have been removed. The stench was abominable. . . .

Once put to bed in the hospital, they got the same medical and nursing care as that given to our own service patients. In nursing, there is no war. Whereas British and Allied senior officers were placed in semi-private wards, no discrimination was shown to the German officers. Majors and captains were in beds next to the lowest ranks. One boy of sixteen years was the only one with the Nazi imprint of hostility on his face. His eyes were forever wary. This youngster, who had only a superficial head wound, ate ravenously and when offered second helpings of bread and margarine, his apparent disbelief was almost comical. . . . The hospital was one of the first to produce penicillin and it was given as unstintingly to the Germans as to our own casualties. In those early days of its use, three-hourly injections were given throughout the twenty-four hours. Most of these wounded Germans had to be taken to the theatre and be anaesthetised before their stinking plasters could be removed. In the theatre at this time we learned to say the first few German numerals as encouragement to the bewildered men to count their way into oblivion as they were given intravenous anaesthetic. I say 'bewildered', as at first it seemed obvious that they did not expect to be treated well. The look of compassion on the face of the efficient Scottish theatre sister stays with me to this day. . . .

Back on the wards, as the Germans settled down to English hospital life, they shyly produced photographs of their families. One young boy had been educated in England and he would rapidly interpret the radio news to his fellow patients. He would mimic Goebbels, monocle and all, and be hilariously funny in doing so. Once recovered, the Germans were sent to prisoner-of-war camps. A few who still needed hospital care were there at Christmas 1944. As we toured the wards, as is usual at Christmas they noticed those of us who had changed the colour of our uniform dresses. They knew by then that it meant we had passed our State Final Examinations, and seemed pleased to congratulate us.   AUDREY BRASINGTON

The approach of victory was not evident in the shops. In December 1944 the Gas industry issued a recipe for a fuel-saving Christmas pudding making use of carrots.

Fuel is very precious – very scarce. We are expected to – and will – save fuel.

Let us have a 'one boil pudding'. Carrot Pudding, which is almost as good as the traditional Christmas one, *will save from five to eight hours' fuel* in every home where it is made.

CARROT (CHRISTMAS) PUDDING

The dry ingredients can be prepared a day in advance. The pudding itself should be mixed first thing on Christmas morning and put on to steam or boil $3 - 3\frac{1}{2}$ hours before required.

1 teacup self-raising flour; 1 teacup fine bread-crumbs; 1 teaspoon mixed spice; $\frac{3}{4}$ teaspoon bicarbonate of soda; $\frac{1}{4}$ teaspoon salt; $\frac{1}{2}$ cup sugar; 2 tablespoons dried egg (dry); 1 teacup shredded suet or margarine; 1 teacup sultanas; $\frac{1}{2}$ teacup chopped raisins; $\frac{1}{2}$ teacup chopped prunes; 1 – 2 tablespoons marmalade or chopped peel; 1 teacup grated raw carrot; 1 teacup grated raw potato; 2 tablespoons syrup; $\frac{1}{2}$ tablespoon liquid gravy browning; lemon squash to mix.

Mix together the first eight ingredients in the order given. Add and mix in the fruit and marmalade, then the carrot, potato, syrup and liquid gravy browning. Finally, add just enough lemon (or orange) squash to make a firm mixture which drops from the spoon when you give it a little jerk.

Mix all very well.

Two-thirds fill a thickly greased pudding basin. Cover with margarine paper and a cloth and boil or steam for 3 – 3$\frac{1}{2}$ hours. Serve with a nice custard sauce.

Note Boil or steam this pudding very hard for the first hour. You can then reduce the heat considerably.

CHRISTMAS FARE, leaflet issued by the Gas Council

The rocket was a terrible weapon. I saw one explode under a lowering grey sky heavy with rain. The burst of flame against the grey clouds, scarlet and orange and lasting an appreciable time, was an unforgettable sight. One further reflection, listening to the beginning of midnight mass broadcast from the solemn quiet of Buckfast Abbey. A rocket exploded in the [Hainault] Forest (without casualties or damage) but the noise reverberated, roared and remained almost suspended in the midnight air. The all-unknowing choir continued their ageless chant *'Et in terra pax hominibus'* – 'peace on earth to men of goodwill'.   JOHN O'LEARY

1945

And when the war is ended
And we needn't look for lights,
We'll have a lot to talk about
Around the fire o' nights.
And when they ask us what we did
To fight for liberty,
We'll tell our grandsons proudly
That we once belonged to 'B'.

Souvenir of 'B' Group Wardens, Harrogate

'I shall celebrate Victory-Day by switching over to asparagus.'

The last winter of the war, like the first, was an exceptionally severe one. Rationing, shortages of all kinds, long hours of work, the flying bombs and rockets and above all the failure to achieve victory in 1944 – indeed the Allied armies had just suffered a sharp reverse in the Ardennes – all combined to produce war weariness. But spring came at last, and with it victory. In April the Allied armies crossed the Rhine, the Russians stormed into Berlin and Hitler killed himself. In May Germany finally surrendered. The splendid summer which followed also recalled 1940, and, as if to compensate for the war in the West having dragged on far longer than anyone had expected, in August victory in the Far East came far sooner than even the most optimistic had dared to hope.

For a few sensitive civilians, though not for the men in the Forces whose lives were saved by it, the defeat of Japan was overshadowed by the means – the dropping of two atomic bombs – which had brought it about. For most people, however, the only emotion was one of relief. Like 1940, too, 1945 included a political sensation, the sudden overthrow of Winston Churchill's government in a general election; a clear indication that whatever other casualties Britain had suffered in the war, British democracy had survived unharmed.

29 December, 1944 – 5 January, 1945 Well, here we are, with another year starting. I think in the first week of the last one I expressed great hopes for the coming year and what did we get? Flying-bombs, turned out of the house from delayed action bombs, phosphorus bombs, and now rockets. . . . Just where I was before, in the same old office, though it's windowless and knocked about a bit. . . . So this year I am hoping for nothing, expecting nothing – and will doubtless get nothing. Oh yes, we will win the war, there's no doubt of that, and away from London I imagine one can see the dawn of victory, but here we are tired and depressed. And this week has been a wonderful foretaste of what is before us . . . fog and ice have been the rule and now a biting wind has added its joy. The rockets are falling much faster and the horrible rolling explosions are now becoming as frequent as our other familiars.   VIVIENNE HALL

Although the maximum age for women to be directed into war work was fifty, many over that age had volunteered to take a man's place. Among them was a woman living in Sussex who now discovered some of the hardships of her new life as a postwoman.

We had a fortnight of snow early in 1945; the first real fall since I had been put on post work. . . .

Soon it came, large flakes falling fast, until in about half an hour the roads and fields were thickly covered, and the hedges already heavy with the fall. . . . It was still quite easy to ride on the main road for, though fairly deep, the snow was soft and one did not skid, and riding in the tracks made by cars it was safe. But very soon in the side roads and lanes it became too deep and, finding that my brakes and wheels were getting clogged, I abandoned my bicycle and set out to walk.

Snow goes through leather boots as though they are blotting-paper, and my feet were soon soaked. . . . Coming back I found my bicycle and parcel bag thickly covered by snow, and I myself looked like a snowman. I mounted again to find that coming downhill the only way to stop was to run into a bank and fall off, the brakes being no use at all. So I walked the rest of the way home.

That night there was more snow. I decided to walk that morning, carrying a small sack on my back with as many little parcels as I could take, and any registered parcels there might be. The registered parcels one must always take, even if it means leaving others behind. . . .

I started up the Rectory Field, a steep path leading to the Rectory and Church Hill – a short cut for a walker. Dawn was just breaking, and the snow, too, helped to make it light. I noticed how very black the trees and houses appeared against the dark grey sky and the whiteness of the snow. The church tower in the trees stood out black on the hill, but the large Rectory looked more friendly with here and there a yellow light shining – the only colour I saw on that grey morning, until later on the landgirls appeared with their gay handkerchiefs and rosy faces. . . .

After three days I think we all began to feel fairly tired. Walking and slithering and carrying a load on slippery and snowy roads for perhaps seven hours on end does make one's back and legs ache. . . .

Not meaning to complain, but rather thinking aloud, I came into the hall of a farmhouse, stamping the snow off my boots.

'Oh, my feet are so wet and cold,' I said.

'Wait a minute,' said the girl who came to meet me.

She ran upstairs, and returned with a pair of gumboots, almost new.

'You can have these if they fit. They are too small for me, and I have another pair.'

They were a little large, but wearable, and I was overjoyed. I thanked her profusely. The thought of dry feet was delightful, and I could hardly be grateful enough. . . .

On Monday night, after a better day with hardened snow on the roads, the wind got up. On waking next morning I went to the window to inspect the weather; to my dismay there had been another heavy fall, and my window-seat and floor were covered with drifted snow. Outside it was deep on the road, and had blown in drifts against the walls. . . .

Picking up my overcoat, torch and gumboots, I went out. The garden gate was stuck, and in trying to open it I slid in the woolly-lined boots I was wearing, and fell flat in the snow. That was a bad start.

To my horror I found, when we reached the Post Office, that I had dropped one of my gumboots when I fell on the garden path. I could not possibly fetch it before starting on my round, and my heart sank.

'I don't see myself getting round North Common in this,' I said; 'what *does* one do on a post round when it is so deep?'

'At our place,' said Mr Collins, 'we reckon we must get round somehow.'

So now I knew what I must do at *our* place. . . .

Whenever I saw a light, and had a letter or parcel for that house or cottage, I tapped on the door, told my sad tale, and asked, 'Can you lend me some gumboots?'

I tried the Police Station, and the kind policeman on duty and Mrs Sanders, the wife of the policeman next door, both racked their brains for a solution of my problem; but all they could produce was a pair of overshoes a size too small. So on I went again to No. 4, where I sometimes had a cup of tea.

'I know,' said Mrs Smith, 'I'll give you a very old pair of my husband's socks, and we'll push them on over your boots.'

It was a struggle to get them on, but the effect was wonderful. The heel got no further than my instep, but this acted as a brake. . . . All went well until, when nearing the Land Army Hostel after four or five miles of walking, my lovely socks came in half at the soles. I arrived at the Hostel with both the toes full of snowballs which beat the ground in front of me as I walked.

The landgirls had just had their dinner. They brought me a cup of tea, and . . . one of them lent me a needle and thread, and helped me to pull off the soaking socks and empty out the snow. After sewing up the holes I started off again. . . .

At last I reached the village street. My socks were again in half, and I flapped back to the Post Office with more snowballs in my toes – and feeling very silly.

Next day the thaw began.   MARGARET STEWART ROBERTS

For women doing their war-work on the canals an even greater adversary was ice.

The ice made an enormous difference to everything. If you tied up at night with a strap [rope] that was needed next day, when morning came, you would find that it was impossible to use it – it was frozen as hard as the branch of a tree. The weather . . . was freezing all day long, so that the ropes would stiffen between one lock and the next; the cotton-line, which we used a great deal for locking, was like a steel hoop with a coating of ice all over it and it stuck to your hands when you picked it up. So did the shaft; the metal part at the end was really painful to handle, giving you a sensation like an electric shock.

It did not matter how carefully we swept down the night before; the remains of the snow and damp had frozen into a thin film of ice on all the sheets by next day. Walking down the top-planks was really tricky . . . We used to spread the ashes from the fire on the gunwale of the motor and on the edge of the butty hatches on which we had to walk and stand. . . .

The cold only worried us really when we had a long pound to do, against driving snow, or, far worse, wind and sleet. Then it did go right through you and your feet would be like blocks of ice, standing steering for a long patch at a time. Working through the locks was nice and warm; I used to start off with all my wraps on and cast them off as the drawing of paddles got my circulation going. The locks themselves were quite incredible in the ice. . . . It took us twenty minutes of concerted effort to get the gates shut so that we could empty the lock.

Lock gates have not got hinges . . . but are hung on the collar and pin principle . . . The collar had frozen solid on to the pin on which it was supposed to turn, and the ice had got to be broken down by brute force before the gate would move. . . .

One of the compensations about this Arctic spell was the hoar frost.

On the Cut it was beautiful. . . . the sky of lowering grey made a perfect background for the white lacery of the frosted trees, every little bunch of twigs on the top-most branches standing out with the delicacy of a Chinese painting. It was the loveliest when there was no sun to give colour to the scene; or in the evening when sometimes the sun was just sufficiently there to redden the sky with its setting glow, and throw a pink shadow on the snow.

And all the day long that wonderful muffled stillness from the thick blanket of the snow.

The quietness was emphasised by the fact that there was very little traffic now. We heard afterwards that most of the boats had tied up at least a day before we did, but we were so determined not to let down the 'weaker' sex by giving up first, that we actually went on longer than most of the others.   SUSAN WOOLFITT

For many the symbol of approaching victory was the reappearance of a luxury fruit which had been scarcest of all.

Just before the end of the war, a girl in my class brought a banana to school. Most of us could not remember having seen one before and she enjoyed making a display of herself. I felt disgusted, as after every nibble, she made comments on its delicious flavour. Most of us felt somewhat jealous and one girl took the rejected peel and began to scratch the pith to try to gather the flavour from this. When I told my mother about this, she felt very angry . . . as she strongly disapproved of any showing off.   EILEEN NIXON

At last, with the spring, came the final Allied advance and the surrender of Germany. The official announcement of the news was delayed, long after it had begun to leak out, to try to please the Russians, who had not yet signed their separate armistice agreement in Berlin. The result in Great Britain was universal frustration. The war which had begun in anti-climax ended in muddle.

On Monday, 7th May, I was due to go back, and spent an agonising day waiting for the news to break so that I need not go. Not that I didn't want to go back to the boats; merely that I could think of nothing worse than having to spend two days' holiday, and such a holiday, down the Newdigate arm, which is scarcely more than a ditch, narrow and malodorous, with coal and cinders on the one hand, and rats in the muddy bank on the other. . . .

Although the evening papers were full of headlines there was still nothing definite by the time I was due at Euston for the 4.25 and I trailed miserably through the station to find my train. Suddenly the loudspeaker said in imperious accents: 'Here is an important announcement!'

Everybody in the whole station stopped dead as if instantaneously petrified. The voice went on:

'The 4.9 for Northampton will leave from Platform 6 and NOT from Platform 7 as stated on the indicator.'

There was – or it felt as if there was – a sort of howl of fury from everyone on the station, including myself; deliverance had really seemed to be at hand and now there was nothing for it but to go back to Coventry, which I duly did. When I got back to where I had left the boats there wasn't a sign of them, but an obliging boater next door said they had moved round to Hawkesbury, 'loaded you this morning, they did'. This meant a walk of half a mile down the towpath carrying my bag and wearing a very uncomfortable pair of heavy boots that my husband had had in the Home Guard. It was also boiling hot.

When I got to Hawkesbury, passing a bean-field in full bloom on the way which partially restored me, the others took one look at my draggled form and said in chorus: 'Whatever HAVE you come back for? Don't you know the war's nearly over and it will be V-Day tomorrow?' . . .

By the time the news did come through, the wireless battery had practically run down, which lent a nightmare quality to everything. We only dared to turn it on for a second at a time, judge by the tone of the voice what the news was, and hastily switch it off again. . . .

In the morning I had a brainwave and suggested that we should all hitch-hike to Stratford-on-Avon and spend our two days there. It took a little while to woo Margaret away from her dancing idea but she finally decided that she would come too. We put everything we could into the cabins, asked a boater friend to keep an eye on the rest for us, locked up and set off with enough food to keep us from starvation if we could not get anything else.

The thing of most importance now was to get to Stratford in time to hear Mr Churchill's broadcast at three o'clock. We only just did it. First there was a walk of a mile or more to the main Coventry road. Then we found there were no buses and had to wait some minutes before we found a car which answered our flagging. He took us to the outskirts of Coventry and almost at once we found another lift to Kenilworth. There our luck changed and we waited for what seemed hours till a large lorry came by. To our joy they were N.F.S. men who were going right to Stratford; we piled into the back and covered the remaining distance at breakneck speed, rattling about in the back of the lorry, with nothing to hold on to, like peas in a pod. But no one minded.   SUSAN WOOLFITT

8 May 1945   We were told on the wireless and in the newspapers and in our office that on VE-Day all work would cease for two days; and we wondered how it would all happen. What did happen was that the announcement was given out after most of we early risers had gone to bed, so that only a few who heard it stayed away from work next morning, and the rest of us turned up as usual.

It was a lovely May morning. We started to set in our letters, wondering all the time what would happen. The telephone bell rang, and Mr Walker went over to answer it.

'Yes. Is it? Now – leave off now? I see. Cheerio!' We all stopped to listen, and as he rang off he turned to us: 'It's over,' he said. 'You can all go home.'

I don't think anyone spoke much. We sat back against our benches, leaving our letters half sorted as they were. It was as though one had been suddenly relieved of a great pain, which left one with a feeling of peace, but still very tired. Someone suggested making tea, and we all went downstairs, and over our teacups we talked quietly.

'How will you go back?' they asked me – it was about 6 am. 'I shall walk,' I said, 'It's such a lovely morning, I shall enjoy it.'

'I'll drive you home,' said Mr Barton. He had recently been made Postman Supervisor. 'Then I'll drive over to Petworth to see the Postmaster and tell him about it all.'

Bessie, my maid, was awake, and came to her window as we drove up in the red van. 'It's over, Bessie,' I called. 'Come down and we'll have breakfast and go for a walk. We'll go and see if Mrs Marjoram is up and wish her good morning.'

We went out over the common, my Scottie dog delighted to have such an early walk. The morning was very fine – a perfect May day; the bright fresh green and blue sky and all the colours of early May, with a faint haze over the Downs, which made everywhere so sweet and quiet and peaceful.

We came down the slope on the far side of the common. 'She's up, then,' I said, as we saw the smoke rising from Mrs Marjoram's chimney. She saw us coming, and came to the window.

'It's over,' we said, 'and we've come to say good morning.'

This led to cups of tea once more, and, after a little rest and chat, we walked up the village street. Flags were being put up already; and later on there was to be a service in the church. People had miraculously found red, white and blue clothing to put on, and rosettes of red, white and blue, or buttonholes of red, white and blue flowers.

Later that day my cousin John came down from London. He looked thin, pale and gaunt after many nights through the war running air raid shelters and roof-spotting for fly-bombs in one of the hottest parts.

He had letters he must write that evening, so I wandered down the road alone. The light was going; the lovely clear sky was still blue, with here and there a star. Over the Downs towards the sea the guns from the coast [firing a victory salute] made flashes against the sky, and looking towards London there was a glow of light from bonfires, and searchlights and flares.

I went back to the cottage, where John sat writing in the window – no blackout now, and the light streaming out over the garden.

'You must come with me now, John, and see the lights!'

He had finished, and put his writing away. We strolled down the street, and stood at the quiet corner, for all the neighbours were down at the far end of the village, where a bonfire was alight on the green in front of the 'Swan'; we could see the glow.

All along the Downs beacons were shining and flickering; more lights flashed from the ships; over towards London the skies were full of lights. We thought of the horror and dread with which we had looked that way not so long ago. The stars were shining as the sky darkened, and near where we stood two nightingales were singing.
MARGARET STEWART ROBERTS

D-Day came and went . . . then one day V-Day arrived. We turned on all the lights, took out the piano, dusted the fairy-lights and strung them on the trees and . . . gave the kids the best party we possibly could. Two of my friends and I walked down to Chorlton with three empty prams and bought bread, jellies, potted meat, anything we could buy, and fitted them until the prams were full to the top. We took tables on to the green, made sandwiches, hot dogs, cooked sausages rolled in buttered bread with mustard on. More of the mothers and wives made cakes and scones and we all brought anything out that would burn and had a gloriously, brightly, burning bonfire. That was the end of our war, the housewives' war. . . .

MARY SMITH

When I had finished my luncheon, I found . . . the whole of Trafalgar Square and Whitehall was packed with people. . . . As Big Ben struck three there was an extraordinary hush over the assembled multitude, and then came Winston's voice. He was short and effective, merely announcing that unconditional surrender had been signed, and naming the signatories. . . . 'The evil-doers,' he intoned, 'now lie prostrate before us.' The crowd gasped at this phrase. 'Advance Britannia!' he shouted at the end, and there followed the Last Post and 'God Save the King' which we all sang very loud indeed. And then cheer upon cheer.

I dashed back into the House and into the Chamber. After the roar and heat outside, it was like suddenly entering an Oxford quadrangle. Cool and hushed the Chamber was, with P.J. Grigg answering questions as if nothing unusual were impending. The clock reached 3.15, which is the moment when Questions automatically close. We knew it would take Winston some time to get to the House from Downing Street in such a crowd. We therefore made conversation by asking supplementary questions until 3.23. Then a slight stir was observed behind the Speaker's chair, and Winston, looking coy and cheerful, came in. The House rose as a man, and yelled and yelled and waved their Order Papers. He responded, not with a bow exactly, but with an odd shy jerk of the head and with a wide grin. Then he started to give us the statement that he had just made on the wireless. When he had finished reading, he put his manuscript aside and with wide gestures thanked and blessed the House for all its noble support of him throughout these years.

Then he proposed that 'this House do now attend at the Church of St. Margaret's, Westminster, to give humble and reverent thanks to Almighty God for our deliverance from the threat of German domination'. The motion was carried, and the Serjeant at Arms put the mace on his shoulder and, following the Speaker, we all strode out.

Through the Central Lobby we streamed, through St. Stephen's Chapel, and out into the sunshine of Parliament Square. We entered St. Margaret's by the West door which was furthest away from us, and that meant a long sinuous procession through a lane kept open for us through the crowd. . . . The service itself was very short and simple, and beautifully sung. Then the Chaplain to the Speaker read in a loud voice the names of those who had laid down their lives: 'Ronald Cartland; Hubert Duggan; Victor Cazalet; John Macnamara; Robert Bernays' – only the names of my particular friends registered on my consciousness. I was moved. The tears came into my eyes. Furtively I wiped them away. . . .

Then back we streamed into the House and adjourned for the day. Winston made a dash for the smoking-room. When he was passing through Central Hall the crowd there broke into loud clapping. He hesitated and then hurried on. A little boy dashed out: 'Please, sir, may I have your autograph?' Winston took a long time getting out his glasses and wiping them. Then he ruffled the little boy's hair and gave him back his . . . album. 'That will remind you of a glorious day,' he said, and the crowd clapped louder than before. In the smoking-room Kenneth Pickthorn produced a bottle of champagne and we clinked glasses. . . .

[That evening] I . . . walked back through the happy but quite sober crowds to Trafalgar Square. The National Gallery was alive with every stone outlined in flood-lighting, and down there was Big Ben with a grin upon his illumined face. The statue of Nelson was picked out by a searchlight, and there was the smell of distant bonfires in the air. I walked to the Temple and beyond. Looking down Fleet Street one saw the best sight of all – the dome of St. Paul's rather dim-lit, and then above it a concentration of searchlights upon the huge golden cross. So I went to bed.

That was my victory day.   HAROLD NICOLSON

8 May 1945

This is VE-Day.

Last night, looking from the same bedroom window from which I saw London burning in the Blitz, and from which we watched the flying-bombs sailing towards us like red stars, we watched London's bonfires celebrating victory. For a brief moment one might have thought London was once again the victim of raiders, though the flickering fires were less and the glow in the sky not so fierce.

This morning the sky was dull, and light rain fell; many a house is sporting its Union Jack. . . . The Russian hammer and sickle can be seen, too. But in my neighbourhood the streets were as quiet as on a Sunday. . . . This afternoon I went into London to walk through Whitehall, Trafalgar Square and Piccadilly. The sun came out, and London was gay, gay and densely thronged but, in a sense, comparatively quiet. I saw only half a dozen people tipsy, and these hung from a second-storey window in Piccadilly Circus, one woman beating time and wearing a large imitation policeman's helmet. American soldiers were throwing oddments down from the windows of their club in Piccadilly; suddenly a great streamer of paper came down, and for a moment we wondered how this had been contrived; then we saw it was a roll of toilet paper, and everybody laughed. Streets were crowded, and looked, from a short distance off, impassable. But in the main one could move about. It was a crowd light-hearted, wearing its red, white and blue rosettes as on a Cup Final Day, and wearing, too, a host of comic little hats, silver cones, tricoloured cones, and in one instance, small royal crowns. Some hats had 'Welcome Home' written on them. Two soldiers sported a badge: 'Pity the poor unemployed'. . . . There was little singing or jigging about, but I heard 'Marching through Georgia' in Whitehall, and the Volga Boatmen's song in the Haymarket. . . . In the heavens a number of Flying Fortresses were moving on, pleasure bent. From Trafalgar Square five or six in formation seemed to be flying up Northumberland Avenue. Over the Admiralty one dropped two cerise flares, and later I saw a Lancaster let fall a Very light over St. James's Park. Girls had climbed on to various clumps of stone and turned themselves into living statues; the lions' heads in Trafalgar Square were being sat upon, and in Whitehall a girl had clambered onto a stone ledge twenty-five feet above the street. In Piccadilly we slipped into a News theatre and here heard the only bitter comment, from the woman taking our tickets who said: 'All celebrating like fools and the war not over.' Maybe she had a husband or a lover in Burma. . . .

Tonight the city was thronged. The King and Mr Churchill have been on to the Palace balcony and have been greeted with the sort of delight shipwrecked mariners bestow on a sail. Buildings have been floodlit so that Admiralty Arch seemed to be rising out of the ground, and Horatio Nelson, standing aloft in a greenish ray of light, was as romantic as even he could have wished. Some of the effects had great beauty, notably when the first light caught the dome of St. Paul's and slowly the cross began to shine. One watched, leaning on a ruined wall in this neighbourhood where so much about the church is ruin and flatness and the old church stands with a massive serenity; and one wondered anew at the miracle of it. One other thing caught the imagination; not far from the Mall some gas jets had been lit, and they flared in the open like Roman torches. And then the heavens were pierced by swords of light as so often they have been pierced by those searchlight beams which sought the enemy. Now they wove in a kind of geometric dance of rejoicing, and we watched the beauty of them and tried to realise, and as for me, found it very hard to realise, that we shall not be bombed again. . . .   JAMES LANSDALE HODSON

Suddenly the war in Europe was over. On Marian's fourth birthday, after the last few days of confusion in Berlin, she and I listened to the wireless announcement of the unconditional surrender of the German armed forces.

'Marian,' I said, 'you must remember this all your life. It's history.'

But the reception was poor; and I could see she would forget at once any word she happened to hear.

In the morning I got the little girls ready for the junketings on the village green. I had washed and ironed clean frocks for them; and I tied up their curls with red, white and blue ribbons. I went down to the kitchen for my own clean clothes. My mother held out her mackintosh to me.

'If you run,' she said, 'you'll just catch the next bus into Eastbourne, and then the train. I'll look after the children.'

'But my clothes –' I said, looking down at my garden-stained cotton frock and sandals.

'It doesn't matter. You look all right. I've put some money in one pocket and some buns in the other. Only hurry!'

I ran with the mackintosh to the bus-stop, and jumped on board as the bus was starting. At Eastbourne station I heard Churchill's victory speech. Crowds came off the train from London. There were only two other passengers on the London-bound train. . . .

All the way up in the train I looked out of the window. There was not a house in town or country without its flag flying for the day. Rural cottages, great Victorian villas, rows of railway-side tenements, how-ever battered they or their surroundings, all had their flags.

In the West End of London the traffic had stopped, and Londoners in summer clothes walked slowly about the streets. Their pace, physically and emotionally, was that of a Sunday stroll. There was no wild excitement, no frenzy.

I guessed that Donald might be at his club, and started to walk towards it through the friendly but lethargic crowd. As I passed Buckingham Palace, a gentle roar went up in salute of the King and Queen coming out on to the balcony. Their slow waving acknow-ledgement echoed the exhausted relief felt by everyone.

'Oh, how I love them today', said a small red-faced old dear at my elbow. 'I come up special to see them, same as the Queen came down special to see me after our building went up.' She cackled at her own joke. 'She did though, and spoke to my neighbour. Ah, but she's a lovely woman.'

To my relief Donald was in his club. Combing London for him on VE-Night would have been no fun.

'I knew you'd come, darling,' he said.

Alan joined us. And, when we had heard the King's speech on the radio, we three went out to walk with the crowds.

As we neared the Palace, the King and Queen came out again. Almost every quarter of an hour that day they appeared on their balcony. We climbed up a heap of Palace coke which was being used as a public grandstand; but still I could not see over the heads of the crowds. Suddenly, Alan, in a burst of patriotism and helpfulness, clasped me round my knees and lifted me off my feet. A number of other patriots rolled down the coke heap with us. . .

Licensing hours were extended, and it was good to see the doors of restaurants and bars and pubs left open with their lights shining out onto the pavement. It was good to be able to saunter in without having to disentangle oneself from the folds of a flapping blackout curtain, which I once heard a soldier describe as like getting mixed up in the skirts of a nun.

By now bonfires had been lit at street-corners. We walked through Soho. There the celebrations had a pattern of their own. Traditional dances of central Europe were being performed with all the skill and seriousness of Highland reels. Foreigners, as grateful for victory as any of us, if not more so, advanced and retired and turned and skipped to their own thin mournful chants. Their old people stood round in the firelight clapping in time.

Donald and I returned to [his] room in Bloomsbury . . . His landlady was in a fine state. Part of her back wall had collapsed.

'Today, of all days!' she exclaimed, at the injustice of life. 'They'll never accept it as war damage now. Why couldn't it have fallen down yesterday?'   VERILY ANDERSON

At last, on May 11th, I was able to tell the School that we were going home . . . I shall never forget their reception of the news and the cheers that welcomed me when I entered the crypt . . .

So, on Monday, May 28th, we came home. We shall not forget that day, nor the fortnight which preceded our homecoming . . . We had to arrange for the transport of furniture and equipment for 300, a dozen pianos, other musical instruments, dinner equipment, science apparatus, art equipment, games equipment, an incredible quantity of books, bicycles, all our own personal belongings (and one accumulates a great deal of junk in five years), 232 children, 28 adults, and a number of cats, dogs and rabbits; and we lived in a world of lorries, railway containers and Weetabix boxes, the latter all bearing the suitable inscription, 'Be brave; courage is catching'. . . .

We shall long remember, too, the send-off which we were given from Llanelly; the journey by special train (shared with the Honor Oak School), and our reception at Paddington, where we were met by . . . the station master, and seen off in special buses; and the reunion in the School Hall with parents. . . . And at last, after we had all joined in singing from our hearts, 'Now thank we all our God', and parents had collected the right children and the right luggage . . . we went home . . . We went out as a school, and it was as a school that we came home.   M. DOROTHY BROCK

Just after the General Election of 1945 a meeting was arranged at the local steelworks where I was employed, where the visitor was Mr George Strauss, Minister of Supply in the new Government. . . . All the local trade union officials, plus minor and senior staff people, were invited to the Board Room to meet the Minister. The chairman of the day was the managing director . . . who was upset by the election result. . . . Questions were asked for from the floor. . . . Statements were made by various union representatives about the shortages of

226

various foods, certain iron ore – and when was clothing to be taken off ration? Then up jumped Joe and asked why there was a shortage of essential things such as alarm clocks, which were wanted by people who have to get up in the morning. All of a sudden the meeting came to life, everybody was talking, from senior staff men to the workmen, 'Why should we be short of these items?' Then the Minister got up. 'Gentlemen,' was the first word he spoke, 'if you are short of this item I will see you get them in the future. Let me have details.'

The Minister was true to his statement, a list was made of people who required clocks, in no time over 230 people were given permits to buy clocks in a local dealers and for months afterwards permits were granted.

To this day the individual who spoke up is known as 'Alarm Clock Joe'.   J. WILLIAMS

For the civilian VE-Day was really the end of the war. The celebrations on VJ-Day, marking Japan's surrender on 14 August, had the air of a repeat performance.

On the first VJ-day [of the two-day holiday], the Wednesday, I suddenly decided, in my bath, that I would like to have some special memory of it. So I raced through my shaving, and hurried in the light drizzle across the Park to the Palace, where a sizeable crowd was collected to see the State procession set off to open Parliament. The guardsmen lining the route seemed to be in the same happy, informal mood as the crowd: then the sudden clap and rattle as arms were presented all down the Mall, the clatter of the black chargers of the Life Guards as they pranced out of the Palace courtyard heightened the tension. They were followed by the open barouche in which were seated the King, looking rather nervous and leaning forward in his Admiral's uniform, with the powder-blue Queen waving and smiling beside him – a cheer from the crowd – more Life Guards – more barouches filled with officials – no cheers. . . . As I walked back, I passed a shabby little old woman stumbling along by herself, a beautiful smile on her face, and muttering 'lovely dresses . . . lovely dresses . . .'

The evening was perfectly clear, warm and still: it was impossible to resist going out to see how London was celebrating, to join in some-how, somewhere. We went down from Carrington House by Whitehorse Street, and as we emerged into Piccadilly, we were confronted by an extraordinary sight: the brilliantly lit street – that was strange enough in itself – was packed with people as far as the eye could see, in both directions, with no wheeled traffic to be discovered anywhere, except one slowly moving car on to which people kept climbing and crowding. As we walked towards the Circus, the mass turned out not to be so impassable as it seemed, because everyone was quietly, happily, aimlessly on the move. One longed for bands and music everywhere; but it was, after all, a totally unrehearsed occasion, and people found their own haphazard way of giving vent to their feelings, as if scarcely able to believe that the long, long horror was over at last, bemused in their joy, with exhaustion suddenly coming over them. There were sailors giving girls endless, passionate kisses in the middle of the street; here and there people threw fire crackers; climbed lamp-posts; occasionally burst out singing; exclaimed to one another delightedly at the display of the searchlights; and most extraordinary of all, suddenly made dancing rings, performing strange, impromptu, atavistic steps, as they might have when the news of Waterloo, or of the Armada's defeat came through; then wandered on again. We made our way past the Athenaeum, where torches were flaming over the portico and all around the Clubs were blazing with lights and hung with flags, down into the Mall, where we were confronted by the same perspective of massed crowds, thickening up to the Victoria Memorial: at the end the great illuminated facade of the Palace, with an enormous, raw half-moon hanging over it. As we came nearer, the noise of singing increased; the crowds were finally jammed beyond movement, and on the Memorial itself people were clustered as thickly as swarming bees. Every few minutes the singing would pause, and the chant would go up: '*We* want the *King* . . . *We* want the *King*. . .'. Until at last the french windows on the far red-draped, fairytale balcony were opened, and the King and Queen, diminutive but glittering figures – the Queen's diamonds flashed into the night under the arc-lights – came out to wave and be greeted by cheer after cheer, waving of hands, and the singing of 'For he's a jolly good fellow'.

Then many dispersed – though many others, insatiable, waited for a later reappearance – and the squashed but happy crowd poured through the gates into Green Park, where the sudden soaring of fireworks lit up the innumerable couples on the grass and under the trees.   JOHN LEHMANN

Food was still rationed when my husband came home from Burma in October 1945. . . . I shall never forget the time I spent my precious points on rice and tinned pilchards, which we had come to regard as a delicacy, and preparing a meal fit for a king, as I thought, only to be told by my husband that he did not really enjoy it, as rice and pilchards were more or less the staple diet when he was cut off by the Japs at Imphal for six months. JOAN BAKER

Husbands returned home, each to his own private welcome. Mine returned on 13 November 1945. When my sons saw him the eldest said, 'Oh, you are my daddy!' The second said, 'You are Mr Smith!' and my youngest, poor frail little thing, said, 'Ooh, 'im?', the first words he had ever said. This was the first time he had ever seen his father. MARY SMITH

A man from a glass works was sent by the Council to ascertain how many broken windows we required replacing. He refused to include the cracked ones, and bent down to speak to my little boy. 'You broke those, didn't you, sonny, with your football?' he said. His method of trying to extract information from a child savoured of Gestapo methods. I had never cheated, and I wouldn't be accused of doing so. I grabbed [him] by the collar of his jacket, and ran him from the back door to the front. I opened the door with my left hand and flung him through the door on to the step. The war was over and I'd had enough of dictators.

In 1939 I wouldn't have said 'Boo' to a goose. By 1945 here I was throwing men about with the nonchalance of a music hall bouncer. I think the war did something for me, most definitely. MAY BECKER

Retrospect

On the morning of 8th May, 1945, I was told Peter [the writer's husband, critically ill after an emergency operation] was out of danger. . . . It was also my twenty-sixth birthday.

That evening, after the children were asleep in bed, I went outside and sat on the low front wall before the house – the wall from which the ornamental iron railings had long since been taken for the 'war effort'. It was a warm, still evening and the long street was quiet. But from almost every window light streamed out, splashing onto the pavement. Curtains had been pulled aside and blackouts had been removed. For the first time in nearly six years we were released from the necessity of hiding out in darkness and people were reacting by letting the lights from their homes shine out.

Too tired to move, I sat thinking of those six years. When they began I'd been twenty, full of the enthusiasms, ambitions, certainties and energy of youth. I'd married and borne children, but the war had stolen from us the simple ordinary joys of a young couple shaping a shared life. Our first home had been burnt to rubble and with it had gone many of the gifts which relatives and friends had given us and which should have been treasured for life, while what had been salvaged would always bear the marks of that night of destruction. We had known the agony of separation and the too rare, too short, too heightened joys of reunions. Apart, we had endured illnesses and dangers and fears for each other. As a family too we had been separated and now must learn to live together, overcoming the barriers set up by experiences which had not been shared. . . .

I thought of those who had been dear to us who had not lived to see this. . . . Of John, who had stood at the altar with us on our wedding day, John, who had . . . been trapped in his cockpit when his plane sank beneath the waves. . . . Of Ron, constant companion of my brother since schooldays . . . who had vanished without trace when the troopship he was on had been sunk by the Japanese; of Peter, my girlhood friend's gay, kind brother . . . who had been shot while trying to escape from the prisoner-of-war camp to which he'd been taken. . . . They were all so young. The youngest died at nineteen, the oldest at twenty-four. I sat thinking of them . . . and then went indoors to stand looking at the sleeping faces of my two little sons, whose lives lay before them in a world at peace.   MEGAN RYAN

LIST OF SOURCES

The sources of extracts are normally listed under author, or, where this is unknown, under their opening words. Others, such as the Ministries, the W.V.S., the R.S.P.C.A., *The Times* and *Housewife* magazine, are listed under those names.

Allingham, Margery. *The Oaken Heart*. Michael Joseph, 1941: 6–8, 45–6
'And when the war is ended . . .' '*B*' *Group Harrogate: Civil Defence Wardens Service Souvenir*. Privately published, n.d. (c.1945): 211
Anderson, Verily. *Spam Tomorrow*. Rupert Hart-Davis, 1956: 99–100, 121–3, 187–9, 224–6.
Angus, (Miss) Helen. Private information: 31–2.
Anti-Gas Protection . . . see Home Security, Ministry of

Baker, (Mrs) Joan. Private information: 229.
Banner, Hubert S. *Kentish Fire*. Hurst & Blackett, 1944: 55–7, 145–8.
Baring, Norah. *A Friendly Hearth*. Jonathan Cape, 1946: 84–8.
'Because of the pail . . .' Quoted by Woolton, Earl of (*q.v.*)
Becker, (Mrs) May. Private information: 160, 229.
Belfrage, Bruce. *One Man in his Time*. Hodder & Stoughton, 1951: 115–16.
Bells, Go Down, The. Anon. Methuen, 1942: 29, 32, 71.
Benson, Theodora. *Sweethearts and Wives*. Faber, 1942: 21–22, 27–9.
Bombs, Weights and Prices. Wings for Victory leaflet in War Savings series. National Savings Committee. n.d. (c.1943): 181.
Brasington, (Mrs) Audrey. Private information: 207–9.
Brewin, (Mrs) Doris. Private information: 95–8, 141.
Brock, M. Dorothy. 'An Unusual Happening'. In *The Story of the Mary Datchelor School, 1877–1957*. Hodder & Stoughton, 1957: 5–6, 226.
Burnie, (Mrs) Gladys. Private information: 38–40.

Calder, Ritchie. *Carry on London*. English Universities Press, 1941: 89–91.
Chandos, Viscount. *The Memoirs of Lord Chandos*. Bodley Head, 1962: 117–18.
Crombie, Lt.-Col. D.C. *History of the Fifth (Bideford) Battalion, Devon Home Guard*. Burleigh Press, Bristol, 1946: 136–7.
Cross, (Mrs.) Pat. Private information: 19–20.

Daily Express, The. 16 February 1938: 3.
Denholm, (Miss) Jean. Private information: 26–7.
Devereux, (Mrs) Brenda. Private information: 171–2, 201–2.

Dicker, (Miss) Kathleen. Private information: 134, 205–6.
Dilly, (Mrs) Rose. Private information: 151–2.

Evans, D.H. Ltd. *Winter Sale Catalogue*. February 1940: 45.
Faviell, Frances. *Chelsea Concerto*. Cassell, 1959: 12–13, 68–71, 80–81, 98–9, 104–12.
Finlow, Clarence. Private information: 180–81.
Fitzgibbon, Constantine. *The Blitz*. Wingate, 1957: 112–13.
Flight, H.E. (ed.) *North-West (London) Frontier, No. 6 Company, 23rd Middlesex Battalion, Home Guard*. Privately printed, 1946: 120–21.
Food, Ministry of. *Let's Talk about Xmas Food*. (Advertisement). December 1941: 135–6.
    'Because of the pail . . .' (Advertisement). No. 150.
– Recipe for Woolton Pie. In Leaflet No. 12, *Cheese*, n.d: 154–5.
– Recipe for Mock Lemon Curd. In Leaflet No. 6, *Carried Meals Snacks and Sandwiches*, Food Advice Service. March 1944: 155.
– Recipe for Carrot Croquettes. In War Cookery Leaflet No. 4.: 155.
Francis, Maclaren. Private information: 173–4.
Fuel, Ministry of. 'In war a strong defence . . .' (Advertisement). December 1941: 139.
– Fuel Communiqué No. 6 (Advertisement). 8 October 1942: 163–4.

Gas Council. *Christmas Fare: More Food – Less Fuel by Helen Burke, the well-known writer and broadcaster on cookery, for Mr. Therm to cook*, 1944: 209–10.
Gielgud, Val. *British Radio Drama 1972–1956: A Survey*. Harrap, 1957: 22–4.
Glover, (Mrs) 'Gym'. Private information: 203–4.
Gow, A.S.M. *Letters from Cambridge*. Jonathan Cape, 1945: 27, 136, 182–3, 185.
Graves, Charles *The Home Guard of Britain*. Hutchinson, 1943: 47–50.
Grisewood, Frederick. *The World Goes By*. Secker & Warburg, 1941: 153–4.

Hall, (Miss) Vivienne. Private information: 24, 189–90, 195–7, 202, 213.
Henrey, (Mrs) Robert. *The Incredible City*. Dent, 1944: 174–7.
Herbert, (Sir) A.P. *The Thames*. Weidenfeld & Nicolson, 1966: 53–4, 198–9.
Hickman, (Miss) May. Private information: 142–5.
History of the 8th (Burton) Battalion, Staffordshire Home Guard. Privately printed. n.d: 60–61.
Hodson, James Lansdale. *The Sea and the Land*. Gollancz, 1945: 222–4.
Home Security, Ministry of. *Anti-Gas Protection of Babies and Young Children*. 1939: 11.
– *Your Brick Street Shelter this Winter*. 1940: 78–9.

List of Sources

Housewife magazine. 'The following were the pre-Blitz arrangements . . .'
   October 1940: 35.
- 'Have you packed a kitbag . . .?' August 1940: 59.
- 'The babies who are being born now . . .' August 1940: 59–60.
- 'Prevent dust forming . . .' December 1941: 135.
- 'When dawn broke . . .' August 1941: 113–15.
Huxley, Professor Julian *see* Woon, Basil.

Ierston, (Miss) Joan. Private information: 150–51.
'If you want to go to heaven . . .' Quoted by Joseph, Shirley (*q.v.*).
Ingersoll, Ralph. *Report on England*. John Lane, 1941: 77–8.

Jackson, (Miss) Florence. Private information: 126–9.
Jobbins, (Miss) Beatrice. Private information: 20–21.
Joseph, Shirley. *If Their Mothers Only Knew*. Faber, 1946: 132.

Kay, (Mrs) Verna. Private information: 125–6.
Kentish, Lt.-Col. L.W. Home Guard: Bux 4. Privately printed. n.d: 118–20,
   141–2.
Kiernan, (Miss) Isabel. Private information: 82–4.
Knappett, Rachel. *A Pullet on the Midden*. Michael Joseph, 1947: 133–4.
Kops, Bernard. *The World is a Wedding*. MacGibbon & Kee, 1963: 65–6.

Lambert, Derek. *The Sheltered Days*. André Deutsch, 1965: 15–19, 40–41,
   103–4, 155–6, 157, 158–60, 160–62.
Lancum, F. Howard. *Press Officer, Please*. Crosby Lockwood, 1946: 151,
   178–9.
'Land Army Song, The'. Quoted by Shewell-Cooper, W.E. (*q.v.*).
'Langton Maltravers Women's Institute, War History of' in *War Record of the
   Dorset Federation of Women's Institutes* (Manuscript). n.d. (c.1945): 53.
Leakey, J.H. *School Errant*. Dulwich College Preparatory School, 1951:
   14–15, 50–51, 173, 182.
Lehmann, John. *I am my Brother*. Longmans, 1960: 227–8.
Lewey, Frank R. *Cockney Campaign*. Stanley Paul, 1944: 74–6.

Macleod, Joseph. *A Job at the B.B.C.* William MacLellan, Glasgow, 1947:
   24–6, 54–5.
Matthews, Post Warden. Quoted by Fitzgibbon, Constantine (*q.v.*).
Meech, (Mrs) D. (deceased). Private information: 191–3, 193–4.
Mikkelsen, (Mrs) J. Private information: 179–80.
Millard, (Mrs) Lily Pearl. Private information: 197.
Miller, (Mrs) Muriel. Private information: 172–3.
Moonen, (Mrs) Rosemary. Private information: 100–102, 123–5, 153.

Morton, H.V. *I Saw Two Englands*. Methuen, 1942: 11–12.

Nicolson, Harold. *Diaries and Letters 1939–45*. Collins, 1967: 221–2.
Nixon, Barbara. *Raiders Overhead*. Scolar Press, 1980: 62–5, 66–8, 88–9.
Nixon, (Miss) Eileen. Private information: 164–5, 217.

O'Leary, John. *Danger over Dagenham*. Borough of Dagenham, 1947: 210.
Priestley, J.B. *Postscripts*. Heinemann, 1940: xii, 51–3, 57–8.

Rathbone, (Miss) Lettice. Private information: 53.
Roberts, (Miss) Margaret Stewart (deceased). Private information from an unpublished manuscript: 213–16, 219–20.
Rodd, (Mrs) Thekla. Private information: 193, 201.
Royal Society for the Prevention of Cruelty to Animals. *Feeding Dogs and Cats in Wartime*, n.d: 156–7.
Ryan, (Mrs) Megan. Private information: 81–2, 152–3, 200–201, 230.

Sackville-West, V. *The Women's Land Army*. Michael Joseph, 1944: 135.
Sansom, William. *Westminster in War*. Faber, 1947: 199–200.
Seth, Ronald. *The Specials*. Gollancz, 1961: 31.
Shewell-Cooper, W.E. *Landgirl*. A Handbook for Volunteers in the Women's Land Army. English Universities Press, 1941: 132.
Short Guide to Great Britain, A. U.S. Department of Defense. Numerous editions from 1942: 169–71.
Smith, Henry. *Bureaucrats in Battledress*. R.E. Jones, Conway, n.d. (c.1945): 204–5.
Smith, (Mrs) Mary. Private information: 220–21, 229.
Speshul, The. Quoted by Seth, Ronald (*q.v.*).
Stork Margarine Wartime Cookery Book. Stork Margarine Co. Ltd: 36.
Supply, Ministry of. 'Rubber Shortage' (Advertisement). 22 July 1942: 162–3.
Swain, George. *Norwich Under Fire*. Jarrold & Sons, Norwich, n.d: 145.

'There'll always be a dustbin . . .' *see* Women's Voluntary Service.
Thompson, Sylvia. Extract from *Housewife*, 35.
Times, The. 'When walking in the blackout . . .' (Letter) 8 November 1939: 31.
– 'Just as common sense dictates . . .' (Advertisement) 21 September 1940: 78.
– 'Now that we are apparently to have a return of the four-poster . . .' (Letter) 15 October 1940: 102–3.
– 'From May 1st all men's and youth's jackets . . .' (News report) 19 March 1942: 158.

List of Sources

– 'Everyone recognises the need for the removal of iron railings . . .' (Letter) 15 September 1942: 163.

Town Children Through Country Eyes (pamphlet). National Federation of Women's Institutes, 1940: 36–8.

Train, Jack. *Up and Down the Line*. Odhams Press, 1956: 142.

Turner, (Miss) Nellie. Private information: 30.

Wadsworth, John. *Counter Defensive*. Hodder & Stoughton, 1946: 91–2.

White, (Mrs Eva). Private information: 152.

Williams, J. Private information: 226–7.

Willis, Jerome. *It Stopped at London*. Hurst & Blackett, 1944: 71–4.

Wilson, Rev. H.A. *Death over Haggerston*. A.R. Mowbray, 1941: 79–80.

Wings for Victory leaflet see *Bombs, Weights and Prices*.

Women's Land Army. Christmas card (verse by F. Young). Quoted by Sackville-West, V. (*q.v.*).

Women's Voluntary Service. 'Our incident was an extensive one . . .' *W.V.S. Bulletin*, May 1944: 190–91.

– 'Rural Dorking's Christmas Toy Exchange . . .' *W.V.S. Bulletin*, February 1944: 183.

– 'There'll always be a dustbin . . .' The Cogs' Song, n.d. 167.

Woodhouse, (Mrs) Vera. Private information: 177–8.

Woolfitt, Susan. *Idle Women*. Ernest Benn, 1947: 129–32, 206–7, 216–17, 217–19.

Woolton, The Earl of. *Memoirs*. Cassell, 1959: 3–4, 148–50.

Woon, Basil. *Hell Came to London*. Peter Davies, 1941: 79.

Worsley, Francis. *ITMA 1939–1948*. Vox Mundi, 1948: 32–5.

ACKNOWLEDGEMENTS

Many wartime books and pamphlets were privately published, often by companies which have now disappeared and, owing to the lapse of time, other copyright-holders have also in many cases proved untraceable. Apologies are offered for any inadvertent breach of copyright and appropriate amends will gladly be made in any future edition.

Grateful acknowledgement is due to the private contributors whose material has been used in this book and whose names are identified as such in the List of Sources. The extracts from official wartime advertisements and leaflets are Crown Copyright and are reproduced by permission of Her Majesty's Stationery Office.

Acknowledgement is also made for kind permission to reproduce extracts from copyright material as follows: to Curtis Brown Ltd London for *The Oaken Heart* by Margery Allingham on behalf of P. & M. Youngman Carter Ltd; to Joyce Weiner Associates and the author for *Spam Tomorrow* by Verily Anderson; to Hutchinson & Co. Ltd for *Kentish Fire* by Hubert Banner; to Norah Baring for *A Friendly Hearth*; to David Higham Associates Ltd for *One Man in his Time* by Bruce Belfrage; to Methuen & Co. Ltd for *The Bells Go Down*; to Faber & Faber Ltd for *Sweethearts and Wives* by Theodora Benson; to The Clothworkers' Foundation for *The History of the Mary Datchelor School* by M. Dorothy Brock; to Hodder & Stoughton Educational Ltd for *Carry on London* by Ritchie Calder; to A.D. Peters & Co. Ltd for *The Memoirs of Lord Chandos*; to A.M. Heath & Co Ltd and the executors of her estate for *Chelsea Concerto* by Frances Faviell; to David Higham Associates Ltd for *The Blitz* by Constantine Fitzgibbon; to Harrap & Co. Ltd for *British Radio Drama 1922–1956: A Survey* by Val Gielgud; to Jonathan Cape Ltd and the author for *Letters from Cambridge* by A.S.M. Gow; to Secker & Warburg Ltd for *The World Goes By* by Frederick Grisewood; to J.M. Dent & Sons Ltd and the author for *The Incredible City* by Mrs Robert Henrey; to Weidenfeld and Nicolson Ltd for *The Thames* by Sir Alan Herbert; to A.D. Peters & Co. Ltd for *The Sea and the Land* by J.L. Hodson; to International Publishing Corporation Ltd for *Housewife* magazine; to Michael Joseph Ltd for *A Pullet on the Midden* by Rachel Knappett; to Granada Publishing Ltd for *The World is a Wedding* by Bernard Kops; to André Deutsch Ltd for *The Sheltered Days* by Derek Lambert; to Crosby Lockwood Ltd for *Press Officer, Please* by F. Howard Lancum; to Dulwich College Preparatory School and the author for *School Errant* by J.H. Leakey; to Longman and the author for *I am my Brother* by John Lehmann; to Stanley Paul & Co. Ltd (c/o Hutchinson Publishing Group Ltd.) for *Cockney Campaign* by Frank R. Lewey; to William MacLellan Ltd for *A Job at the B.B.C.* by Joseph Macleod; to Methuen & Co. Ltd for

I Saw Two Englands by H.V. Morton; to William Collins Sons & Co. Ltd for *Diaries and Letters 1939–1945* by Harold Nicolson; to Scolar Press in association with Gulliver Publishing Co. for *Raiders Overhead* by Barbara Nixon; to William Heinemann Ltd and the author for *Postscripts* by J.B. Priestley; to Michael Joseph Ltd for *The Women's Land Army* by V. Sackville-West; to Faber & Faber Ltd for *Westminster in War* by William Sansom; to Unilever Ltd for the *Stork Wartime Cookery Book*; to Jarrold & Sons for *Norwich under Fire* by George Swain; to *The Times* for various extracts; to the National Federation of Women's Institutes for *Town Children Through Country Eyes*; to Hodder & Stoughton for *Counter Defensive* by John Wadsworth; to the Hutchinson Group for *It Stopped at London* by Jerome Willis; to A.R. Mowbray & Co. Ltd for *Death over Haggerston* by the Rev. H.A. Wilson; to Ernest Benn Ltd for *Idle Women* by Susan Woolfitt; to A.D. Peters & Co. Ltd for *Memoirs* by the Earl of Woolton; to The Women's Royal Voluntary Services for the *W.V.S. Bulletin*; to Peter Davies Ltd for *Hell Came to London* by Basil Woon.

ILLUSTRATION ACKNOWLEDGEMENTS

The photographs are reproduced by courtesy of:
B.B.C. Hulton Picture Library: plate nos 1, 2, 3, 4, 7, 8, 10, 11, 12, 13. Forman Newspapers, Nottingham: no. 16. Imperial War Museum: nos. 5, 6, 15. Women's Royal Voluntary Services: no. 14.

Grateful acknowledgement is made to the proprietors of *Punch* for permission to include the following cartoons:
'Don't dance about on it, Winnie, . . .' (25 October 1939): p.2.
'But apart from this, life is going on . . .' (13 September 1939): p.10.
'My husband got a load of sand . . .' (15 July 1942): p.44.
A suit of armour. (25 February 1942): p.94.
'I say – WHAT a persuasive man.' (7 July 1943): p.140.
'Are you ready to cut the cake, Madam?' (10 January 1945): p.168.
'Now in the next game . . .' (n.d.): p.186.
'I shall celebrate Victory-Day . . .' (2 May 1945): p.212.

INDEX

Main references are in italic. Page-references for all contributors will be found in the List of Sources, p. 231.

Index

Index

V.A.D./s (Voluntary Aid Detachment:
auxiliary nurse) 13, 71, 111
 see also Nurse; First Aid *etc*
Versailles, Treaty of (1919) 3
V-1/V-2 *see Flying-bomb*

W.A.A.F. (Women's Auxiliary Air
Force) (*now* W.R.A.F.) 55
War:
 declared 24, 26–7
 VE (Victory in Europe) Day 217–26
 VJ (Victory over Japan) Day 227–8
Warden, Air-raid 12–13, 64, 66–8, 211
 blackout 30, 34
 Cambridge 27
 invasion preparations 46
  see also Blitz; Air-raid *etc*
War Savings Certificates 141, 181
War Transport, Ministry of 129–30
Water tank 88
Wedding/s 179–80
Winston *see* Churchill
W.L.A. *see* Land Girl

Women:
 'called-up' (conscripted) 95, 101, 123, 213
 canal-boats 129–32, 206–7, 216–17
 factories 123–6, 127, 128
 office 126–9
 postwoman 213–16, 219–20
 training 101, 123, 130
  see also Land Girl; W.V.S. *etc*
Women's Institute/s (W.I.) 53
Women's Land Army *see* Land Girl
Wood, Sir Kingsley (Chancellor of
 Exchequer 1940–3) 117–18
Woolton, Baron Frederick J.M.
 (Minister of Food 1940–3) 97, 148, 149
 Pie 154–5
  see also List of Sources
W.R.N.S. (Women's Royal Naval
 Service) (Wrens) 129
W.V.S. (Women's Voluntary Services)
 (*now* W.R.V.S.) xiii, 75–6, 84, 88,
 183, 190–91

Y.M.C.A. (Young Men's Christian
 Association) 148